MOTIVATING

HUMANS

To my father,
a master theorist who has spent his life
facilitating positive and productive goals,
emotions, and personal agency beliefs
in those around him.

MOTIVATING
HUMANS

Goals, Emotions, and Personal Agency Beliefs

Martin E. Ford

SAGE Publications
International Educational and Professional Publisher
Newbury Park   London   New Delhi

For information address:

SAGE Publications, Inc.
2455 Teller Road
Newbury Park, California 91320
E-mail: order@sagepub.com

SAGE Publications Ltd.
6 Bonhill Street
London EC2A 4PU
United Kingdom

SAGE Publications India Pvt. Ltd.
M-32 Market
Greater Kailash I
New Delhi 110 048 India

Printed in the United States of America

Library of Congress Cataloging-in-Publication Data

Ford, Martin E.
  Motivating humans: goals, emotions, and personal agency beliefs/
Martin E. Ford.
    p. cm.
  Includes bibliographical references (p. 258-283) and index.
  ISBN 0-8039-4528-0 (cloth).—ISBN 0-8039-4529-9 (pbk.)
    1. Motivation (Psychology) I. Title.
  BF501.F67 1992
  153.8—dc20   92-27865

96 97 98 99 00 01 10 9 8 7 6 5 4 3

Sage Production Editor: Diane S. Foster

Contents

Preface

THE WRITING OF THIS BOOK was motivated by the urgent need for a clear, coherent, and useful theory that could guide the efforts of scholars, professionals, and students concerned about, and interested in learning how to better address, real-world problems with strong motivational underpinnings—problems such as academic underachievement and school dropout, low levels of work productivity and job satisfaction, social irresponsibility in youth, family conflict and child/spouse abuse, and chronic emotional distress. Consistent with this objective, *Motivating Humans* is organized in a uniquely integrative manner. Specifically, rather than highlighting differences between motivational theories and research programs, *Motivating Humans* emphasizes their common elements and themes, thus providing the reader with a unified description of the basic nature of motivation and its impact on human functioning and competence development. It does so through the creation of a new theory of motivation called Motivational Systems Theory (or MST for short) that was constructed by combining the basic formulation represented in a larger, comprehensive theory of human functioning and development (i.e., the Living Systems Framework) with the best that other, more specialized theories in psychology, education, and business have to offer. *Motivating Humans* thus resolves the long-standing "identity crisis" in the field of motivation, explicates how motivational processes interact with other psychological, behavioral, and environmental factors in organizing human behavior, and shows how all other theories of motivation can be understood within the integrative framework of MST.

Motivating Humans goes beyond integrative theorizing, however. It also provides readers with a set of principles for facilitating positive and productive motivational patterns, and shows how these principles can be applied to a diversity of practical problems in education, business, and human development. It thus provides scholars and practitioners in these fields with a framework that can enhance efforts to conceptualize and design both research and intervention activities.

Several strategies are used in an effort to make *Motivating Humans* as readable and accessible as possible. First, the book does not get bogged down in theoretical jargon, excessive detail, or masses of data. This makes it possible to present information in a clear, concise, and straightforward manner. Of course, the tradeoff in adopting such an approach is that only a limited amount of detail can be provided about specific research studies and specialized theoretical approaches. To address this limitation, *Motivating Humans* provides the reader with hundreds of references and suggestions for further reading that can facilitate efforts to pursue in greater depth particular concepts, theories, and research programs. Supplementary empirical support for Motivational Systems Theory is contained in many of these references (keeping in mind that MST capitalizes on, rather than competes with, empirical research generated under the rubric of other theories), as well as in the two-volume set of books describing the conceptual framework in which Motivational Systems Theory is anchored (i.e., the Living Systems Framework; D. Ford, 1987; M. Ford & D. Ford, 1987; see also D. Ford & Lerner, 1992). In addition to this focused presentation strategy, *Motivating Humans* provides a wide variety of concrete, real-world examples for each new concept, and frequently uses tables, lists, summaries, and other organizing devices to assist the reader in digesting and remembering key information.

Motivating Humans is designed to serve as both a reference and conceptual tool for scholars and professionals and as a textbook for graduate students and upper-level undergraduates. With respect to both uses, the book is organized in component parts that can be reshuffled or even pulled out of the overall book to meet the needs of a particular class or audience. Chapter 1 briefly characterizes why the need for precise, integrative theorizing is so urgent in the field of motivation. Chapter 2 summarizes the comprehensive, "whole-person" Living Systems Framework in which MST is anchored, and Chapter 3 applies this framework to the problem of defining human motivation and its role in effective functioning. Chapters 4 and 5 describe the basic concepts and principles involved in "motivational headquarters"—personal goals, personal agency beliefs, and emotional arousal processes. Chapter 6 summarizes the core ideas of 31 other theories and categories of theories of motivation of historical and contemporary significance in psychology, education, and business, and offers readers an integrative chart that shows how these theories can be understood in terms of the basic MST categories of goals, emotions, and personal agency beliefs. This chart may be particularly useful to instructors who wish to supplement *Motivating Humans* with additional readings. Chapter 7 translates the information presented in the preceding chapters in an effort to address the problem of how to "motivate" people, providing readers with a set of 17 principles for motivating humans. Finally, Chapter 8 provides a summary of the basic concepts and principles of Motivational Systems Theory that can serve as a study guide for students and a basic reference for scholars and professionals.

In a course on motivation in education, business, or psychology, *Motivating Humans* can be used with at least three different teaching strategies: (a) it can be used to help students learn the integrative MST approach to understanding and influencing human motivation; (b) it can be used as a framework for the analysis and comparison of several different approaches to motivation (e.g., by selecting representative approaches from the chart in Chapter 6 and examining the basic concepts and propositions in those theories in relationship to Motivational Systems Theory); and/or (c) after becoming familiar with the basic MST framework, students can be asked to develop a possible approach to resolving a specific motivational problem, either through a class paper or an in-class presentation that facilitates the development of skill in using MST to deal with real-world problems. Thus, *Motivating Humans* can be effectively used in motivation courses with either a theoretical or applied emphasis.

The creation of Motivational Systems Theory and *Motivating Humans* was facilitated by a number of students, colleagues, and professionals. Collaborators Nick Nichols, Christopher Chase, and Chris Barden were particularly influential in stimulating my thinking and increasing my understanding of the fundamental nature of human motivation, as were those who conducted research contributing to the formulation and/or application of the ideas described in this book: Chip Benight, Christi Bergin, David Bergin, Rosa Casarez-

Levison, Peggy Estrada, Shifteh Karimi, Deborah Loesch-Griffin, Robin Love, Teresa McDevitt, Irene Miura, Jerry Pattillo, Kathy Wentzel, and Deborah Wood. Special thanks also go to Bernie, Louise, and Janis Guerney for their comments and insights regarding the motivational assessments described in Chapter 4 and the potential utility of Motivational Systems Theory for clinical and counseling work. Finally, I am particularly indebted to my wife, Sheri Ford, for her pragmatic advice and immediate reactions to ideas and examples; to my brother Cameron Ford, for his expert guidance with regard to the literature on motivation in business; and to Donald Ford, for providing both the intellectual foundation for Motivational Systems Theory and thorough substantive and editorial feedback on earlier drafts of *Motivating Humans*.

CHAPTER ONE

Rationale for Motivational Systems Theory

The marvelous richness of human experience would lose much rewarding joy if there were no limitations to overcome.

Helen Keller

A TYPICAL STRATEGY ADOPTED in many books on motivation is to begin with an example of some shocking or bizarre behavior—for example, a shooting spree by a deranged killer or intentional starvation by an anorexic teenager. Such examples are intended to dramatize the need for a scientific understanding of human motivation by compelling the reader to ask, "What could possibly cause a person to act that way?" Various motivational "explanations" are then offered in the form of a survey of the scientific literature on motivation. Because the focus of this survey is usually on major theorists and the prototypical experiments supporting their ideas, however, there is a tendency to lose track of the real-life problems that "motivated" the survey in the first place. Moreover, the natural inclination to portray theorists as rivals competing for the honor of having the "best" explanation of human behavior obscures the fact that complex behavior patterns are usually multidetermined—that is, they are the product of a diversity of interacting motivational and nonmotivational factors (D. Ford, 1987).

In an effort to address the limitations of the "survey-of-theories" method of familiarizing readers with the field of motivation, the present book was written with a somewhat different strategy in

mind. Rather than highlighting the differences between specific theories and research programs, this book attempts to provide the
reader with a coherent, unified description of the basic substance of
human motivation—what it is, how it works, and how it impacts
what people do and how well they do it. The scholarly field of
motivation and its major "players," both historical and contemporary, are comprehensively covered in this book, but this is accomplished by organizing the major theories and theorists around *categories of motivational processes* rather than assuming that a linear
presentation of each of these theories will somehow "add up" to
produce a clear picture of the processes and principles involved in
human motivation. Thus the present book emphasizes the need to
integrate separate but generally compatible ideas into a systematic
understanding of what motivation is and how it operates. Implications of this perspective for the content and design of research are
also noted in several places.

This is not just a book about theory and research, however. Practical utility is also a central concern. Indeed, a major purpose of this
book is to persuade students, scholars, and professionals interested
in human behavior and development that motivation is at the heart
of many of society's most pervasive and enduring problems, both as
a developmental outcome of demotivating social environments and
as a developmental influence on behavior and personality. Consistent with this objective, concrete examples from a variety of life
domains are liberally supplied throughout the book in an effort to
bridge the gap between the world of abstract theory and the world
of practical human affairs. In addition, Chapter 7 of this book is
devoted entirely to the task of explaining "how to motivate people"—both in terms of general principles and in terms of specific
applications to a selected set of enduring, real-life concerns in child
and adolescent development, education, business, and counseling
and everyday living: (a) promoting social responsibility and caring
behavior in youth, (b) increasing motivation for learning and school
achievement, (c) understanding and facilitating the links between
job satisfaction and work productivity, and (d) helping people lead
an emotionally healthy life.

The integrative conceptualization of motivation described in this
book is called **Motivational Systems Theory** (or **MST** for short). It
is designed to represent all three sets of phenomena that have traditionally been of concern in the field of human motivation: the selective *direction* of behavior patterns (i.e., where people are heading and
what they are trying to do); the selective *energization* of behavior

patterns (i.e., how people get "turned on" or "turned off"); and the selective *regulation* of behavior patterns (i.e., how people decide to try something, stick with it, or give up). Although most theories of human motivation focus on only one or two of these phenomena, many definitions of motivation include all three (Kleinginna & Kleinginna, 1981). For example, according to Franken (1988), "The study of motivation has traditionally been concerned with the arousal, direction, and persistence of behavior" (p. 3), and Beck (1978) states that "Motivation is broadly concerned with the contemporary determinants of choice (direction), persistence, and vigor of goal-directed behavior" (p. 24). Steers and Porter (1987) believe that "When we discuss motivation, we are primarily concerned with (1) what energizes human behavior; (2) what directs or channels such behavior; and (3) how this behavior is maintained or sustained" (pp. 5-6). Mitchell (1982) says that "Motivation [represents] those psychological processes that cause the arousal, direction, and persistence of voluntary actions that are goal directed" (p. 81), and, according to Bandura (1991a), "Motivation is . . . a multidimensional phenomenon indexed in terms of . . . the determinants and intervening mechanisms that govern the selection, activation, and sustained direction of behavior" (p. 158).

In Motivational Systems Theory, **motivation is defined as the organized patterning of three psychological functions that serve to direct, energize, and regulate goal-directed activity: personal goals, emotional arousal processes, and personal agency beliefs.** These motivational components and their integrated patterning are defined in more precise terms in subsequent chapters of this book. In the present chapter I provide the reader with an overview of the major issues and concerns that led to the creation of Motivational Systems Theory.

Obstacles Facing Efforts to Apply Scholarly Work on Motivation to Real-World Problems

One might suppose that a century of theory and research on motivation would have led to significant advances in society's ability to respond to practical human problems; however, it is difficult to identify many such advances (Appley, 1990; Cofer & Appley, 1964; Franken, 1984; Geen, Beatty, & Arkin, 1984; Landy & Becker, 1987; McCombs, 1991a; Mook, 1987; Petri, 1991; Pinder, 1984; Weiner,

1980, 1990, 1992). Recent contributions from a number of distinguished research programs have raised hopes for a more productive future (e.g., Abramson, Metalsky, & Alloy, 1989; Ajzen, 1985; C. Ames & R. Ames, 1984a, 1985, 1989; R. Ames & C. Ames, 1984; Bandura, 1986, 1989, 1991b; Brophy, 1987; Cantor & Fleeson, 1991; Covington, 1992; Csikszentmihalyi, 1990; deCharms, 1984; Deci & Ryan, 1985, 1987, 1991; Dweck & Leggett, 1988; Elliott & Dweck, 1988; Emmons, 1986, 1989; Halisch & Kuhl, 1986; Harackiewicz & Sansone, 1991; Heckhausen, 1991; Izard, 1991; Kanfer & Kanfer, 1991; Klinger, 1987; Kuhl & Beckmann, 1985, in press; Langer, 1989; Lazarus, 1991a, 1991b, 1991c; Little, 1989; Locke & Latham, 1990a, 1990b; Lord & Hanges, 1987; Maehr & Ames, 1989; Maehr & Kleiber, 1987; Maehr & Midgley, 1991; Maehr & Pintrich, 1991; Markus & Nurius, 1986; Markus & Ruvolo, 1989; McCombs, 1991a, 1991b; Nicholls, 1984a, 1984b; Pervin, 1989, 1991; Peterson, Seligman, & Vaillant, 1988; Plutchik, 1980; Powers, 1989; Schunk, 1984, 1990a, 1991a, 1991b; Seligman, 1991; Slavin, 1984, 1987; Sorrentino & Higgins, 1986; Vroom, & Deci, 1992; Weiner, 1986; Wentzel, 1989, 1991a, 1991b; Wood & Bandura, 1989). Nevertheless, trying to make a case for the central role of motivation in real-world problems by cataloguing the practical contributions of past scholarly work on motivation is a challenging, if not impossible, task. In fact we reached our conclusion regarding the importance of motivational processes in spite of this disappointing history. Only when we were able to view the field of motivation through the clarifying lens of D. Ford's **Living Systems Framework** (LSF) were we able to recognize and appreciate the possibilities for constructing a scientifically sound and pragmatically useful theory of human motivation. Thus Motivational Systems Theory emerged from an iterative process of integrating the basic framework provided by the LSF with the concepts and data provided by existing work on motivation (both historical and contemporary).

Historical Overview

A brief review of the history of scholarly work on motivation reveals numerous obstacles to the application of motivation theory and research to real-world problems (a more extensive overview of the evolution of motivational theorizing is presented in Chapter 6 of this book). The most fundamental of these obstacles is an "identity crisis" centering on the problem of how to define and delimit the field of motivation. This problem has been recognized for many years but never really resolved (Hilgard & Atkinson, 1967; Kleinginna &

Kleinginna, 1981; Pinder, 1984). For example, Brown (1961) characterized the "ubiquity of the concept of motivation" as "surprising when we consider that its meaning is scandalously vague" (p. 24). Mowrer (1952), in the first issue of the *Annual Review of Psychology* to include a chapter on motivation, similarly commented that "considering its prominence in present-day psychology, the concept of motivation has had a surprisingly meager history" (p. 419). An even more pessimistic assessment was made by the next author to contribute an *Annual Review* chapter on motivation (Cofer, 1959), who concluded that "if present trends continue, motivation as a distinctive concept, coordinate to other psychological concepts, may well disappear" (p. 194). Some psychologists would no doubt applaud such a development, agreeing with Dewsbury (1978) that "the concept of motivation tends to be used as a garbage pail for a variety of factors whose nature is not well understood" (p. 172).

The nature and depth of the problem of defining and delimiting the field of motivation is difficult to summarize in a concise way; however, Pinder's (1984) analysis of the problem provides a good initial overview:

> It is only a slight exaggeration to say that there have been almost as many definitions of motivation offered over the years as there have been thinkers who have considered the nature of human behavior. . . . Some writers view motivation from a strictly physiological perspective, while others view human beings as primarily hedonistic, and explain most of human behavior as goal-oriented, seeking to gain pleasure and avoid pain. Others stress the rationality of humans, and consider human behavior to be the result of conscious choice processes. Some thinkers stress unconscious or subconscious factors. (p. 7)

The consequences of this identity crisis for students, scholars, and professionals attempting to learn about the field of motivation have been well summarized by Mook (1987):

> The topic of motivation has long had an anomalous status in psychology. What is motivation, anyway? One can define it so broadly that is encompasses all of psychology, or so narrowly that it threatens to vanish entirely. . . . It seems to me that most textbook treatments leave the reader still wondering, "Yes, but what is the field of motivation *about?*" Readers of these treatments will be in (temporary) possession of masses of data and of specialized interpretations, but little in the way of overview. (pp. xvii-xviii)

Some contemporary theorists have responded to the identity crisis in the field of motivation by essentially abandoning the term in favor of more precise concept labels representing component processes (e.g., deCharms, 1987; D. Ford, 1987; Powers, 1989, 1991). Such theorists argue that " 'motivation' is clearly an overused term" and that "it is not clear to what it uniquely applies. The burden of meaning is too heavy for the beast" (deCharms, 1987, p. 1). Moreover, when the term motivation is used, it often does not serve as a major organizing construct. For example, many motivation scholars emphasize the currently more fashionable labels of "self-system" or "self-regulation" (e.g., Bandura, 1989; Harter, 1983; Kuhl, 1985; Markus, Cross, & Wurf, 1990; McCombs & Marzano, 1990; Raynor & McFarlin, 1986); others highlight concepts related to goals and goal-setting processes (e.g., Elliott & Dweck, 1988; Locke & Latham, 1984, 1990a, 1990b; Nicholls, 1984a, 1984b; Pervin, 1983, 1989); and still others focus primarily on emotional processes (e.g., Ekman, 1972; Frijda, 1988; Hoffman, 1986; Izard, 1977, 1979, 1991; Plutchik, 1980). This fractionation of the field makes it increasingly less accessible and useful to people who are looking for answers to practical questions framed in motivational terms.

In addition to the general problem of defining and delimiting the field of motivation, there are a number of more specific features of motivation theory and research (as historically defined) that have contributed to the field's uncertain scientific status and limited practical utility. These are discussed next.

Machine Model of Motivation. Most early theories of motivation viewed humans as machine-like entities driven by internal or external forces beyond their control (Weiner, 1992). Although motivation scholars have begun to appreciate the capability of humans for self-direction and self-regulation, concepts such as needs, drives, incentives, reinforcers, and the like—concepts that dominated the field for many years—continue to influence contemporary theorizing. Moreover, public understanding of "how to motivate people" is still dominated by simplistic, mechanistic conceptions of human motivation. This can be seen, for example, in college textbooks that continue to feature outdated theories of biological and situational determinism; in business seminars based on decades-old conceptions of motivational needs and incentives; and in administrative and managerial practices and procedures that fail to respect the capacity of ordinary people (e.g., students, teachers, patients, employees) for self-direction, autonomous decision making, and personal responsibility.

Emphasis on Biological Mechanisms. During the middle part of the twentieth century progress in understanding motivational contributions to complex, real-world problems came to a virtual standstill as researchers focused on the principles governing the behavior of caged animals in states of biological deprivation and on theoretical formulations that represented all other aspects of motivation as indirect manifestations of these biologically based mechanisms (e.g., "derived motives" and "secondary drives"). Only gradually did it become apparent that these principles were of limited utility for understanding the everyday problems of humans. We now have a much more profound appreciation of the complexity and context-sensitivity of human behavior—an appreciation that has set the stage for renewed progress in theory and research on human motivation.

More generally, as Petri (1991) states, it has become evident that "the processes that undergird the physiologically important motives are different from the processes that undergird psychological motives" (p. 22). These two sets of phenomena have (appropriately) evolved into separate fields of study, as evidenced by the fact that for over a decade chapters on motivation in the *Annual Review of Psychology* have focused either on biological processes *or* on psychological and social processes, but not both. Biological functioning does, of course, provide a foundation for behavioral functioning— for example, illness, fatigue, or extreme hunger can short-circuit even the most compelling goals and plans. Nevertheless, the biological subsystems of a person represent a qualitatively different level of analysis and are best understood not as motivational processes per se, but, rather, as facilitating and constraining boundary conditions for motivational processes and problems at the level of the person-in-context. As D. Ford (1987) has warned:

> The functioning of primitive organisms is dominated by material and energy exchange processes. When that is the case biological determinism can explain much of such organisms' behavior. As more complex organisms evolved, however, the growing ability to collect, organize, interpret, transform, and use information to deal with the natural world made organisms decreasingly dependent on the physical-chemical, "here and now" conditions of their environments. . . . The human brain, with its massive capabilities for using information in self-constructing ways, often can override the more primitive components that control behavior in lower organisms. Therefore, generalization from the characteristics of other animals to humans, or vice versa, is risky business; it must be done with great care, particularly if information-based processes are involved. (pp. 183-184)

Isolation of Emotion Theory and Research. Although the relevance of emotional experience to motivation has long been recognized, the tendency has been to view emotions as a separate source of motivational energy rather than as an integrated part of motivational patterns. For example, in textbooks on human motivation there is usually a single, isolated chapter on emotions near the beginning or end of the book, with little mention of emotional processes in other chapters. This is largely a reflection of the fact that few cognitively or behaviorally oriented theories of motivation incorporate emotional processes in a meaningful way, and few theories of emotion deal with cognitive motivational processes beyond the role they play in initiating and maintaining emotional states. Thus concepts that should be richly integrated are, instead, awkwardly juxtaposed like preadolescent boys and girls at a school dance—in the same place but hardly ever interacting with each other.

Philosophical Extremism. Theories of motivation have generally been based on rather divergent and often extreme images and assumptions about the nature of humans (D. Ford, 1987; McCombs, 1991a; Pintrich, 1991; Urban & Ford, 1961; Weiner, 1991, 1992). Some have portrayed humans as "robots" whose every thought and action is determined by "animal instincts," biologically based needs and drives, or powerful external forces that are largely beyond their control (e.g., Freud, 1915/1957; Hull, 1943; Skinner, 1953). In contrast, humanistic scholars have emphasized individuals' capacity for envisioning and striving toward self-chosen ideals of personal fulfillment and self-actualization (e.g., Maslow, 1943; Rogers, 1951). Still others have emphasized the logical side of humans, portraying them as "scientists," "judges," or "pilots" actively steering a course toward well-defined objectives using systematic and rational methods of planning and evaluation (e.g., Atkinson & Birch, 1970; Fishbein & Ajzen, 1975; Miller, Galanter, & Pribram, 1960; Vroom, 1964; Weiner, 1974). Because there is some "truth" in all of these perspectives, more recent theories of motivation have been based on more sophisticated combinations of these images (e.g., Bandura, 1986; Csikszentmihalyi, 1990; Deci & Ryan, 1985; Dweck & Leggett, 1988; Elliott & Dweck, 1988; Emmons, 1989; Kuhl, 1986; Locke & Latham, 1990a; Maehr & Braskamp, 1986; Markus & Ruvolo, 1989; Seligman, 1991). Nevertheless, the ancient battles between free will and determinism, between conscious and unconscious forces, and between situational and personality influences on behavior continue to distract motivation scholars from the basic task of understanding how the person and context work together as a unit to produce coherent, goal-directed behavior patterns.

Conceptual Confounding. Vagueness and ambiguity have characterized efforts to define and conceptualize motivation throughout the history of psychology. For example, early theories about human instincts and basic needs (e.g., Freud, 1915/1957; McDougall, 1933; Murray, 1938), although rich in content, were lacking in predictive or explanatory value because they tended to confound motivation and action (i.e., the evidence for a need or instinct was identical with the behavior it was designed to explain). Consequently, these theories were primarily useful only as devices for labeling behavior that had already occurred. Such labeling required either the reduction of diverse classes of behavior to a few motivational categories (e.g., Freud's life and death instincts), or the invention of new instincts or needs for each new class of behavior to be explained (e.g., McDougall added a number of "minor" instincts to his original taxonomy to account for behaviors such as scratching, sneezing, urinating, and the like, and considered adding many others). As Holt (1931) complained:

> If he goes with his fellows, it is the "herd instinct" which activates him; if he walks alone, it is the "anti-social instinct"; . . . if he twiddles his thumbs, it is the "thumb-twiddling instinct"; if he does not twiddle his thumbs, it is the "thumb-not-twiddling instinct." Thus everything is explained with the facility of magic—word magic. (p. 428)

Another kind of conceptual problem that has limited the value of motivational research is the confounding of motivation—an internal psychological phenomenon—with features of the external environment. The idea that motivation is somehow "out there" rather than within the person is pervasive even among scholars. For example, discussions of intrinsic and extrinsic motivation often imply that motivation resides in *activities* rather than in *people* (e.g., "drawing is an intrinsically motivating activity" rather than "Christopher is intrinsically motivated to draw"). Similarly, in research on goal-setting processes, goals are often described as if they were a part of the task context rather than a product of the person's thinking about that context (e.g., "the goal of this task is to complete the puzzle" rather than "your goal in working on this task should be to complete the puzzle"). Research testing the basic propositions of equity theory has also failed to carefully distinguish between the psychological experience of inequity and objective conditions of inequality—conditions that may or may not have any significance for a particular worker or research subject (Huseman, Hatfield, & Miles, 1987; Pinder, 1984). This lack of conceptual precision contributes to a mechanistic and oversimplified conception of human motivation. The implications of this confounding for the assessment and experimental control of motivational processes are also quite profound (e.g., one cannot simply assume that seemingly straightforward task or social manipulations will necessarily produce their intended motivational consequences).

Yet another type of conceptual confounding that has greatly exacerbated the identity crisis in the field of motivation is the tendency of some scholars to equate motivation with behavioral causation—that is, to assume that virtually anything that causes or influences behavior is an aspect of motivation (e.g., Lefrancois, 1980; Young, 1961). This is what has given motivation its reputation as an overly inclusive, all-encompassing concept (Cofer & Appley, 1964; D. Ford, 1987; Powers, 1991). For example, biological processes and environmental incentives and contingencies are often included under the rubric of motivation because they can influence what a person tries to do and how vigorously they try to do it in very powerful and obvious ways. The history of motivational theorizing, however, suggests that if motivation is to be a unique and useful concept, it must be restricted to the *psychological* processes involved in the direction, energization, and regulation of behavior patterns. Thus in Motivational Systems Theory motivation represents only one of four sets of influences to be accounted for in human behavior patterns: (a) biological influences, (b) environmental influences, (c) motivational influences, and (d) nonmotivational psychological and behavioral influences. In some circumstances motivation may be a dominating influence, and in other circumstances motivation may be the least salient of these influences (e.g., circumstances in which a person is biologically deprived, physically coerced, severely ill, or significantly constrained by social, behavioral, or developmental limitations).

Conceptual Narrowness. As part of a more general trend toward scholarly specialization, contemporary motivational theorizing has become more precise but also more restricted in scope. Indeed, many theories are anchored around a single concept or component process. Although some may regard this as an inevitable and perhaps even healthy trend (e.g., Landy & Becker, 1987; Pinder, 1984; Pintrich, 1991), a basic premise of Motivational Systems Theory is that both precision *and* scope are needed to address complex, real-world problems effectively. As Hyland (1988) has argued, "motivational research is now at a stage when the different theories need to be brought together. Predictions should be made from a consideration of how the system operates as a whole rather than being based on just one aspect of the system" (p. 650). The utility of such an integrative approach is suggested by the growing tendency of motivation scholars to include constructs representing multiple perspectives in their research designs (e.g., Bandura & Cervone, 1983; Eccles, Adler, & Meece, 1984; Locke, Frederick, Lee, & Bobko, 1984; Locke & Latham, 1990b; Meece, Wigfield, & Eccles, 1990; Miura, 1987; Pintrich & DeGroot, 1990; Wentzel, 1991b; Wood & Bandura, 1989).

Conclusion

Some of the problems that have contributed to the limited practical utility of scholarly work on motivation have been or are currently being resolved in productive ways. There is still an urgent need, however, to address the lack of consensus, cohesion, and integration in the field of motivation. As Appley (1990) has commented:

> In recently trying to assess changes in the field of motivation over the past 25 years . . . I was struck by the enormous growth in the size of the literature . . . particularly . . . by what seemed to be a replacement of broad issues by narrower—and in many cases, relatively trivial—issues. (p. 11)

Thus what is needed is a clear, coherent, and comprehensive conceptualization of motivation that can retain the detail and precision of specialized theories but that can also integrate these "minitheories" into a broader theory focusing on the basic substance and overall organization of motivational patterns. Such a theory also needs to be embedded within an even larger framework that can specify how motivational patterns operate as one of several kinds of factors influencing the fundamental unit of interest in real-world applications—the whole person-in-context.

Motivational Systems Theory is designed to meet these criteria. It is an integrative theory that focuses on the content, processes, and relationships involved in the three basic components of motivational patterns—personal goals, personal agency beliefs, and emotional arousal processes. Although MST adds a variety of new ideas and concept labels to the literature, it is generally compatible with existing theories of motivation and does not try to replace them. Rather, it attempts to bring coherence to the field by recognizing and capitalizing on the strengths of existing theories and showing how they can be organized into a common framework. In doing so it addresses the kinds of questions and concerns raised by Staats (1991) in his essay calling for theoretical unification:

> We will never achieve a related, meaningful, coherent, compact, and parsimonious field of knowledge if we do not relate and organize the phenomena studied. . . . As an example, consider phenomena such as interests, attitudes, emotions, values, reinforcement, hedonic value, preferences, motivation, and evaluative meaning. . . . Are there any relationships among these phenomena? Could theory bridges of common underlying principles be constructed? (pp. 905-906)

Motivational Systems Theory is derived from D. Ford's Living Systems Framework (D. Ford, 1987; M. Ford & D. Ford, 1987), a comprehensive theory of human functioning and development that is designed to represent all of the component processes of the person and how they are organized in complex patterns of unitary functioning in variable environments. The anchoring of MST in this broader framework makes it possible to describe how motivational processes interact with biological, environmental, and nonmotivational psychological and behavioral processes to produce effective or ineffective functioning in the person as a whole. The LSF thus provides the foundation for constructing a conceptualization of motivation that has broad theoretical, empirical, and practical utility.

Objectives of Motivational Systems Theory

As may be evident from the preceding discussion, Motivational Systems Theory was created with five major objectives in mind.

Conceptual Clarity. In this book considerable effort is devoted to the task of resolving the identity crisis that continues to plague the field of motivation. Three strategies are used to accomplish this goal. First, consistent with Pintrich's (1991) assertion that "one of the most important issues for the future viability of the field of motivational theory and research is the theoretical and definitional clarity of the constructs" (p. 200), a great deal of emphasis is placed on conceptual clarity and precision. A guiding principle of Motivational Systems

Theory is that there be no ambiguity about the boundaries that separate motivational and nonmotivational phenomena and no confusion about the defining features of specific motivational concepts. Second, MST tries to focus on the basic substance of motivational phenomena rather than the variety of "specialized interpretations" (Mook, 1987) that have been offered to account for these phenomena. This speaks to Bolles' (1975) criticism that "what one proposes as a definition of motivated behavior seems to depend more on [one's] theoretical commitments than upon anything in the behavior itself" (p. 1). Finally, basic motivational concepts are explicated primarily through examples and illustrative studies that deal with real-world problems rather than through "masses of data" (Mook, 1987) that focus primarily on abstract theoretical problems. (For those interested in applying MST concepts to broader segments of the empirical research literature, suggestions for further reading are provided at the end of each chapter, and numerous references representing virtually all of the major streams of motivation theory and research, both historical and contemporary, are provided in Chapter 6 and throughout the book.)

Theoretical Integration. The field of motivation is like an orchestra in which each musician is playing his or her own favorite song— some nice individual melodies are being played, but the overall impression is one of discord and confusion. Landy and Becker (1987) have summarized with unusual clarity what needs to be done to repair this "state of disorder":

> We have more than enough theories of motivation and more than enough data on motivational phenomena. What is needed is a new synthesis of both theory and data. We need to be more clever with what we already have. (pp. 3-4)

It should be noted that at least some degree of theoretical integration is being attempted by a number of contemporary motivation scholars (e.g., Abramson, Metalsky, & Alloy, 1989; Bandura, 1986; Campion & Lord, 1982; Carver & Scheier, 1982; Hyland, 1988; Kanfer & Kanfer, 1991; Klein, 1989; Kuhl & Beckmann, 1985; Locke & Latham, 1990a, 1990b; Lord & Hanges, 1987; Maehr & Braskamp, 1986; Markus, Cross, & Wurf, 1990; McCombs & Marzano, 1990; Pervin, 1983, 1991; Wentzel, 1991b). This suggests not only that productive cross-fertilization is occurring, but also that theoretical survival depends in large part on the degree to which diverse motivational concepts can be incorporated into one's theory.

For example, Locke and Latham (1990b) have strengthened their position of leadership in the field of work motivation by expanding their goal-setting theory to include concepts from expectancy theory, social cognitive theory, and theories of job satisfaction. Similarly, the popularity of Bandura's (1986) social cognitive theory can be attributed in part to his "cleverness" in using concepts from other theoretical frameworks and research programs to elaborate his own theory (e.g., goal theory concepts from Locke and Dweck; systems theory concepts from D. Ford and others). This means that MST is unique not so much because it embraces multiple processes, but because it uses a "top-down" rather than a "bottom-up" approach to identifying and representing motivational phenomena. That is, rather than starting with a few core constructs and expanding in somewhat piecemeal fashion, MST starts with a comprehensive conceptualization of the whole person (i.e., the LSF), and then focuses in on the subset of processes that are motivational in character. This approach yields a representation of motivation that is theoretically coherent and logically complete, with clear boundaries and a strong emphasis on patterns of organization. It also enables one to specify in a precise way the relationships between motivational processes and other aspects of person-in-context functioning.

Heuristic Utility for Guiding Research. MST can facilitate the work of motivation scholars in several ways (M. Ford, 1987a). Because it provides a clear and comprehensive taxonomy of motivational concepts (and specifies how other theories can be translated into these terms), it can serve as a guide for reviewing and interpreting diverse, often confusing literatures. It can also help researchers avoid the unproductive arguments and artificial barriers that often accompany theoretical competition and isolation. In terms of methodological implications, MST's emphasis on motivational *patterns* suggests that research designs and data analysis techniques that focus on configurations of multiple variables are likely to be particularly informative in revealing the nature of motivation and its impact on a person's functioning (Pintrich, 1991). The MST assumption that motivational patterns are idiosyncratically organized within individuals further implies that, whenever possible, research should be designed to collect information representing the functioning of each person being studied on multiple occasions of measurement (Nesselroade & Ford, 1987; Pervin, 1983). Such designs yield unusually rich information and provide a sound basis for generalizations within and across individuals.

Practical Utility for Addressing Real-World Problems. MST is designed to help people understand and deal with problems of learning, behavior change, and effective performance in themselves and others. The major examples in this book focus on problems of concern to parents, teachers, business managers, and counselors; however, the concepts and principles of MST are relevant to almost anyone interested in influencing human behavior or facilitating competence development, including their own (e.g., writers, artists, actors, athletes, coaches, politicians, lawyers, medical and health professionals, marketing and sales personnel, etc.).

Chapter 7 deals most directly with the practical problem of trying to "motivate" people. However, the goal of providing readers with a truly useful theory of human motivation influenced the organization and presentation of information throughout this book, as evidenced, for example, by the frequent use of heuristic "formulas," lists, and summaries. Thus Chapter 7 is designed to be the culmination of a logical progression through the preceding chapters rather than a disconnected attempt to say something that might be significant to people other than motivational scholars.

As the preceding paragraph implies, an underlying assumption of this book is that the practical utility of any theory of motivation will be largely dependent on how well the objectives of conceptual clarity and theoretical integration are attained. For example, the conceptual confounding of motivational processes with external influences on motivation has contributed to the tendency of interventionists to focus primarily on the *contexts of change* rather than the *change process* itself as it is governed and experienced by the individual. By untangling person characteristics from context characteristics, MST provides a way of thinking about motivation that can accommodate individual differences in how people respond to efforts to motivate them. Moreover, by specifying the precise nature of these person characteristics and how they are organized, MST provides interventionists with a clear understanding of how to tailor their change efforts to the motivational patterns of particular individuals.

Infusing the Field of Motivation With a Developmental Orientation. Historically, motivation has been viewed either as a variable state that has little enduring significance (e.g., a state produced by a temporarily aroused drive or set of environmental contingencies) or as a stable trait representing a relatively fixed part of an individual's personality (as illustrated by concepts such as need for achievement and locus of control). A major objective of this book is to add a

developmental orientation to these traditional perspectives on motivation. Specifically, MST views motivation in terms of dynamic "steady
state" patterns that exhibit both stability and variability within
boundaries. These motivational patterns are usually neither fixed
nor fleeting; rather, they often endure and gain strength over time,
while still retaining considerable potential for significant change.

A related and equally important objective of MST is to infuse the
field of developmental psychology with a motivational orientation.
The fact that most textbooks on child and adolescent development
do not include a chapter on motivation or even have motivation as
an index term, speaks volumes about the gap between actual and
potential accomplishments in the field of motivation. Thus one of the
most important messages in this book is that **motivation provides
the psychological foundation for the development of human competence in everyday life.** This implies that a critically important
objective of parents, teachers, child care workers, and helping professionals should be to assist people (especially young people) in
building a strong motivational foundation for the academic, vocational, social, and personal challenges and opportunities that await
them.

Suggestions for Further Reading

Cofer, C. N., & Appley, M. H. (1964). *Motivation: Theory and research.* New York: John
    Wiley.
Heckhausen, H. (1991). *Motivation and action* (2nd ed.). New York: Springer-Verlag.
Petri, H. L. (1991). *Motivation: Theory, research, and applications* (3rd edition). Belmont,
    CA: Wadsworth.
Pinder, C. C. (1984). *Work motivation: Theory, issues, and applications.* Glenview, IL: Scott,
    Foresman, and Company.
Steers, R. M., & Porter, L. W. (Eds.) (1987). *Motivation and work behavior* (4th ed.). New
    York: McGraw-Hill.
Weiner, B. (1992). *Human motivation: Metaphors, theories, and research.* Newbury Park,
    CA: Sage.

CHAPTER TWO

Theoretical Foundation: The Living Systems Framework

If we did all the things we are capable of doing, we would literally astound ourselves.

Thomas A. Edison

Purpose of This Chapter

As NOTED IN CHAPTER 1, one of the unique characteristics of Motivational Systems Theory is that it is anchored in a comprehensive conceptualization of the whole person. The purpose of this chapter is to summarize that conceptual framework so that it can then be used as a basis for: (a) defining and delimiting the substantive domain of motivation, (b) specifying how motivation operates in conjunction with other influences to produce effective and ineffective behavior patterns, and (c) describing how motivational processes provide a foundation for the development of human competence.

Origins of the Living Systems Framework

Throughout his rich and varied career in counseling, psychotherapy, research, teaching, and administration, Donald Ford has been concerned with the problem of how to facilitate efforts to understand and improve the human condition. His vision of a multidisciplinary, multiprofessional approach to this problem has been an inspiration to many students, scholars, and practitioners. Because this approach runs counter to the segregating forces of academic and professional specialization, however, progress has been uneven and has required considerable patience and persistence. Indeed, it was only after spending 10 years experiencing the rewards and frustrations of serving as an academic dean responsible for the creation of a new interdisciplinary college (the College of Health and Human Development at the Pennsylvania State University) that D. Ford fully appreciated the need for a major integrative theoretical effort. This experience convinced him that communication and collaboration across diverse groups of scholars and practitioners could be greatly facilitated if some common framework for thinking about human behavior and development could be synthesized from the empirically limited but conceptually rich insights of personality and psychotherapy theories and the conceptually narrow but empirically rigorous contributions of analytic science.

The roots of the LSF were firmly established three decades ago when D. Ford and Hugh Urban, after devoting several years to the task of analyzing and comparing influential theories of psychotherapy, published their classic work, *Systems of Psychotherapy: A Comparative Study* (Ford & Urban, 1963). Based on this effort and his subsequent experiences in scholarly, professional, and administrative work, D. Ford formulated the core ideas of the LSF in the late 1970s. These ideas were consistent with a much broader trend in the physical, biological, and behavioral sciences characterized by increasing appreciation of the complexity of functional organization and change processes and increasing recognition of the need for systems theoretical approaches to handle such complexity (e.g., Ackoff & Emery, 1971; Buckley, 1967; Hoffman, 1981; Jantsch, 1980; Koestler, 1967, 1978; Laszlo, 1972; Miller, 1978; Powers, 1973, 1989; Prigogine, 1976; Prigogine & Stengers, 1984; von Bertalanffy, 1968).

After several years of elaborating, refining, and testing this integrative conceptual framework, a two-volume set of books was published describing the LSF and illustrating its utility for stimulating theoretical advances, guiding research, and facilitating the work of health and human service professionals (D. Ford, 1987; M. Ford & D. Ford, 1987). The LSF has since produced two theoretical offspring— Motivational Systems Theory and Developmental Systems Theory (DST; Ford & Lerner, 1992)—each of which was created by integrating major components of the LSF with other recent theoretical advances.

Due to space limitations, what follows is an abbreviated description of the LSF that necessarily ignores much of the history and logic underlying the framework and most of the evidence supporting it. To obtain a more complete understanding of the LSF and its potential utility for scholars and practitioners, the reader should consult *Humans as Self-Constructing Living Systems: A Developmental Theory of Behavior and Personality* (D. Ford, 1987) and *Humans as Self-Constructing Living Systems: Putting the Framework to Work* (M. Ford & D. Ford, 1987). To avoid repetitive citations of these volumes, they are not referenced in the remainder of this chapter. The reader should understand, however, that they are the source of much of the information included in this chapter.

Objectives and General Strategy of the Living Systems Framework

Objectives

The LSF is a comprehensive theory of human functioning and development that integrates scientific and professional knowledge about the characteristics of people in general (nomothetic knowledge) and the organization and operation of these characteristics in individual persons (idiographic knowledge). Perhaps its most distinctive feature is that it is designed to represent, at the person-in-context level of analysis, *all* aspects of being human, not just some particular attribute or process. Thus the LSF is intended to provide researchers and practitioners with an overall framework for guiding efforts to interpret and build upon existing knowledge, thereby addressing a need that has been noted by many observers. For example, Bevan (1991) points out that:

> Our view of the forest is forever obscured by the trees. Yet specialized knowledge derives its meaning . . . from the context of larger perspectives and questions. When it loses touch with that larger context, it loses its coherence and meaning. (p. 475)

In addition, Staats (1991), explains that:

> Psychology suffers from a crisis of disunity. . . . Psychology has so many
> unrelated elements of knowledge with so much mutual discreditation,
> inconsistency, redundancy, and controversy that abstracting general
> meaning is a great problem. . . . We need many unified theorists to save
> us from ever-increasing redundancy and artificial diversity. . . . Sheer
> production must be counterbalanced by an equally strong investment
> in weaving the unrelated knowledge elements together into the fabric
> of organized science. . . . Psychology has enormous potential power in
> its building materials, but that potential will only be realized by adding
> the architectural direction of unification efforts. (pp. 899, 905, 910)

Overview

To account for the organized patterning, dynamic flow, and overall complexity of human functioning and development (Pervin, 1983,
1991), the LSF is composed of a variety of integrated conceptualizations representing three basic kinds of phenomena:

1. the unitary functioning of the whole person-in-context;
2. the functioning of the component parts of the person; and
3. stability and change in the functioning of the component parts of the
   person and the person-as-a-whole.

Thus the LSF not only provides a way of thinking about specific
"pieces" of the person (e.g., their goals, emotions, perceptions, actions, etc.), it also describes how these component processes work
together in organized patterns and how these patterns can "add up"
over time and across contexts to produce a unique, self-constructed
personality and developmental history. Moreover, it describes how
behavior patterns can be strengthened or altered through a diversity
of change processes.

Basic Strategy

Science and practice often advance by taking a model of demonstrated utility in one field and transforming it in a way that makes it
applicable and useful for some other field. As has become increasingly popular in the social and behavioral sciences in general and the
field of motivation in particular, the starting point for the construction of the LSF was the familiar model of a control system (Ashby,
1956, 1962; Campion & Lord, 1982; Carver & Scheier, 1981, 1982,

1985, 1990; Hollenbeck, 1989; Hyland, 1988; Klein, 1989; Lord & Hanges, 1987; Lord & Kernan, 1989; Miller, Galanter, & Pribram, 1960; Powers, 1973, 1989; N. Weiner, 1948). In a *simple control system* (e.g., a thermostat), activity is generated whenever a discrepancy is perceived between current conditions and some desired state or consequence. In other words, the system is designed to "control" some variable that is being monitored by an information collection function and evaluated by a comparator or regulatory function based on the command of a directive function. This is a flexible arrangement but limited in several important ways. For example, such systems are unable to invent new goals, to construct new action capabilities, or to alter or repair their "hardware" or "software" if they are no longer able to produce the desired consequence. They are designed to function in one way, and can never function in any other way.

By adding multiple options to one or more components of a simple control system (e.g., multiple goals, plans, regulatory rules, or action capabilities), one can construct an *adaptive control system* in which increasingly complex and flexible functional patterns are possible (e.g., chess playing by a computer; automatic piloting of an airplane). Such systems can not only react to current conditions (using "feedback" information from a variety of sources), they can also anticipate possible future consequences (using "feedforward" information) and adjust their behavior accordingly. Nevertheless, an adaptive control system, no matter how sophisticated, is still just a "fancy machine."

In contrast, human beings not only have the properties of an adaptive control system, they also have two additional capabilities that enable them to transcend the fundamental limitations of a mechanistic control system: *biological self-constructing capabilities* and *behavioral self-constructing capabilities*. In other words, unlike a "fancy machine," people can construct, elaborate, and repair their own "hardware" or biological structure (e.g., through biological growth and maturation and repair of damaged tissue), as well as construct, elaborate, and revise their own "software" or behavioral repertoire (e.g., through learning and skill development). That is how a young infant can develop into a mature adult, how a novice can become an expert, and how people can change major components of their basic "personality." Thus a **human being is a self-constructing adaptive control system**, or, in simpler terms, a *living system*.

A basic premise of Motivational Systems Theory is that behavioral (information-based) self-construction is guided primarily by motivational processes. The reasoning behind this proposition is that: (a) behavioral self-construction requires selective informational exchanges between persons and environments, as well as the selective activation of internal constructive processes (Ford & Lerner, 1992), and (b) the influence of motivation on a person's activity occurs largely through such selective processes. For example, selective attention—a basic prerequisite for the self-construction of new knowledge (learning)—is governed primarily by motivational processes. Selective action, which is a fundamental prerequisite for the self-construction of new behavior patterns (e.g., skill development through practice and rehearsal), is also governed primarily by motivational processes. Thus **motivation provides the foundation for learning, skill development, and behavior change by determining how, where, and to what ends people will invest their capabilities for behavioral self-construction.** This theme is repeated and elaborated throughout this book and is the primary focus of Chapter 7.

The Unitary Functioning of the Whole Person-in-Context

The Principle of Unitary Functioning

A key assumption of the LSF is that a person always functions as a unit in coordination with the environments in which they are functioning. This is the Principle of Unitary Functioning.

How can unitary functioning be achieved among the diversity of biological systems, thought processes, emotional states, motor skills, communicative patterns, and other functions that comprise a person? Organization is the key. Indeed, organization is the essential defining property of a system. Organization exists when various components are combined in such a way that the whole is different than the sum of the parts. This "difference" involves both gains and losses. In one sense, the whole is *greater* than the sum of the parts because new qualities or capabilities emerge from the relationships among the parts that none of the parts could accomplish on their own (e.g., a fancy vehicle can emerge from a box of Lego building blocks; a more secure and intimate relationship can emerge from a marriage). In another sense, however, the whole is *less* than the sum of the parts because the functioning of each of the parts has been restricted by virtue of being "locked in" to a particular organizational form (e.g., the Lego pieces can no longer be used in some other creation; the spouses will need to accept certain restrictions on their personal freedom).

Relationships between system components that yield new properties and possibilities are called *facilitating conditionalities*. Relationships between system components that reduce the range of possibilities to some smaller subset are called *constraining conditionalities*. These interrelated concepts are vitally important in Motivational Systems Theory because motivational problems often involve trade-offs between facilitating and constraining conditionalities (e.g., giving up one goal in order to pursue some other goal). These concepts also provide a useful way of thinking about the impact of motivation on other component processes of the person. For example, by helping a person selectively attend to personal strengths and opportunities rather than to limitations and obstacles, motivational patterns can be altered so that they are more likely to facilitate than to constrain a person's activity.

The Concept of Behavior Episode

If we want to understand a person rather than just some part of a person, then we need some practical way of representing the organized flow of their complex behavior patterns. The LSF uses the concept of *behavior episode* to represent coherent sequences of unitary person-in-context functioning. Informally, a behavior episode can be thought of as a "slice of life." In more technical terms a behavior episode is defined as a context-specific, goal-directed pattern of behavior that unfolds over time until one of three conditions is met:

1. the goal organizing the episode is accomplished, or accomplished "well enough" (sometimes called "satisficing");
2. the person's attention is preempted by some internal or external event and another goal takes precedence (at least temporarily); or
3. the goal is evaluated as unattainable, at least for the time being (Pervin, 1983; Simon, 1967).

For example, a textbook-reading episode initiated by a college student in her dorm room may continue until: (a) she has finished reading the required material; (b) she is distracted by hunger, a fun-loving roommate, or some other compelling event; or (c) she decides she is unable to complete the assignment, at least for now (e.g., because she doesn't understand the material or is too tired to keep her eyes open).

The goal of the episode (i.e., the person's cognitive representation of what they would like to achieve) provides direction for that episode and triggers an organized pattern of cognitive, emotional, biological, and perceptual-motor activity that, in coordination with the opportunities and constraints in the environment, is designed to attain the goal. Thus **goals and contexts are the anchors that organize and provide coherence to the activities within a behavior episode.** These activities or *behavior patterns* are often varied and complex because many behavior episodes involve the simultaneous pursuit of multiple goals in somewhat unpredictable environments. Indeed, it is impossible to understand most human activities without understanding the goals and contexts that organize them (Schutz, 1991).

Because a person is always doing something (i.e., behavior episodes are always occurring), behavior episodes are like stories on a television news show that is on 24 hours a day, every day. One episode follows another, each one coherent in its own right. Some episodes are long; some are short; some are funny; some are sad; some are meaningful; and some are forgettable. Some episodes build upon one another to tell a larger story (i.e., a news program's coverage of a war or a baseball pennant race); other episodes are isolated, one-of-a-kind events that have little to do with the rest of life's activities (i.e., coverage of a freak accident or special human interest story). Occasionally there are dramatic life events that receive a great deal of attention for a period of time (such as special news coverage of some major event), but most behavior episodes, like most news stories, are pretty mundane, even repetitive. On the other hand, it is always possible to "preempt" such episodes when something important does happen (analogous to a news bulletin).

Three different types of behavior episodes can be distinguished. In an *instrumental episode*, the person is actively engaged in some motor or communicative activity ("output") designed to influence their environment in some way and is actively seeking feedback information ("input") from the environment about the results of that activity. In an *observational episode*, the person is actively seeking relevant informational "input" from the environment about someone else's instrumental activity. There is no "output" to speak of because the person is not trying to influence the environment. In a *thinking episode*, both the output and input processes associated with instrumental activity are inhibited, and no effort is made either to influence or watch others influence the environment. The purpose of a thinking episode is, rather, to experience, enjoy, or try to improve the organization of some information in a person's repertoire or to construct or rehearse a plan for future action from such information.

Activities such as reading, mental rehearsal, and dreaming illustrate such episodes.

All else being equal, instrumental episodes provide the most salient kind of experience. For example, learning by doing generally has more impact than observational or "book" learning. Similarly, personal participation in an event is generally more compelling than simply seeing or thinking about that event. However, because different kinds of episodes tend to focus one's attention on different component processes (e.g., sensory-perceptual processes in observational episodes versus cognitive processes in thinking episodes versus transactional processes in instrumental episodes). Different kinds of episodes may be particularly useful for different purposes. For example, observational episodes provide a particularly efficient means of facilitating social learning outcomes (Bandura, 1986). Overall, though, the most memorable experiences will generally be those that involve a combination of all three kinds of behavior episodes. For instance, a three-episode science lesson in which students first read about the results of an experiment, then observe the teacher demonstrating the experiment, and then conduct the experiment themselves will probably yield deeper and more transferable learning than would repeating the same kind of episode three times (e.g., observing three different demonstrations). Similarly, in trying to teach a child not to engage in some hurtful behavior, a combination of providing negative consequences for the behavior, having the child observe other people receiving negative consequences, and explaining why the action is hurtful may have more impact than many repetitions of a single kind of learning experience.

Behavior episodes are often organized in nested hierarchies in which the *goal* of one episode is the *means* for attaining some broader goal (Powers, 1989). For example, a golfing episode guided by the goal of winning a match can be broken down into 18 subepisodes, each representing one hole of play. The subgoal of earning a good score on each hole is the means by which the larger goal can be attained. One could also take these smaller episodes and break them down into subepisodes representing each time a shot is played. Playing a good shot is simultaneously the goal of each of these subepisodes and the means by which a good score on each hole can be attained. Similar examples can easily be generated for other complex activities such as writing a book, planning a vacation, raising a child, or getting a college degree. For example, the goal of passing a calculus exam is a means for achieving the goal of earning credit for a calculus course, which is a means for accumulating the credits needed to earn a college degree. Thus the hierarchical organization of behavior episodes is a ubiquitous phenomenon. It is also a very important concept in Motivational Systems Theory because several different techniques for enhancing motivation capitalize on this property of behavioral organization (e.g., Bandura & Schunk, 1981; Barden & Ford, 1990, 1991; Harackiewicz & Sansone, 1991; Locke & Latham, 1984, 1990a; Schunk, 1991b).

The Concept of Behavior Episode Schema/Schemata

Behavior episodes are temporary phenomena that come and go like stories on a news program, but with one notable exception—it is impossible to rerun a behavior episode. And yet people do guide their behavior in new episodes by using experiences from past episodes. That is possible because people can remember past episodes and combine them with memories of similar episodes. Thus behavior episodes provide the raw materials from which people can construct a complex repertoire of enduring behavior patterns. The concept of *behavior episode schema/schemata* (BES) is used in the LSF to represent the product of this behavioral self-construction process. A BES is an integrated internal representation of a particular kind of behavior episode experience or, more commonly, a set of similar behavior episode experiences (including episodes that have only been imagined or observed). "Similarity" is in the eye of the beholder, but it is primarily a function of the degree to which different behavior episodes involve the pursuit of similar goals in similar contexts (recall that goals and contexts are the anchors that organize behavior episodes).

A BES represents the functioning of the whole person-in-context because that is what is involved in any given behavior episode. The BES concept is therefore similar to concepts such as motor schema (e.g., Schmidt, 1975), perceptual schema (e.g., Arbib, 1989), cognitive schema (e.g., Neisser, 1976), or self-schema (e.g., Markus, Cross, & Wurf, 1990), and contributes to the historically prominent stream of theory and research that has featured the schema concept in various forms (e.g., Piaget, 1954). The idea of a behavior episode schema is somewhat broader than its predecessors, however, in that it represents an integrated "package" of thoughts, feelings, perceptions, actions, biological processes, and relevant contexts. Some parts of a BES are accessible to consciousness and some are not. Moreover, the parts that are consciously accessible may vary across BES.

Functionally, a BES provides guidance—sometimes very specific guidance, sometimes more general guidance—about what one should pay attention to and how one should think, feel, and act in a specific behavior episode. In this sense it is analogous to Neisser's (1976, 1985) concept of anticipatory schema. The quality of this guidance can vary tremendously, however (Arbib & Hesse, 1986). The organization of a BES is therefore a primary factor in determining the effectiveness of a behavior pattern. For example, a well-trained soldier—that is, a soldier who has constructed a highly organized repertoire of soldier BES—will know precisely what to do when given an order to accomplish some military objective under a particular set of circumstances. A football coach or chess player who has carefully studied his opponent will know just what play to call or move to make in a given situation. A student who has extensive experience with the format and content of standardized tests will be able to call upon a large and reliable repertoire of test-taking BES when faced with an important exam. A physician or counselor specializing in a particular type of problem will be able to proceed with great efficiency and confidence when a patient or client presents a familiar symptom pattern.

Conversely, if the best available BES for a given situation is weak or disorganized, the person's activity is likely to be erratic, tentative, or inappropriate for that situation. For example, a company experiment with self-managed teams may yield disappointing results if the affected employees lack training or experience in cooperative self-management. A statistics instructor with a well-developed repertoire of procedural routines may have difficulty understanding the haphazard solution attempts of a statistical novice. A father with little experience in providing emotional comfort and support may respond insensitively to episodes of distress among members of his family. A teenager who has recently learned to drive may display poor judgment or react slowly to a situation that a more experienced driver could handle easily and automatically.

Just as with the behavior episodes from which they are constructed, **BES are anchored by goals and contexts**. Consequently, even though each person has many BES available in their repertoire, only those BES that include goal and context characteristics similar to those of the current behavior episode will be potentiated and available for use in organizing that new episode. Arbib and Hesse (1986) also emphasize this point in discussing their related concept of schema:

We must specify the goal of the actor and the environmental situation . . . to be able to specify the action appropriate within a particular schema. The execution of the action brings with it certain expectations as to consequent changes in the environment; and the match or mismatch that results will determine the ensuing course of action. (p. 68)

Understanding the anchoring role of goals and contexts in behavior episodes and BES can help explain a diversity of behavior patterns that may seem ineffective or inappropriate to an observer, but that are actually quite sensible and productive given what the person is trying to accomplish. For example, a politician may engage in unethical practices that are potentially damaging to his political career if the payoff is sufficiently large and he believes that such practices are standard procedure for people in his position. A normally responsive parent may respond harshly and abruptly to a misbehaving child if the transgression is unusually severe (e.g., running out into the street), or if her primary concern at that time is the completion of some urgent task. A student who is perfectly capable of answering a teacher's questions may avoid doing so if he believes that his peers disapprove of academic effort or accomplishment, and he cares more about the approval of his peers than the approval of his teacher.

The principle that behavior patterns are organized around goals and contexts can also help account for the commonplace finding that people often do not use the capabilities they have learned in one situation in other seemingly relevant situations. For example, educators and psychotherapists have found that transfer of training (i.e., application of a learned skill to new situations) is unlikely to occur unless one explicitly attempts to promote such transfer (Goldstein & Kanfer, 1979). Child development researchers have also been misled by the pervasive belief that skilled performances should be highly consistent across situations. Because the initial BES that young children construct tend to be goal-, behavior-, and context-specific, researchers often mistakenly infer that a child lacks some capability on the basis of evidence that he or she failed to display that capability on a particular experimental task. Yet in many cases it may simply be that the experimental task is sufficiently different from the kinds of episodes normally experienced by the child that it does not activate the child's relevant BES (Borke, 1971; Demetriou & Efklides, 1981; M. Ford, 1979; Maratsos, 1973; McDevitt & Ford, 1987; Menig-Peterson, 1975).

As the preceding examples illustrate, the anchoring of BES to goals and contexts, while facilitating the process of constructing clear and specific guides to behavior, can constrain the process of transferring useful BES components to other relevant BES. To overcome this limitation, humans have developed the capability of constructing cognitive representations of BES components and component relationships, typically called *concepts* (or constructs) and *propositions* (or rules or theories), respectively. Concepts and propositions are powerful tools in learning and communication because they are much less constrained by the contexts, goals, and activities involved in the BES from which they were constructed. This property of *functional autonomy* allows them to be integrated into other BES and combined with other concepts and propositions with relative ease. This not only facilitates behavioral self-construction within the individual, it also plays a key role in the cultural transmission of knowledge. That is because it is much easier to construct shared meanings from abstracted BES components, which tend to be relatively simple and general, than from whole BES units, which tend to be complex and somewhat idiosyncratic.

On the other hand, it is important to understand that concepts and propositions, by themselves, lack personal significance precisely because they have been divorced from particular goals, contexts, and activities. **It is only when concepts and propositions are embedded back into a personalized and contextually anchored BES that they become infused with personal meaning and utility.** This is the "missing link" in much of education—information is taught in the form of abstract concepts and propositions to facilitate communication and generalization, but is too often left unconnected to the real-world contexts and purposes for which it can be used. Having students use concepts and propositions in personally meaningful behavior episodes helps bring their meaning to life.

For example, in teaching courses organized around the Living Systems Framework, I have discovered that students can achieve a deeper understanding of the framework and its utility if they have an opportunity to apply the LSF to their own interests and experiences—as illustrated by a natural childbirth instructor describing techniques for facilitating a smooth labor and delivery, a day care provider discussing the problem of biting behavior in two-year-olds, an elementary school teacher describing how she is helping her colleagues update their approach to mathematics instruction, a campaign manager revealing his successful strategies for winning a statewide election, and a young woman describing how she helped a suicidal friend cope with her troubled past. Pedagogical techniques such as the use of classroom demonstrations and laboratory exercises also illustrate how observational and instrumental episodes can be used to imbue abstractions with meaning.

Once a BES has been constructed, it can be elaborated or combined with other BES and BES components. Over time this can yield a very powerful BES encompassing a diverse repertoire of optional behavior patterns organized around a related set of goals and contexts. By combining a number of such BES together, a qualitatively superior kind of expertise called *generative flexibility* can emerge. This ability to generate effective options for achieving a particular set of goals quickly and flexibly under challenging conditions is characteristic of exceptionally resourceful people such as experienced politicians, clever lawyers, imaginative chefs, elusive NFL quarterbacks, expert video game players, and highly skilled auto mechanics. Generative flexibility does not guarantee success (as illustrated by Wile E. Coyote of Road Runner cartoon fame), but it can prove to be a crucial element in success when circumstances are variable and unpredictable.

BES can also be elaborated by linking them together in sequential fashion to produce a "script." A script serves as a template for a stereotyped sequence of events (Abelson, 1981), as illustrated by the performance of a musician in an orchestra, a politician giving a speech, or a gymnast executing a routine. Well-rehearsed scripts (sometimes also called habits) can greatly facilitate the execution of precise, efficient behavior patterns; however they tend to be lacking in generative flexibility. In fact the essential value of "automated" scripts or habits is to eliminate such variability! Scripts are therefore most effective in contexts that require close conformity to a set of rules or conventions (e.g., behaving properly in school or church) and in repetitive situations where efficiency is highly valued (e.g., driving to work, shopping for groceries, putting the kids to bed).

The Concept of Personality

The field of personality psychology seeks to distinguish itself from other domains by its focus on enduring patterns of functioning at the person level of analysis. Unfortunately, traditional methods of representing such patterns (e.g., traits, dispositions, attitudes) have been of limited utility because they have failed to deal adequately with the context specificity and functional variability characterizing most behavior patterns (Mischel, 1968). Personality theorists have successfully addressed this problem by identifying cognitive and social-cognitive processes that are variable in content but that nevertheless may play a major role in organizing an individual's functioning (e.g., goal orientations, beliefs about personal agency, self-regulatory skills, coping strategies, etc.). This approach, however, has left many wondering what happened to the "person" in personality. The BES concept resolves these dilemmas by providing a way of representing both the consistency and variability in the functioning of the whole person-in-context. Specifically, **personality is defined in the LSF as the person's repertoire of stable, recurring BES.** By defining personality in these terms, one can account for cases in which there is a high degree of situational consistency and temporal stability (e.g., people who have highly generalized "habits" or "scripts"; people who live in highly structured contexts regulated by strict norms), as well as cases in which there is a great deal of situational and temporal variability (e.g., people involved in an unusually diverse range of activities and social groups; people with addictive or multiple personality disorders).

One strategy that can be used to describe an individual's repertoire of stable, recurring BES is to focus on the BES units as a whole and how they are organized. For example, Markus' concept of "self-schemas" (Markus & Nurius, 1986), Schlenker's notion of "desired identities" (Schlenker & Weigold, 1989), and Cantor's conception of "life tasks" (Cantor & Fleeson, 1991; Cantor & Langston, 1989) are all designed to represent broad, goal-directed patterns of activity or potential activity. Alternatively, one can focus on BES components that pervade the person's overall repertoire of BES (e.g., the emotional or thought patterns of a very shy person). This is the basic strategy of most cognitively based personality theories; however, such theories are limited in how effectively they can apply this strategy because they generally lack a broader conception of unitary functioning in which to anchor their major constructs. Indeed, this is currently the major barrier to progress in the field of personality psychology. Without some way of representing how the component processes of the person function as a unit, personality researchers cannot put their "person variables" together to make a person. For example, Mischel's cognitive social learning theory (Mischel, 1973) and Bandura's social cognitive theory (Bandura, 1986) offer a rich menu of person variables, but no clear set of propositions specifying how these variables operate in an organized fashion to represent the person-as-a-whole.

The LSF resolves these problems by providing a comprehensive "map" of all of the components of unitary functioning. This model of system components is described next. In Chapter 3 the components of this model that are used to represent the concept of motivation are identified and defined in greater detail. In addition, this conceptualization of motivation is anchored to the concepts of *achievement* and *competence*, which are used in Motivational Systems Theory to represent the effective functioning of the whole person-in-context system.

The Components of Unitary Functioning

Structural Components

The term *structure* is often used in the human sciences to refer to the functional organization of a living system (e.g., social structure, cognitive structure, personality structure). Unfortunately, such labeling makes it difficult to avoid attributing "thinglike" properties such as rigidity and permanence to phenomena that are intrinsically variable and dynamic. Consequently, organized functional units are called *patterns* rather than structures in the LSF. The term *structure* is restricted to organized physical units (i.e., body structures).

All body structures are composed of organized combinations of cells, each of which is itself a complexly organized living system. Indeed, the biological self-construction processes involved in producing the approximately 75 trillion cells that comprise the adult human body provide a dramatic illustration of the differences between an adaptive control system and a living system. Starting from the same basic cell, many different kinds of specialized cells evolve during embryological development to produce the complexly organized skeletal and organ systems of the person, all of which are organized in amazingly intricate ways to support unitary biological and behavioral functioning.

Overview of Functional Components

The physical structure and organization of living systems makes possible four basic sets of functions. These can be summarized as follows.

1. *Biological Functions*: (a) Life-sustaining biological processes—growth, maintenance, operation, and repair of the biological structure; energy production; maintenance of biological steady states (e.g., body temperature, blood pressure, concentration of minerals and hormones, etc.) and (b) Providing a biological foundation for psychological and behavioral functioning.

2. *Transactional Functions*: (a) Exchange of materials essential for biological functioning (i.e., ingestive and eliminative actions); (b) Information collection (i.e., sensory-perceptual actions); (c) Body movement (i.e., motoric actions); and (d) Information transmission (i.e., communicative actions).

3. *Governing (Cognitive) Functions*: (a) System organization and coordination—Directive function (i.e., personal goals); Regulatory function (i.e., evaluative thoughts); Planning and Control function (i.e., problem-solving thoughts); and (b) Information processing and Memory functions.

4. *Arousal Functions*: (a) Management of energy production, distribution, and use—Attention and consciousness arousal (i.e., energizing of cognitive functions); Activity arousal (i.e., energizing of transactional functions); and Emotional arousal (i.e., energizing and regulating attention and activity arousal patterns in contexts involving prototypical adaptive problems and opportunities).

Figure 2.1 provides a pictorial overview of the component functions of the person-in-context and how they are organized to produce unitary functioning. This figure summarizes the most significant details of the framework in an easily interpretable form. One problem with trying to portray a complex, dynamic system in a static, two-dimensional space, however, is that it is difficult to represent the simultaneous patterning of mutually influential processes. Consequently, the reader should be careful not to interpret the sequencing of boxes and arrows in Figure 2.1 to mean that processes are occurring one-at-a-time in a predictable, linear fashion. In most behavior episodes a person's functioning is guided by a BES that activates a *pattern* of activity involving the continuous functioning of all of the components of the person. This way of understanding the dynamics of human functioning is analogous to the idea in cognitive psychology and artificial intelligence of highly distributed cooperative computation in which networks of specialized subsystems operating in parallel are organized in such a way that they are able to function both autonomously and as a unit (Arbib, 1989; Arbib & Hesse, 1986; Rumelhart & McClelland, 1986). In such an arrangement

34

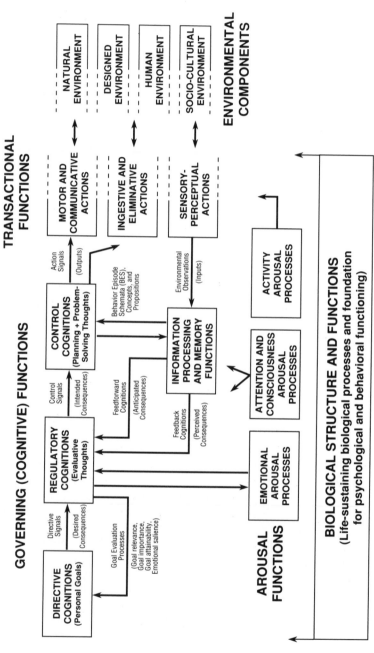

Figure 2.1. Component Functions of the Person-in-Context.

there is some sequencing of processes, but influences tend to be multiple and reciprocal rather than simple and unidirectional. It is our limited capacity to attend to more than a single influence at a time that produces the impression of simple linear causality.

Biological Functions

Biological functioning is comprised of two different kinds of components, each of which serves a fundamental but different purpose. Some components undergird the *material/energy-based operations* that are responsible for the person's basic biological existence and healthy functioning. These include physiological systems responsible for respiration, digestion, blood circulation, waste elimination, energy production, cell repair and replacement, protection against infection and disease, and many other life-sustaining processes. Other components undergird the person's *information-based psychological and behavioral operations* (i.e., nervous system processes, including brain functions). These components enable a person to represent their behavior episode experiences internally, and to construct BES from this information that can later be reconstructed for use in guiding future activity. This capability enables humans to adapt quickly to a wide range of circumstances (including novel, unfamiliar circumstances), and thereby transcend the limitations of evolutionary built-in adaptive potentials (Ford & Lerner, 1992).

Transactional Functions

Because an individual's actions are the only component functions that are directly observable by other people (i.e., they capture the attention of observers), they are often assumed to be the central organizing force in behavior patterns—the component being "served" by the thoughts, feelings, and biological processes of the person. Actions, however, are more accurately understood to be the *servants* supporting the person's biological, information processing, and self-construction activities. In control system terms, what is being "controlled for" in a particular behavior episode is the material-energy and informational *consequences* of action, not the actions themselves (Powers, 1989). In other words, action patterns are constructed as a more or less flexible means of producing desired consequences (Kuhl & Beckmann, 1985). One implication of this fundamental principle is that behavior patterns characterized by a great deal of action variability may actually be quite consistent with regard to the desired consequences of those actions (i.e., the current goals of the system). Failure to appreciate the principle that behavior patterns involve variable patterns of activity anchored by goals and contexts has resulted in considerable confusion and misdirected effort in the psychological literature, as illustrated by the extensive and heated debate in the personality literature regarding the issue of whether human behavior patterns tend to manifest consistency or specificity across situations.

Ingestive and Eliminative Actions. Ingestive actions (e.g., eating and breathing) are the primary means by which the person takes in materials essential for biological growth and functioning. Eliminative actions (e.g., sweating, urination, respiration) are the primary means for moving unnecessary and potentially dangerous materials out of the body. These actions have particularly important consequences for the person's arousal functions, which are heavily dependent on energy availability and the balance of important materials in the body. For example, improper water intake and poor nutrition can greatly constrain the ability of a student or worker to draw upon and efficiently use energy resources during the ebb and flow of his or her daily activities. Ingestive and eliminative actions can also disrupt a person's ability to think clearly and efficiently, as illustrated by the effects of drug and alcohol use.

Sensory-Perceptual Actions. The function of sensory-perceptual actions is to collect accurate information about the environment, the person's relationship to the environment, and the internal states of the person. Sensory-perceptual processes are analogous to ingestive actions, except that in this case *informational* rather than material forms are being brought into the person (i.e., "food for thought"). Just as people are selective in what they eat, they are also quite selective in what they attend to and perceive. Indeed, if they were not, they would be overwhelmed by the immense amount of information available in their surroundings. Selective perception is guided by selective attention, which is, in turn, guided by the person's goals and contexts—the anchors of the person's current behavior episode. In other words, people can only perceive information if they pay attention to it (i.e., if they are conscious of its existence), and they will only pay attention to it if it is relevant or potentially relevant to their personal goals, or if it is such a salient part of their context or their own functioning that it cannot be ignored (e.g., a disgusting smell, painful sensation, or unexpected loud noise).

Attention and perception are linked in another fundamentally important way. Not only is attention a prerequisite for perception, perceptibility is a prerequisite for attention. In other words, **a person cannot attend to something or be conscious of it unless it is in a perceptible form**—that is, something they can see, hear, smell, taste, touch, or feel. This highlights an important and often confused distinction between *perceptions* and *conceptions*, or thoughts. People are always conscious of what they perceive, but very often are not conscious of everything involved in their current thought processes. In fact, most cognitive processing occurs outside of awareness. Information surfaces in consciousness primarily on a "need to know" or "alarm" basis, similar to the way a chief executive seeks information about the functioning of a nation or large corporation.

The practical implications of this link between perception and cognition are enormous. Essentially, it is impossible to bring information into consciousness without first putting it into some perceptible form. Mental images commonly serve this purpose, but a more flexible tool for bringing thoughts into consciousness is language. Because words (and other symbols) can be seen or heard or touched, and yet do not have any intrinsic meaning, they can be attached to any idea that the user desires. Moreover, if a group of people can agree about what words to attach to particular ideas, they can communicate about abstract concepts that they would otherwise be unable to bring into consciousness. That is why language is such an important human capability, and why having a shared language is such an important factor in facilitating learning and cooperative group functioning (as many people involved in bilingual education have discovered).

Because it is difficult for people to focus their attention on more than one pattern of events at a time, perception (and conscious thought processing) often operate at a relatively slow pace when a behavior episode involves multiple or multifaceted event patterns. Like a television news anchor trying to integrate information from several different reporters in a variety of locations, the person must selectively attend first to one set of perceptions, then another, and so on until the "story" is adequately covered, all the while monitoring the overall situation (through peripheral attention) so that a "reporter" with "breaking news" can be put "on camera" (in focal attention) at any time. This is one key reason why it is so useful for people to retain information about familiar behavior episodes in BES form. If they already "know" (i.e., can anticipate) what information will be present in a particular behavior episode, they can proceed efficiently and effectively without having to spend much time perceiving that information or consciously thinking about it (Neisser, 1976).

Motoric Actions. Motoric actions enable people to manipulate and move around in their environments as one means of producing consequences of value to them. For example, an infant who has learned to walk can explore closets, cupboards, and cabinets that were previously beyond her "sphere of influence." A gymnast or pianist with refined motor skills may be able to accomplish feats that a very few humans have ever achieved. In contrast, a disabled person who is unable to manipulate objects with his hands must rely on other people to accomplish relatively simple actions such as getting dressed, taking a bath, preparing a meal, or operating a household appliance.

Motoric actions are most likely to produce their intended consequences when they are guided by a well-constructed and well-rehearsed BES that is a good match for the current context. Under such conditions action patterns can be "run off" with little conscious effort, much like executing a subroutine in a computer program or replaying a prerecorded performance. For example, when athletes say they were "zoning" or "playing in a zone," they usually mean they were able to perform with remarkable ease and efficiency without paying attention to the details of their performance. Indeed, paying too much attention to a well programmed BES may disrupt it and produce performance variability and errors, as when an athlete suffers "paralysis through analysis." On the other hand, even routine performances require careful coordination of "feedforward" information (what one expects to happen), feedback information (perceptions of what is actually happening), and semiautonomous action patterns. For example, a commuter driving along a familiar route may be able to drink a cup of coffee and listen to the radio while traveling to work, but he or she will still need to be vigilant for unexpected hazards and obstacles.

Communicative Actions. Whereas motoric actions provide a means of directly influencing the environment through physical processes, communicative actions provide a way of indirectly influencing the environment through information-based processes. This is accomplished by saying or doing something that causes the recipient of the communication to activate and use a BES that includes the information being conveyed. That BES may then influence the thoughts, feelings, and actions of the recipient of the communication.

In at least one respect communicative actions are more complex than other kinds of actions because a coding phase must occur between the process of conceptualizing a goal and constructing and executing the physical action on which the information is to be coded (e.g., speech, writing, hand or mouth movements, facial expressions). Moreover, the person or persons to whom the communication is directed must understand the code being used to represent the information (although they need not necessarily be able to communicate with that code themselves, as illustrated by the ability of young children to understand the meaning of many words before they can say or write those words). Consequently, successful communication requires knowledge of a socially shared symbol system as well as skill in performing the actions that convey that symbolic code.

The symbolic coding phase of communicative actions involves three component processes:

1. the selection of a BES to guide the process of organizing the information to be conveyed (i.e., the meaning of the message), called the semantic component;
2. the selection of the symbols (e.g., words) to be used to convey the information, called the lexical component; and
3. the organization of symbolic patterns to convey the meaning intended, called the syntactic component, according to rules called the grammar of that particular coding system. The coding of the information on an action pattern (e.g., speech) is called the articulatory expression.

Sequences of communicative actions are not totally preplanned; rather, they are constructed and modified as they are being executed, with guidance from a combination of feedforward and feedback information (just like sequences of motoric actions). For example, a child trying to excuse his irresponsible behavior may change the details of his story as he progresses if his parents appear to be unimpressed by what he is saying. Similarly, participants in a business meeting may alter the tone and content of their comments as the meeting progresses based on their perceptions of what is occurring (feedback) and their expectations about where the meeting is going (feedforward).

There is yet another element contributing to the complexity of communicative transactions. As researchers in linguistics, communication, and artificial intelligence have demonstrated, understanding the intended meaning of a communicative action depends on more than just knowing the symbol system being used to convey that information. It also involves shared knowledge about the context of the communication and the ways in which meanings can change as a function of the communicative context. In other words, effective communication requires the activation of a BES in the recipient of the communication that provides the appropriate frame of reference for interpreting the meaning of the communication. If the BES activated by the communication enables one to decode the message but not to anchor that understanding to relevant context information, miscommunication and communicative failures will result. For example, a child might not understand the intended meaning of a humorous or facetious comment even though he understands the words being spoken. Similarly, a local politician who is unfamiliar with the communicative habits and traditions of the various ethnic groups represented in her district may find it difficult to communicate with those constituencies in a clear and convincing manner.

Governing (Cognitive) Functions

During the past two decades cognition has become the central phenomenon of interest for many subfields of psychology, and justifiably so—the most distinctive characteristic of human functioning is the capability for using thought to construct informational forms that can represent the past, present, and possible futures (including ideas that transcend past, present, and future existence), and then using those self-constructed representations to guide current behavior in complex, variable environments. Progress in understanding the role of cognitive processing in human functioning and development has been greatly impeded, however, by the pervasive tendency of scholars and practitioners to view cognition in an undifferentiated way. Moreover, the historical tradition of treating cognition, emotion, and "conation" (i.e., motivation) as separate topics for psychological study has led to the rather bizarre situation in which, at the same time that cognition is becoming an increasingly dominant focus of motivational theorizing, cognition and motivation continue to be regarded as separate fields of study (e.g., Kuhl & Beckman, 1985; Pervin, 1989; Sorrentino & Higgins, 1986). As the LSF makes clear, **motivation represents the integrated patterning of a subset of cognitive and arousal processes, not a qualitatively distinct kind of psychological phenomenon.** The persistent view that motivation is fundamentally different from both cognition and emotion is probably as responsible for the enduring identity crisis in the field of motivation (described in Chapter 1) as any other single factor.

Information Processing and Memory Functions. Humans have developed several behavioral (information-based) self-construction capabilities that enable them to go beyond the information available through perceptual processes and thereby transcend the limitations of time and space. The construction of *behavior episode schemata* from related sets of behavior episode experiences is one such capability. Another is *concept formation*, which involves the self-construction of generalized informational forms from a set of related perceptions or conceptions (including conceptions that have no relationship to perceptions), each of which was initially a component of some BES. These two capabilities are roughly analogous to Arbib's (1989) distinction between episodic learning and skill learning.

Concept formation can occur at virtually any level of abstraction. First-order imagistic concepts are symbolic prototypes of perceived objects and events that are constructed in perceptual codes and therefore can enter into consciousness (e.g., I can think about Chopin's Polonaise in A Major). Second-order abstract concepts are symbolic prototypes of a related set of imagistic concepts (e.g., I can think about "Chopin music"). Abstract concepts are useful because they can represent a great deal of information all in one component. However, for that very reason, they are usually harder to define in precise terms than imagistic concepts. Higher-order abstract concepts can also be constructed from related set of lower-order abstract concepts (e.g., I can think about classical music, or simply music in general). However, because abstract concepts are represented in nonperceptual codes, they cannot enter into consciousness unless they are put into some perceptible form. For example, although I cannot mentally listen to a generalized piece of classical music, I can become conscious of indicators of the abstract idea by "hearing" some specific examples of classical music in my head, or by putting that concept into concrete words ("classical music"). Through such processes I am able to think consciously about the variety of phenomena that fits under that label, as well as discuss the idea of classical music with someone else who labels that concept in a similar way (e.g., "Do you like classical music?").

Imagine how limited this discussion would be, however, if people did not have some shared way of representing their abstract ideas in conscious form. Consequently, *linguistic representations* are the primary tools that people use to make abstract concepts accessible to themselves and others for conscious thought and the communication of ideas. A language is a set of arbitrary but agreed upon perceptible symbols (and rules for organizing those symbols) that can be used as surrogates for abstract concepts (or anything else the user desires). Thus as Arbib and Hesse (1986) explain, "language is . . . a way of giving us an imperfect representation of the schema assemblages each of us has" (p. 15), not only for the purpose of communication, but also as a "way in which a person alone can make his thoughts available to consciousness, to work on them, play with them, (or) to create new thoughts from them" (p. 64). In other words, by "attaching" linguistic images (whether visual, auditory, or tactile) to cognitive abstractions, it becomes possible to manipulate those inherently unconscious abstractions by manipulating their perceptible linguistic "handles." Like a handle on a closed drawer, the words or symbols representing an abstract concept (i.e., the contents of the closed drawer) can be used to "pull the concept out" where the person—and other people— can get a good "look" at it and, if desired, try to manipulate its contents. In this way, people can quickly learn about the ideas that others have created and build upon them. That is a primary mechanism by which education, socialization, and cultural advancement occurs. It is also the foundation of verbal psychotherapy, a process in which clients' verbalizations are used to try to bring troublesome imagistic and abstract representations into operation during a therapy episode, where they can be more easily explored and potentially modified.

Self-constructed concepts, propositions, and behavior episode schemata would be relatively useless if they could not be remembered and reactivated in future behavior episodes. The capability for organizing information patterns in such a way that they can be reconstructed under appropriate future conditions is called *memory*. The information that actually triggers the process of reconstructing a BES or BES component can be almost anything in the person's current stream of consciousness, but goal and context information—the anchors for all BES—are the primary triggers. That is why the use of analogies, advance organizers, clear instructions, and other techniques for "framing" the task at hand are so useful. Recall also appears to be heavily influenced by emotional arousal components, which can amplify or dampen the vividness and detail of informational constructions and organize the content of what is recalled (Hoffman, 1986). Because people remember information *patterns* rather than isolated bits of information, much of what is remembered does not and need not enter into consciousness. This is particularly true for well-learned BES, which can function mostly automatically without focal awareness.

Directive Cognitions (Personal Goals). Goals are thoughts about desired (or undesired) states or outcomes that one would like to achieve (or avoid). Such thoughts may represent a diversity of potential future consequences—for example, experiencing a pleasurable feeling, acquiring a useful piece of information, engaging in a meaningful social interaction, successfully mastering a task, or virtually anything else that a person can imagine. Goals may also vary in content from moment to moment as the person focuses on different details of what needs to be accomplished, and they can evolve into more complex forms as they are applied in different contexts and coordinated with other goals in the person's repertoire of BES. Consequently, goals are dynamic and versatile sources of information about the desired consequences of person-in-context functioning.

Although goals specify the general "conditions of satisfaction" for system activity (Searle, 1981), they do not specify the content or form of the activity itself. Goals may become "fused" (Ford & Lerner, 1992) with other cognitive functions that do specify such content, as emphasized by Tubbs and Ekeberg (1991); nevertheless, once a goal has been activated, there is often little need to attend to it more than periodically, if at all (recall that most cognitive processing occurs outside of awareness). Consequently, observers often fail to appreciate the importance of goals in human functioning and development, focusing instead on the more visible components that are responsible for carrying out the "orders" specified by the directive process (e.g., problem-solving and action components). Yet, by supplying the organizing "themes" or frames of reference for a person's activity, goals provide the basis for the selective operation of all other system components, thereby serving as anchors for all behavior episodes and behavior episode schemata.

The fact that humans are capable of imagining possible and desirable futures does not guarantee that they will do so in effective ways (i.e., in ways that will help produce those futures). As elaborated in subsequent chapters of this book, goals are sometimes formulated in ways that detract from their potential ability to direct and organize an effective pattern of activity. For example, people often spend too much time thinking about large, distal goals that are daunting and demotivating (e.g., getting a Ph.D.) rather than concentrating on smaller, short-term goals that can enhance their motivation and provide a clear guide to action (e.g., doing well on a particular exam) (Bandura, 1986; Harackiewicz & Sansone, 1991; Schunk, 1991b). Often the goals directing an individual's activities are too vague or transient to sustain an effective course of action (Locke & Latham, 1984,

1990a, 1990b). Sometimes the goals that capture a person's attention
are virtually impossible to achieve (e.g., dating an unavailable partner, becoming a famous athlete, getting rich quick). Such goals may
be a source of satisfaction in thinking episodes, but they may also
lead to a great deal of unproductive activity and significant emotional and self-evaluative damage. Sometimes the person's commitment to a goal may not be strong enough to keep the goal active in
the face of obstacles and temptations (Kuhl & Beckmann, 1985). At
other times the commitment may be so powerful that other important goals are neglected (Pervin, 1991). People in hostile or capricious
circumstances may have difficulty maintaining or formulating any
personally meaningful goals, resulting in profound feelings of depression and hopelessness and a strong tendency to withdraw from
daily life activities (Abramson, Metalsky, & Alloy, 1989). Conversely,
people who are heavily invested in many different kinds of goals
may have difficulty resolving goal conflicts, resulting in frequent
episodes of anxiety and frustration.

Despite these common kinds of problems, it is the ability to formu-
late and pursue self-constructed personal goals that enables people
to experience a sense of purpose and meaning in their lives. Indeed,
the coherence, strength, and productivity that can emerge from the
effective balancing and alignment of meaningful short-term and long-
term goals is a wondrous thing to behold, not only at the level of the
individual (Csikszentmihalyi, 1990; Winell, 1987), but in social systems
as well (e.g., self-managed work groups, school-community partner-
ships, successful football teams, effective political action committees).

Regulatory Cognitions (Evaluative Thoughts). Regulation is a complex concept that is often used to refer to the entire range of processes
involved in a control system (e.g., goal setting, planning, monitoring
of feedback, etc.). In the LSF the concept of regulation refers to a
narrower range of phenomena, namely, processes that evaluate system functioning and facilitate "staying on track" toward a goal in the
context of distractions, obstacles, and other perturbations. In humans, biological functioning is regulated primarily by biochemical
processes that help maintain a diversity of biological variables within
preset boundaries, a process called homeostasis by Cannon (1939).
Behavioral functioning is regulated through a combination of affective and cognitive processes.

Cognitive regulation involves several different kinds of evaluative
thoughts designed to help people make wise and effective choices
among alternative goals, plans, and actions. Regulation therefore

does not include the processes involved in defining *what* is to be accomplished (directive function) or *how* these goals are to be accomplished (control function); rather, it is an evaluative decision-making function that is responsible for determining *whether* a pattern of activity should be initiated, altered, or terminated given a variety of relevant factors: the person's goals, values, capabilities, emotions, and bodily states; and the facilitating and constraining conditions currently operating in the environment.

Specifically, cognitive regulation involves the following four kinds of evaluative thoughts:

1. *Goal Evaluations*—evaluations of the goals being pursued (or contemplated) in terms of their continuing or potential relevance and priority ("Is there something interesting/desirable/compelling in this situation?" "Is this goal still important to me?" "Which goal is more important to me right now?").

2. *Means Evaluations*—evaluations of the means being used (or contemplated) to pursue a goal in terms of their conformity with social, moral, legal, and procedural rules, norms, and standards ("Am I doing the right thing?" "Is this the best way to proceed?" "Would that be a good thing to do?").

3. *Performance Evaluations*—evaluations of goal-related progress against relevant (and often implicit) standards for goal attainment ("Have I accomplished my goal? How far do I have to go?").

4. *Personal Agency Beliefs*—anticipatory evaluations (i.e., expectancies) about whether one can achieve a goal, including: (a) *Capability Beliefs*—expectancies about whether one has the personal capabilities needed for effective action ("Am I capable of achieving this goal? Do I have what it takes to accomplish this goal?"); and (b) *Context Beliefs*—expectancies about whether the environment will be responsive to one's goal-attainment efforts ("Does my context afford the *opportunity* to try to achieve my goal? Will my context make it easier or harder for me to attain my goal? Can I trust this context to support me or cooperate with me in what I try to do, or will I be ignored/rejected/attacked?").

Thus the regulatory process coordinates feedback and feedforward information from several different sources in an effort to determine how things are going and how they are likely to go in the future. The results of these evaluations are used to maintain or initiate activity designed to improve the match between desired and perceived (or anticipated) consequences, or to inhibit activity if the preferred state is evaluated as unattainable due to constraints imposed by personal inefficacy, environmental unresponsiveness, or a combination of personal and contextual limitations.

Another important feature of cognitive regulation is that it is the primary mechanism by which emotions are aroused. Although emotional patterns can also be activated through biochemical mechanisms and direct perception (Hoffman, 1986), most emotional responses are triggered by cognitive evaluations of perceived, remembered, or imagined persons, objects, or events that are relevant to the person's current or potential future activity. Once triggered, however, emotions can influence cognitive evaluations in dynamic patterns of mutual influence (e.g., in motivational patterns involving interdependencies between goals, emotions, and personal agency beliefs) (Hoffman, 1986; Pervin, 1991; Pintrich & Garcia, 1991).

As should now be clear, the regulatory process is a focal point for much of the activity involved in the unfolding of a behavior episode. It takes "orders" from the directive process regarding the system states and outcomes to be evaluated; places boundary conditions on the control process through the application of a wide variety of rules, norms, and standards; triggers emotional processes to help facilitate effective action; monitors the results of system activity; and tries to evaluate the potential consequences of future activity. It also helps determine what orders it gets by regulating goal selection and prioritization.

Given the central role that evaluative thoughts play in a person's functioning, it is perhaps not surprising that self-regulation has become such an important theme in contemporary psychological theorizing. "Underregulation" can result in careless, impulsive, immoral, inappropriate, inadvisable, or inefficient behavior, whereas "overregulation" can produce inflexible, perfectionistic, conflicted, repressed, or even paralyzed behavior patterns. On the other hand, it is important to understand that regulatory functioning is often highly automatized and trouble-free. That is because in most behavior episodes, the BES guiding the person's activity will already include the results of many of the evaluations that need to be conducted to ensure "smooth sailing." Problems are most likely to arise under conditions of unfamiliarity or uncertainty (e.g., "What's going on here?" "What am I supposed to do?" "What's going to happen to me?"), or when there are conflicts among different goals, values, or rules either within the person or between the person and the environment (e.g., "I want to, but should I?" "I should, but do I have to?" "Is this really important?" "Is this good enough?").

Control Cognitions (Planning and Problem-Solving Thoughts). Control thought processes are responsible for determining how one can achieve the goals specified by the directive process within the constraints imposed by the regulatory process, given the biological and contextual facilitating and constraining conditions that are currently operative as perceived and evaluated by the individual. This is the process most closely associated with the concept of *intelligence*, although an alternative view in which intelligence is defined in terms of goal attainment is better able to represent the unitary nature of goal-directed activity and the diversity of processes that contribute to effective functioning (M. Ford, 1986, 1992). Plans and problem solutions are constructed by integrating perceptual information with the information represented in the person's knowledge base and behavioral repertoire (i.e., in their repertoire of BES and BES components). This involves three basic steps, which may occur sequentially or simultaneously depending on the extent to which they are already integrated in BES form (e.g., in the form of a script):

1. *Problem Formulation.* The basic task of the control process is to figure out how to transform the current system state into a preferred state (or how to prevent the current state from being transformed into a less preferred state). Thus the first step in control processing is to try to represent these alternative states as clearly as possible. This requires a precise specification of the desired state from the directive process as well as a clear representation of the current state from perceptions and evaluations of the context. This process of defining the "anchors" for the current behavior episode enables the person to reconstruct a BES that can guide the person's functioning within that episode. Indeed, clear goals and accurate feedback are often the key to successful problem solving (Bandura & Cervone, 1983; Earley, Northcraft, Lee, & Lituchy, 1990; Locke & Latham, 1984, 1990a, 1990b). In contrast, if the goals to be accomplished are vague or ambiguous ("I don't know what I want"; "I don't know what I'm supposed to do"), or if the current state is poorly understood ("I don't know what's going on"; "I don't know where I stand"), problem-solving efforts are likely to be misguided and ineffectual.

Compared to novices, expert problem solvers typically have a much more elaborate repertoire of solution-relevant BES to draw upon (i.e., they have more experience with the problem domain);

however, they also tend to spend more time considering whether they have selected the best available BES for defining the problem. In other words, they invest more time in the initial step of "framing the problem" or "mapping the problem space." This can greatly increase the efficiency of problem solving by enabling the person to avoid unproductive activity and costly mistakes (e.g., repeatedly using an incorrect algorithm, creating an expensive line of unwanted products, habitually "turning off" potential friends).

2. Problem Solving and Plan Formulation. The BES activated in the problem formulation phase provides a set of "design criteria" for the control process and makes certain kinds of information from the person's knowledge base and current context more salient and available for further cognitive processing. Such information may include the emotional components of the activated BES, thereby enabling emotions to influence problem-solving and planning activity. Control processing then proceeds through the selection and integration of informational components from perception and memory.

In familiar, routine situations, effective solutions and plans are likely to be readily available components of the BES being used to frame the problem. In such circumstances the most efficient thing to do is to proceed directly to the action phase of the behavior episode— sophisticated reasoning and problem-solving processes are unnecessary and may even be counterproductive. In situations that are less familiar or predictable, however, it is often useful to consider alternative solutions and plans before choosing one and acting on it. This involves several interrelated skills: (a) generating alternative approaches to a problem (either by considering optional components of the activated BES or by framing the problem with different BES), called *alternative thinking* by Spivack, Platt, and Shure (1976); (b) intentionally delaying action until these alternatives can be evaluated in thinking behavior episodes, a skill sometimes called *consequential thinking* (Spivack, Platt, & Shure, 1976); and then (c) formulating a detailed solution or plan for at least one of these alternatives, commonly called *means-ends thinking* (Spivack, Platt, & Shure, 1976). Because children and immature people often manifest generalized deficits in these areas, a variety of educational and clinical interventions have been devised that focus on the development of these skills (e.g., Camp & Bash, 1980; Shure & Spivack, 1978, 1980; Urbain & Kendall, 1980).

3. Solution/Plan Execution. After formulating and selecting a solution or plan from among the alternatives considered (if any), the control process proceeds to organize a behavior pattern aimed at producing the intended consequences. Under conditions of uncertainty, problem-solving and planning thoughts will continue to guide activity through an iterative process in which feedback and feedforward information are used to revise currently operating solutions and plans and, if necessary, to generate new solutions and plans. The ability to generate effective options quickly and flexibly under challenging conditions, defined earlier as *generative flexibility*, is an especially important skill in situations requiring mental agility, quick reactions, and resourceful action (e.g., classroom teaching, fast-paced business meetings, a job interview, a basketball game).

Arousal Functions

All functioning must be fueled by some sort of energy. Energy production is accomplished by biological processes, but additional capabilities are needed to manage the process of selectively activating these energy production capabilities and selectively distributing energy resources to organize and execute ongoing behavior patterns. Three basic kinds of arousal subsystems evolved to handle these tasks: (a) *Attention and consciousness arousal* processes energize the information-based functions of perception and cognition; (b) *activity arousal* processes energize material-energy transactions (e.g., biological and motor activity); and (c) *emotional arousal* processes serve to regulate (i.e., amplify or attenuate) attention and activity arousal patterns in the context of prototypical adaptive problems and opportunities.

Attention and Consciousness Arousal. The phenomena of attention and consciousness are manifestations of a person's ability to selectively energize particular aspects of perceptual, cognitive, and action functioning to facilitate coordinated unitary functioning. The general subjective experience of *consciousness* indicates that the nervous system is sufficiently activated to carry out its information collection and self-construction functions, as opposed to a state of being unconscious (e.g., in a coma or deep sleep). Given a sufficient level of consciousness, attentional processes can then selectively activate relevant neural circuits to facilitate the highly targeted and efficient use of information in organized patterns of thought, perception, and action.

Attention is a prerequisite for perception and learning—one cannot introduce new information into the system without first attending to that information. Once an informational component has been perceived or learned, however, it can (potentially) be reconstructed and used to facilitate system coordination without the person having to invest further attentional energy into that process. Indeed, as noted earlier, most cognitive processing occurs outside awareness. As Arbib and Hesse (1986) state: "consciousness, if active at all, is active as a monitor rather than as a director of action" (p. 77). The information that does enter into consciousness is just the tip of the BES "iceberg" that is currently being used to maintain organized and effective behavior patterns.

Activity Arousal. Humans have the ability to adjust the amount of energy being produced and utilized in appropriate body locations based on their interpretation of the degree of effort required in a particular situation. When one considers the variability in the amount of energy needed to fuel different kinds of activities (e.g., sunbathing versus fighting the waves to save a drowning child; sleeping versus concentrating furiously on an exam question), and the fine-tuning that is required to ensure that energy resources (e.g., blood supplies) are distributed in precisely the right amounts to precisely the right body parts, it is clear that this is a rather remarkable capability. It requires a continuous flow of accurate feedback and feedforward information at both the cognitive and biochemical levels of functioning.

Because activity arousal is such a highly automated process, it can usually proceed with little or no investment of attentional energy. However, some aspects of the biological processes involved in activity arousal can enter into consciousness, where they can facilitate the effective regulation of activity. In addition to location-specific information such as heart rate or fullness of the bladder, five subjectively recognizable feeling states called *nonemotional affects* can be identified:

1. relaxed-contented-drowsy
2. alert-restless-energetic
3. sluggish-tired-fatigued
4. physical discomfort
5. pain

Emotional Arousal. A variety of emotion patterns evolved to help humans mobilize and deploy their energy resources rapidly and efficiently in circumstances involving pervasive, prototypical adaptive tasks (Izard, 1991; Plutchik, 1980). Some emotions serve to regulate the initiation, continuation, repetition, or termination of behavior episodes (e.g., excitement and satisfaction). Others help people regulate their efforts to cope with potentially disrupting or damaging circumstances that arise during an episode (e.g., fear and anger). Interpersonal bonding is regulated by several social emotions (e.g., loneliness and love); other social emotions regulate conformity to or cooperation with social expectations and patterns of social organization (e.g., resentment and guilt). Each of the 14 basic emotional patterns identified in the LSF is described in greater detail in Chapter 5 of this book.

Emotions are organized functional patterns consisting of three components: (a) *affective* (neural-psychological) (i.e., the general subjective feeling part of the emotion); (b) *physiological* (i.e., a supporting pattern of biological processing), and (c) *transactional* (i.e., a pattern of motor and communicative actions designed to facilitate goal attainment). Thus emotions help people deal with varying circumstances by providing evaluative information about the person's interactions with the environment (affective regulatory function) and by supporting and facilitating action designed to produce desired consequences (energizing function). Emotions provide a very potent mechanism for regulating behavior because affective experience has an immediacy to it that is hard to ignore (Frijda, 1988; Pervin, 1991; Zajonc, 1980, 1984), and because emotional states are sufficiently flexible and generic that they can be linked to almost any conceivable context (Hoffman, 1986). On the other hand, because emotions are usually triggered by evaluative thoughts, they can be heavily influenced by cognitive regulatory processes. A variety of educational and therapeutic strategies in counseling and clinical psychology capitalize on this connection (e.g., Beck, 1976; Beck & Freeman, 1990; Ellis, 1982; Ford & Urban, 1963).

Environmental Components

Because humans are open systems whose existence, functioning, and development depend on material-energy and information exchanges with relevant contexts, the environment is always an integral part of their functioning. Even when a person is merely engaging in a thinking episode, that episode will be guided by a BES anchored, in part, by context information. Moreover, material-energy exchanges with the environment (e.g., breathing) continue to occur in all kinds of episodes. That is why the unit of analysis in the LSF is not the person, but, rather, the person-in-context.

The properties of environments are highly variable, and so they may be classified in many different ways depending on one's purposes. For example, a child might think in terms of physical behavior settings, a politician in terms of constituencies, a television executive in terms of markets and demographics, and a meteorologist in terms of dynamic weather units. At a more general level, environments can be subdivided into four basic categories:

1. *Natural environment.* Included in this environmental component are products of nature such as plants, animals, land, rocks, oxygen, gravity, air pressure, rain, clouds, planets, etc. These phenomena are of primary interest to disciplines and professions such as agriculture, botany, zoology, ecology, geology, mining, meteorology, astronomy, and physics.

2. *Designed environment.* This environmental component includes physical and symbolic environmental forms created by humans rather than by "Mother Nature"—for example, houses, cars, roads, books, computers, television programs, tools, machines, musical instruments, toys, furniture, clothing, prepared foods, medicines, and works of art. These phenomena are of primary concern to fields such as the engineering professions, various manufacturing enterprises, chemists, communication and transportation industries, and the arts.

3. *Human environment.* This component refers to the people in an individual's environment—family members, friends, neighbors, teachers, coworkers, teammates, mail carriers, politicians, sports figures, television personalities, and so forth. Illustrative disciplines and professions that focus on this aspect of the environment include child and adolescent development, social psychology, family sociology, communication, family counseling, group therapy, human resources, and leadership training.

4. *Sociocultural environment.* This environmental component includes social and cultural institutions and traditions that influence behavior and development in ways that are largely independent of the individuals participating in those institutions (e.g., languages, religions, social and cultural norms, laws, governments, schools, industries, hospitals, etc.). Illustrative disciplines and professions concerned primarily with this aspect of the environment include history, philosophy, law, religion, sociology, cultural anthropology, political science, economics, business administration, policy planning, community development, and health and human services administration.

The education profession is unique in that it is centrally concerned with all four environmental components just described.

Summary

Because the person always functions as a unit in a context, human motivation must be defined and understood in terms of that larger person-in-context unit. Some of the processes that influence an individual's functioning will be motivational in character, but non-motivational psychological processes as well as biological and contextual facilitating and constraining conditionalities will also play a major role in shaping behavior patterns. D. Ford (1987) has concisely summarized this living systems perspective:

> Behavior patterns differ because people vary in what they want, how they decide to go about producing the desired consequences, what they actually do, the ways they anticipate and evaluate their progress, the emotions that are aroused in relationship to the activity, the conditions of their biological functioning, the kinds of environments in which they interact, and the attributes of those environments upon which they selectively focus their transactions. If any of those functions are ignored, a person's behavior cannot be fully understood. (p. 145)

Processes and Principles of Change and Development in Living Systems

Variability and change are ubiquitous phenomena in humans. Consequently, they are a major focus of the LSF, which attempts to represent all aspects of being human within a single framework. Recently the LSF concepts representing processes and principles of development have been merged with Richard Lerner's metatheoretical framework in *Developmental Systems Theory: An Intergrative Approach* (Ford & Lerner, 1992). Much of the remainder of this chapter relies on that source of information, in addition to the original LSF theoretical volume (D. Ford, 1987).

A major premise of Motivational Systems Theory is that motivation plays a major role in producing variability and change in behavior patterns, and thus in shaping the course of human development.

It is therefore important to have a precise understanding of the meaning of different change-related concepts.

Basic Concepts Representing Variability and Change

When a person is behaving in a familiar, routine manner, doing the "same old things" or engaging in "business as usual," there is consistency but also some variability in the stream of thoughts, feelings, and actions that occur. This kind of variability is called *steady state variability*. It reflects the unfolding of events in a behavior episode according to predictable parameters defined by an established BES, producing variability within stable boundaries. Because this kind of variability is an intrinsic part of all behavior patterns, and does not alter those patterns, it is distinguished from change and regarded instead as a property of functional organization in living systems.

When a person does something differently, tries something new, or has a new or unusual experience, this reflects a change in their functioning. If the change is reversible and transitory, it is called a *temporary change*. Examples of temporary changes include getting a 24-hour flu bug, going on a short-lived diet, being named "student of the week," abstaining from alcohol or smoking for a few days, and cramming for a test but then forgetting it all later. In contrast, if the change is irreversible or persists over time, it is called an *enduring change*. Examples of enduring changes include learning the meaning of an unfamiliar word, developing a bad habit, initiating a new friendship, taking up a new sport, losing one's eyesight, and being promoted at work.

Elaborative and Decremental Change. Enduring changes can be either elaborative or decremental. An *elaborative change* increases the magnitude, diversity, or complexity of some aspect of the person's structure or functioning (e.g., physical attributes, motor skills, knowledge base, self-concept, behavioral opportunities, interpersonal relationships, etc.). A *decremental change* reduces the magnitude, diversity, or complexity of some aspect of the person's structure or functioning (e.g., physical strength, short-term memory capacity, life goals, behavioral activities, social networks, etc.). Typically, elaborative changes are evaluated positively (as connoted by terms such as growth, maturation, and learning), and decremental changes are evaluated negatively (as implied by terms such as disability, regression, and forgetting). Elaborative changes can, however, sometimes lead to negative outcomes (e.g., becoming overcommitted with new responsibilities, learning how to cheat, developing a malignant tumor); and decremental changes can sometimes lead to positive outcomes (e.g., reducing drug and alcohol use, withdrawing from a time-consuming relationship, forgetting a bad habit).

Capability and Performance Change. Behaviorally, elaborative and decremental changes can be manifested in two ways. *Capability change* represents an enduring change in the person's behavioral repertoire. Such change can involve: (a) the creation of a new BES or BES component (e.g., learning a new concept, acquiring a new motor skill); (b) the reorganization of existing elements into new patterns (e.g., figuring out how to play a new kind of game, learning how to program a VCR); or (c) the loss of some capability (e.g., forgetting how to solve a particular kind of problem, suffering deterioration in some refined motor skill as a result of disuse). *Performance change* reflects the enduring use of some existing BES or BES component in a different context (e.g., applying a standard rule or technique to a new kind of problem, using parenting strategies learned as a child to deal with one's own children). Performance change is the goal of efforts to promote transfer of training in education, counseling, and psychotherapy. Such change is facilitated when: (a) the BES or BES component has been used recently and frequently (*response availability*), (b) the BES or BES component has already been used in a diversity of situations (*stimulus variability*), and (c) the similarity between the current context and the contexts represented in the BES or BES component to be "transferred" is maximized (*identical elements*) (Goldstein & Kanfer, 1979). Understanding the principles and processes involved in performance change can greatly facilitate efforts to help people maximize the use of capabilities they already possess.

Incremental and Transformational Change. Elaborative and decremental change can occur through two somewhat different processes. When organized steady state patterns are altered in such a way that the original pattern remains, but in a somewhat different form, that is called *incremental change* or change by "evolution." The concepts of differentiation and elaboration in developmental biology, classical and operant conditioning in learning theory, and accommodation in Piagetian theory all represent incremental change processes. When organized steady state patterns are altered in such a way that the original pattern is supplanted or superseded by a significantly different steady state pattern, that is called *transformational change* or change by "revolution." This kind of change process is illustrated by concepts such as metamorphosis, insight, identity crisis, emotional decompensation, personality reorganization, and religious conversion. The terms *quantitative change* and *qualitative change* are also sometimes used to refer to incremental and transformational change processes, respectively, although they are not precisely synonymous (e.g., a qualitative change can result from either a transformational change or a succession of incremental changes).

In addition, the concept of *stability maintenance* is used in the LSF to refer to change-resisting processes that function to maintain or restore existing steady state patterns in the face of discrepancies and disturbances. This is similar to the biological concept of homeostasis (Cannon, 1939), Piaget's (1954) concept of assimilation, Festinger's (1957) concept of dissonance reduction, and Freud's (1923/1947) concept of defense mechanisms. In many behavior episodes involving adaptation to new circumstances or new information, incremental or transformational change processes "kick in" only after stability maintenance processes have failed to resolve the "problem" at hand. The human capacity for information-based self-construction, however, enables people to *create* as well as respond to problems and discrepancies, as emphasized by Deci (1975; Deci & Ryan, 1985) in his descriptions of how people are motivated to "seek and conquer" challenges that fit their interests and capabilities, and by Bandura (1986, 1989) in his discussions of "proactive control" through intentional discrepancy production. Thus humans appear to be designed to seek a balance between stability and variability or change.

The Concept of Development. Ford and Lerner (1992) define the concept of *development* with unusual precision, limiting it to relatively enduring elaborative change. Specifically, they define development as follows:

> Individual human development involves incremental and transformational processes that, through a flow of interactions among current characteristics of the person and his or her current contexts, produces a succession of relatively enduring changes that elaborate or increase the diversity of the person's structural and functional characteristics and the patterns of their environmental interactions while maintaining coherent organization and structural-functional unity of the person as a whole. (p. 49)

They also make the fundamental point that no change can manifest itself in future behavior episodes unless it creates enduring change in the person's biological structures or processes or in some BES or BES component that can be reactivated when the need arises. For example, evidence of temporary performance change in students as a result of instruction does not ensure that any learning has occurred in the sense of developmental change.

As illustrated by concepts such as socialization, learning, skill development, and personality change, a central objective of many of the problem domains highlighted in this book (e.g., education, child and adolescent development, counseling and health psychology) is the intentional creation of enduring, elaborative change (i.e., development). These domains are therefore particularly well suited to the task of illustrating how motivational patterns can provide a psychological foundation for the development of human competence.

Stability Maintaining Processes

People have two basic mechanisms for maintaining existing steady state patterns of organization: *negative feedback* processes and anticipatory *feedforward* processes. Negative feedback processes serve to eliminate discrepancies resulting from the disruption of an existing steady state pattern, or to prevent such discrepancies from exceeding certain limits. This is accomplished by comparing the disrupted state with the preferred state, and then using the results of this evaluation to activate or inhibit whatever control and transactional activity is needed to maintain organized functioning (e.g., steering a misdirected car back onto the road, cleaning up a messy room, taking action to keep a budget deficit or a classroom of active children from getting out of hand).

Stability maintaining feedforward processes function in a similar way except that the disrupted state that is being compared to the preferred state is a cognitive representation of an anticipated or feared outcome, not a perception of a current state. Thus the discrepancy that the person is trying to reduce is one that does not exist— yet. This is an incredibly powerful and important capability, as it enables people to make *proactive* decisions based on predictions about the future (e.g., driving defensively, saving money for the future, anticipating problems that may disrupt a social or business relationship). Because feedforward processes are heavily involved in the dynamics of motivational functioning, considerable emphasis is placed on the concept of feedforward in this book.

Incremental Change Processes

Humans have four basic mechanisms for modifying their organized patterns of functioning to take advantage of ongoing opportunities and to adapt to changing conditions and circumstances: *performance change* resulting from stability maintaining processes, *goal setting, positive feedback*, and *biological maturation*.

When negative feedback and feedforward processes fail to remove or prevent the occurrence of some disruption in steady state functioning, people will often begin searching—sometimes systematically, sometimes desperately—for something in their behavioral repertoire that can effectively deal with the disruption. If they find a BES or BES component that works in that situation, that "connection" is "reinforced" (i.e., it is evaluated positively by cognitive and/or affective regulatory processes and incorporated into the BES currently operating in that behavior episode). This learned connection may then be applied in similar contexts in the future. This process of *selection by consequences*, which is the focus of the operant conditioning paradigm (Skinner, 1984), is one way that performance change can occur.

Selection by consequences is also an important feature of incremental change produced by goal setting. As noted earlier, a goal is a cognitive representation of some desired (or undesired) state or outcome. When this imagined future state is different than the current steady state, activity is required to reduce that *self-constructed* discrepancy. Such activity produces consequences. When these consequences are either: (a) the intended consequences (discrepancy removal), (b) consequences that indicate that progress is being made toward the intended consequences (discrepancy reduction), or (c) unintended consequences that are nevertheless valued by the person (e.g., consequences that activate and satisfy some other personal goal), the activity that produced those consequences is incorporated into the BES guiding the person's functioning in that behavior episode (i.e., the activity is learned). Such consequences are called *positive reinforcing consequences*. Consequences that *increase* the discrepancy between the current and desired state are called *negative reinforcing consequences*.

An important implication of this way of understanding reinforcement-based learning is that, by understanding the nature of a person's current and potential future goals, one can predict, often with considerable accuracy, what kinds of experiences will be reinforcing (i.e., it is not necessary to rely solely on after-the-fact observations, as operant learning theory requires). It also becomes possible to a certain extent to "engineer" contexts in terms of the goals they afford so that "what works" in a particular context is what the "engineer" wants a person to learn. One must be cautious, however—a behavioral engineering approach that fails to respect the goals that a person brings to the situation may produce unintended developmental consequences, as illustrated by the extensive literature documenting the potentially negative impact of external rewards on intrinsic motivation (e.g., Deci, 1975; Deci & Ryan, 1985; Lepper, 1981; Lepper & Greene, 1978). Nevertheless, such engineering also has the potential to produce a mutually satisfying alignment of goals between cooperating social partners, especially if each partner understands and appreciates the goals of the other person. That is a primary rationale for MST's strong emphasis on goal alignment as a key process in motivating humans.

Goal setting can also produce incremental change by motivating activity that produces *capability change*. In fact, this is an almost inevitable outcome when the desired consequences cannot be produced using one's current behavioral repertoire. For example, a student who wants to earn a good grade on a test will need to learn the material covered on that test to accomplish her goal. A teenager who wants to become a basketball star will need to spend considerable time and energy elaborating his repertoire of basketball skills. A manager who wants to head up a new division will need to learn how that division operates and develop relationships with a new set of employees and customers.

A third mechanism through which incremental change can occur is *positive feedback*. Informally this term is often used to mean "feedback information that is valued positively by the individual;" however, this usage is unrelated to the technical meaning of positive feedback. Just like the word "negative" in "negative feedback," the term "positive" in "positive feedback" refers not to the valence of the information, but, rather, to what happens to the perceived or imagined discrepancy as a consequence of the person's activity. Positive feedback processes serve to *increase* rather than *decrease* the size of the discrepancy between the original steady state and the current state. As Ford and Lerner (1992) explain, "when a process and its consequences are continually amplified by the effects of their own activity, the essence of positive feedback is present" (p. 188).

Whereas negative feedback serves to maintain functional organization, positive feedback is a source of *disorganization*. Indeed, small initial deviations can be amplified into rather profound changes through positive feedback processes, as illustrated by the progression of a neurotic compulsion, the growth of a romantic relationship, the escalation of an interpersonal disagreement, and the expansion of an activity or interest. That is why positive feedback processes are usually coupled with negative feedback processes that limit the rate or amount of discrepancy that is allowed. When positive feedback processes are permitted to operate unchecked, the results are usually quite dramatic—the functional organization of the system is either transformed into a qualitatively different, more stable pattern of organization (i.e., transformational change is precipitated), or that organization is destroyed. For example, disturbing emotions or thought patterns that are unconstrained by stability maintaining processes can result in mental illness, the destruction of valued relationships, and even suicide. Similarly, individuals or businesses that pursue profit or power in an unconstrained manner are very likely to create the conditions for their own premature demise.

Except for a few major transformational periods, *biological maturation* occurs in an incremental fashion through a combination of biochemically based positive and negative feedback processes that permit controlled elaboration of biological structures and functions. Positive feedback processes enable physical growth and development to occur, and negative feedback processes help ensure that such changes do not get out of control (as occurs in cancerous growth). Biological maturation facilitates and constrains behavioral development in many direct and indirect ways by altering the biological structures and functions underlying the person's cognitive, arousal, and transactional functional capabilities.

Transformational Change Processes

When people experience a discrepancy between their existing steady state patterns of organization and current, anticipated, or desired future consequences, they will normally attempt to deal with that discrepancy through a combination of stability maintaining and incremental change processes. When the discrepancy is very large, however (i.e., when the person is "far from equilibrium" [Prigogine & Stengers, 1984]), these processes may not be powerful enough to restore stable organization. Under such conditions, it may be impossible to maintain unitary functioning without some major reorganization or transformation of the functional pattern or patterns that have been disorganized. There are two basic mechanisms that can produce this "far from equilibrium" condition and subsequent discontinuities in development: *unconstrained positive feedback* processes and *traumatic, confusing, emotionally intense, or otherwise highly disorganizing life events.*

Biological transformations resulting from instability-producing positive feedback processes include puberty, menopause, and other periods of developmental discontinuity. For example, in describing the nature of fetal development, Prigogine and Stengers (1984) note that "when we observe development on film, we 'see' jumps corresponding to radical reorganizations followed by periods of more 'pacific' quantitative growth" (p. 171). Biological transformations (both good and bad) can also be precipitated by disorganizing life events such as severe accidents (e.g., those causing blindness or brain damage), crash diets, or the ingestion of powerful drugs (e.g., dangerous narcotics or life-saving medicines).

The psychological experience of being far from equilibrium is usually accompanied or signalled by subjective feelings of intense distress or excitement (e.g., "I'm so confused;" "I'm so angry/excited I feel like I'm going to explode;" "I'm so happy/unhappy I feel like I'm going to die"). Psychological transformations resulting from unchecked positive feedback processes are surprisingly common, as illustrated by troubled people undergoing an "identity crisis," "midlife crisis," or "personality change"; highly motivated people who have been inspired by a creative idea or new life purpose; "converted" people who have significantly altered their life-style to conform to some philosophy, religion, or cultural practice; and infatuated or sexually absorbed people who begin behaving in a bizarre or dangerous manner because they are unable to stop thinking about their love object. Psychological transformations resulting from intense or traumatic life events can be seen in people trying to deal with victimization, war, or the death of a loved one; people trying to deal with major life transitions such as divorce, retirement, or becoming a parent; and people trying to make sense out of information that shatters strongly held beliefs about a familiar person or experience.

Unlike incremental change produced by selection by consequences, transformational change is very difficult to "engineer" in a systematic manner, either by an outside change agent or the person being changed. That is because systems that are far from equilibrium are very unstable and can be dramatically affected by minor perturbations that normally would be handled rather easily by stability maintaining processes. For instance, an annoyance that would seem trivial to an outside observer might be "the straw that broke the camel's back" for a highly stressed mother or an emotionally distraught husband. The ultimate outcome of these triggering events is also not easily anticipated. For example, a family therapist who intentionally highlights a conflicted relationship pattern in an effort to facilitate transformational change may trigger a healing process or bring the family even closer to disintegration. Thus transformational change is somewhat unpredictable both in terms of the events that precipitate change and the outcomes they precipitate.

On the other hand, the increased variability and uncertainty associated with significant disorganization can also make people more open to change, especially if they have accepted the fact that the old familiar patterns are no longer functional. For example, an alcoholic who recognizes that he has a serious problem (i.e., is far from equilibrium) will be easier to treat than one who persists in using stability maintaining denial processes. This openness to change is called *disorganization flexibility*. Under such conditions it may be possible to facilitate significant change that the disorganized person would not even consider under more stable conditions. That is a primary rationale for crisis interventions; however, any intervention in which the individual being treated is in a state of disorganization must be implemented with great care because even minor disturbances can trigger a major reorganization under such conditions (e.g., a misinterpreted remark by a suicide hotline worker could lead to fatal consequences).

One way to help reduce the distress that a disorganized person experiences and to facilitate successful reorganization is through *transition protection* processes. For example, social support can help crime victims manage their feelings of anger and helplessness and give families coping with the loss of a loved one an important source of strength and guidance (Casarez-Levison, 1991; McCan, Sakheim, & Abrahamson, 1988). The work of a scholar struggling to piece together a disorganized pattern of ideas and evidence can be greatly facilitated if large blocks of uninterrupted time can be scheduled. People who are suffering from emotional stress or a debilitating illness may be able to recover much more quickly if they can withdraw from the everyday demands of work and family life for a while.

The transition from disorganization to reorganization is also influenced by the *stability-instability ratio*—that is, the range of life goals and contexts that are disorganized relative to those that remain in a stable steady state. When disorganization is limited to a relatively narrow range of goals and contexts, the probability of successful reorganization is increased. For example, a child who can stay in the same home and go to the same school while her parents are getting a divorce is likely to fare better than a child who has all of these aspects of her life disrupted. Similarly, a manager planning to reorganize the staffing and operation of his business can minimize resistance and stress by emphasizing the stable patterns that remain, or by phasing in change so that disorganization occurs in only a few components at a time.

Next Steps

The theoretical framework summarized in this chapter, combined with the historical background and statement of objectives outlined in the first chapter, provides the reader with the foundation of information needed to understand: (a) the basic concepts and principles that comprise Motivational Systems Theory, (b) the ways in which these ideas are linked to other theories of motivation, and (c) the significance of motivational patterns in human functioning and development. Chapters 3, 4, and 5 describe the basic concepts and principles of Motivational Systems Theory, including more detailed information about the three component processes that constitute the substance of motivational patterns. Chapter 6 summarizes how 31 other theories and categories of theories of motivation can be organized around the basic MST concepts of personal goals, personal agency beliefs, and emotional arousal processes. Chapter 7 offers a set of 17 general principles for motivating humans, along with several examples of how the basic concepts and principles of Motivational Systems Theory can be applied to real-world problems in child and adolescent development, education, business, and counseling and everyday living. Finally, Chapter 8 provides a concise summary of MST concepts and principles that can be used to help readers organize and review the information covered in this book.

Suggestions for Further Reading

Ford, D. H. (1987). *Humans as self-constructing living systems: A developmental perspective on behavior and personality.* Hillsdale, NJ: Lawrence Erlbaum.

Ford, M. E., & Ford, D. H. (Eds.) (1987). *Humans as self-constructing living systems: Putting the framework to work.* Hillsdale, NJ: Lawrence Erlbaum.

Ford, D. H., & Lerner, R. M. (1992). *Developmental systems theory: An integrative approach.* Newbury Park, CA: Sage.

CHAPTER THREE

Defining Motivation and Its Role in Effective Functioning

Whatever the mind can conceive and believe, it can achieve.
Napoleon Hill

Purpose of This Chapter

CHAPTER 2 SUMMARIZED the overall framework in which Motivational Systems Theory (MST) is anchored, thereby providing the reader with the conceptual foundation needed for understanding the ideas that comprise MST. The present chapter, which is designed to serve as a bridge between the concepts and principles of the Living Systems Framework and those that comprise MST, is divided into two parts. First, several concepts representing the effective functioning of the whole person-in-context are introduced. This provides the reader with a simple but powerful set of tools for linking motivational processes and patterns with other person and environment components and the person-in-context system as a whole. Second, criteria for distinguishing between motivational and nonmotivational processes are explicitly defined. This leads directly to a theoretically precise definition of motivation involving the integration of three sets of component processes and also establishes clear boundaries for excluding processes that contribute to effective functioning in ways that are not primarily motivational in character. The basic concepts and principles of Motivational Systems Theory are then described in Chapter 4 and 5, which focus on the content and functional characteristics of personal goals, personal agency beliefs, and emotional arousal processes, as well as the nature of their organization into motivational patterns.

Motivation and Effective Person-in-Context Functioning

The Concepts of Achievement and Competence

In Chapter 2 the concepts of *behavior episode* and *behavior episode schema* were introduced as a way of describing the functioning of the whole person-in-context unit. Behavior episodes represent coherent sequences of goal-directed activity that unfold over a bounded period of time. Behavior episode schemata (BES) are the learned patterns that are constructed from a set of similar behavior episode experiences.

Because behavior episodes and BES are anchored by goals and contexts, it makes sense to define *effective* person-in-context functioning primarily in terms of these anchors. Two concepts are used in Motivational Systems Theory to define effective functioning. At the situational (i.e., behavior episode) level of analysis, effective functioning is represented by the concept of *achievement*, which is defined as **the attainment of a personally or socially valued goal in a particular context.**

In other words, achievement is a concept representing the successful completion of a behavior episode (recall that behavior episodes may be terminated in three ways: (a) the goal anchoring the episode is achieved, (b) something else takes precedence, or (c) the goal is evaluated as unattainable). For example, one could achieve a state of relaxation, a feeling of accomplishment, an experience of unity, an understanding of a complex situation, a victory in a competition, a good grade on a test, a triumph of justice, a sense of belongingness, or any of a number of other desired outcomes. Evaluations of achievement therefore require more than an assessment of the objective "facts" in a particular set of circumstances—they also involve a subjective frame of reference that specifies (often implicitly) the criteria against which the facts are to be evaluated. Consequently, individuals and social groups may vary in their interpretations of their own and others' achievements either because (a) they disagree about what has been accomplished (e.g., they question the validity of an assessment procedure) or (b) they do not value the same outcomes.

At the personality (i.e., BES) level of analysis, effective functioning is represented by the concept of *competence*. Because evaluations of effectiveness at this level of analysis must take into account consequences for behavior episodes beyond the immediate episode, ethical and developmental boundary conditions are added to the anchoring criteria of goals and contexts. Competence is defined as: **the attainment of relevant goals in specified environments, using appropriate means and resulting in positive developmental outcomes.**

Thus, according to this definition, a person could *achieve* a great deal in some domain but not be regarded as particularly *competent* if desired outcomes are being achieved using methods that are immoral, illegal, highly inefficient, or otherwise "out-of-bounds" (e.g., a student who earns good grades by cheating or cramming for tests without learning the material), or if the attainment of these goals produces negative long-term consequences for the person (e.g., health problems, legal difficulties, or damage to valued social relationships).

Because these definitions of effective functioning lack specific content, it is easy to underestimate their utility for guiding evaluations of achievement and competence. Yet it is precisely because they explicitly define where value-laden content must be added that they are so useful. For example, many people implicitly restrict the definition of *achievement* to task goals or competitive goals attained in academic or occupational contexts, without recognizing that value judgments are involved in the process of specifying these goals and contexts (Maehr, 1974; Stein & Bailey, 1973). By requiring evaluators to make their values explicit, it is much easier to understand that in any given assessment some achievements count (i.e., those valued in a particular cultural context or by a particular individual or institution), and others do not (Langer & Park, 1990). This also makes it easier to discuss what achievements *should* count for a particular evaluative purpose and how such achievements should be prioritized.

In addition, the "skeletal" approach to defining effective person-in-context functioning helps promote a differentiated view of competence in which trait-like labels that imply generalized competence or incompetence are rejected in favor of descriptions anchored in particular contexts and value systems that specify what goals are "relevant," what means are "appropriate," and what developmental outcomes are "positive." The importance of adopting such a perspective is particularly evident in cases involving conflicting norms and value systems (Ogbu, 1981). Consider, for example, the following individuals:

1. A successful manager and caring mother who places her infant son in a corporate day care center for 10 hours each day so that she can avoid losing her seniority and opportunities for career advancement. (Is she prioritizing the "right" goals? Is extended day care an "acceptable" means of child care for an infant? What are the likely developmental outcomes for the mother and child? For example, would a decision to accept a lower standard of living be in the best long-term interests of the child?)

2. A college athlete who has gained fame and fortune for himself and his institution through hard work, great physical skills, and the careful use of steroids. (Is the "careful" use of an illegal but commonly used performance enhancement drug an acceptable means? To what extent do the short-term achievements justify the long-term health risks associated with steroid use?)

3. A prostitute with a high income, happy customers, and good working relationships with her employer and local authorities. (Is prostitution an acceptable means to financial success under these conditions? Does the answer depend on the context—for example, whether the business is in Ohio or Nevada? Are the developmental outcomes of this life-style inevitably negative?)

Examples such as these underline the importance of specifying the criteria for defining and assessing achievement and competence *before* trying to identify the processes underlying effective person-in-context functioning or trying to help people behave in a more effective manner. In some instances this may require the specification of alternative sets of criteria involving multiple or conflicting values. In any case, the *normative problem* of determining what criteria should be used to define and assess achievement or competence must be resolved before one can address the *empirical problem* of trying to explain observed patterns of effective or ineffective functioning, or the *developmental problem* of determining how to intervene to promote more effective functioning (Maehr, 1974).

With this principle firmly in mind, it is now possible to turn to the problem of identifying the motivational processes of the person and how they contribute to effective person-in-context functioning.

A Heuristic Scheme for Classifying the Processes Contributing to Effective Functioning

Whereas the LSF is designed to provide people with a precise and comprehensive "map" of system processes, the scheme described in this section is designed to give people a concise tool with which to begin their efforts to apply the LSF as well as a framework for keeping the person-in-context unit in mind when attention is being focused on the motivational processes of the person.

In any behavior episode, there are four major prerequisites for effective functioning:

1. The person must have the *motivation* needed to initiate and maintain activity until the goal directing the episode is attained.
2. The person must have the *skill* needed to construct and execute a pattern of activity that will produce the desired consequence. (This category includes all of the nonmotivational psychological and behavioral processes of the person.)
3. The person's *biological structure and functioning* must be able to support the operation of the motivation and skill components.
4. The person must have the cooperation of a *responsive environment* that will facilitate, or at least not excessively impede, progress toward the goal.

Thus at a broad level it is possible to describe the processes contributing to effective person-in-context functioning as follows:

$$\text{Achievement/Competence} = \frac{\text{Motivation} \times \text{Skill}}{\text{Biology}} \times \text{Responsive Environment}$$

In other words, effective functioning requires a motivated, skillful person whose biological and behavioral capabilities support relevant interactions with an environment that has the informational and material properties and resources needed to facilitate (or at least permit) goal attainment. If *any* of these components is missing or inadequate, achievements will be limited and competence development will be thwarted.

For example, a musically gifted child who has little interest in learning how to sing or play an instrument will probably never come close to achieving her potential in this domain of competence, even with expert instruction. Similarly, a socially and therapeutically supported client who is perfectly capable of changing a maladaptive behavior pattern will probably maintain that pattern if he is not sufficiently motivated to change.

Skill deficits can also prevent people from achieving their goals. For example, an eager football recruit who lacks the speed needed to perform at the college level will probably achieve little more than benchwarmer status, even with excellent coaching. A toddler who is being potty trained will achieve little success if she lacks the necessary motor control skills, even if she receives exemplary instruction and is a cooperative participant in such training.

Finally, unresponsive environments often cut off promising behavior episodes and developmental pathways. For example, a bright, motivated worker who must constantly deal with antiquated equipment or an uncooperative or incompetent boss will be able to accomplish little. An emotionally stable, socially competent child who is physically or sexually abused by a family member may suffer severe and lasting consequences.

The basic principle that **achievement and competence are the result of a motivated, skillful, and biologically capable person interacting with a responsive environment** summarizes in a concise way how motivational processes fit into the overall person-in-context system. It also provides interventionists with a simple way of framing their efforts to understand and alter dysfunctional behavior patterns and explaining those efforts to students, clients, or employees. For example, an AIDS prevention program that provides emotionally charged information about the deadly consequences of the disease and detailed training in "safe sex" practices can be characterized as an effort to facilitate the motivational and skill components contributing to good health outcomes in the context of a responsive educational environment. This same description could also be applied to a career counseling program that helps young people clarify their vocational interests and develop specific plans and strategies for pursuing those interests.

The consequences of failing to include one or more of these factors in analyses of human competence can be rather dramatic. For example, consistent with research on the fundamental attribution error (Nisbett & Ross, 1980), Schermerhorn (1986) found that supervisors were likely to attribute their own poor performance to an unsupportive environment, but tended to attribute poor performance by subordinates to a lack of effort or ability on the part of those employees. This common tendency to focus attention on one component of the problem rather than "getting the big picture" is a primary rationale underlying the development of the Living Systems Framework (D. Ford, 1987).

The potential utility of the MST formula for effective functioning is supported by the fact that other researchers and professionals have invented similar heuristic devices to guide their thinking about the processes contributing to achievement and competence development. For example, Krug (1989) used a comparable formula to organize his research on the qualities of effective school leaders:

$$\text{Achievement} = \text{S (Situational Factors)} \times \text{P (Personal Factors)} \times \text{M (Motivational Factors)}$$

Schermerhorn (1986) framed his work on managerial effectiveness using an analogous heuristic called the "individual performance equation":

$$\text{Performance} = \text{Ability} \times \text{Support} \times \text{Effort}$$

Pinder's (1984) text on work motivation begins with a summary of the "three basic determinants of business productivity": employee ability, employee motivation, and large-scale (context) factors. Similarly, McCombs' analyses of self-regulated learning and educational empowerment are framed in terms of three broad sets of influences: will, skill, and social support (McCombs, 1991b; McCombs & Marzano, 1990).

It is important to understand that the multiplication signs in the MST formula for effective functioning (and in subsequent formulas) do not represent formal mathematical statements about the relationships among component processes. Such statements are far too ambitious at this stage of theory development, as illustrated by a number of historically prominent attempts to develop such equations (e.g., Atkinson, 1957; Hull, 1943, 1951, 1952; Lewin, 1935, 1936, 1951; McClelland, Atkinson, Clark, & Lowell, 1953; Spence, 1956, 1958). Moreover, the precise way in which these components interact may vary dramatically in linear and nonlinear ways as a function of the current behavior episode and the BES repertoire the person brings to that episode. For example, the weight given to each component may vary in a highly dynamic and somewhat idiosyncratic fashion. Causal influences may also become "fused" (Ford & Lerner, 1992) in a way that defies assignment of a separate number to each component. Thus the MST formula for effective functioning is only intended to represent the general idea that system components interact in a way that requires consideration of both the independent and interdependent functioning of each component. Even with this limitation, however, this formula can function as a powerful and flexible tool for framing problems of human competence development.

Of course this simple heuristic device serves only as a starting point for a more detailed consideration of the processes that contribute to effective functioning. That more detailed analysis is conducted next for the motivation part of the formula.

Defining and Delimiting the Domain of Human Motivation

Criteria for Distinguishing Between Motivational and Nonmotivational Processes

As noted in Chapter 1, there is no clear consensus about how to define and delimit the field of motivation (Kleinginna & Kleinginna, 1981). A major goal of this book is to try to contribute to the building of such a consensus. Consequently, rather than simply asserting that some processes are motivational and others are not, the rationale underlying the MST resolution of this definitional task is explicitly described along with the resolution itself. This will enable readers who believe that motivation should be defined in some other way to pinpoint areas of disagreement, thereby inviting productive debate about real theoretical differences rather than superficial criticism based on seemingly arbitrary choices.

There are three recurring themes that can be abstracted from the psychological literature on motivation and used as criteria for distinguishing motivational processes from nonmotivational processes.

1. *Motivational processes are qualities of the person rather than properties of the context.* Although some historically prominent theories define motivation partly or primarily in terms of contextual processes (e.g., operant learning theory), there is considerable consensus in the contemporary literature that motivation resides within the person rather than in the context of the person (Pinder, 1984; Weiner, 1990). This distinction is not always explicitly stated or carefully maintained (as noted in Chapter 1), but there no longer seems to be much disagreement about this aspect of human motivation.

2. *Motivational processes are future-oriented rather than being focused on the past or present.* Motivation is an anticipatory and preparatory phenomenon (Cofer & Appley, 1964)—that is, motivational processes help people imagine or predict future events and consequences that are relevant and meaningful to them, thereby preparing

them to act or react in ways intended to produce desired futures and avoid undesired futures. Psychological processes that focus on past or current events and consequences are therefore regarded as falling under the rubric of skill-related processes rather than motivation.

3. *Motivational processes are evaluative rather than instrumental in character.* Motivational processes help people decide whether to try to maintain or restore an existing state or to strive for new or improved outcomes. They are not, however, directly involved in the task of changing the current state into a preferred state. In other words, motivational processes identify and "size up" problems and opportunities, but they are not responsible for solving those problems or turning those opportunities into reality. The biological, skill, and environmental components of the person-in-context system carry that burden.

Motivational Components of the Living Systems Framework

There are three component processes in the LSF that meet all of the criteria just described:

1. *Directive Cognitive Processes.* Goals are psychological processes that are anticipatory and evaluative in character—that is, they represent desired future states and outcomes and prepare the person to try to produce those desired futures. Goals also provide the regulatory process with criteria for evaluating the effectiveness of the person's activity. In addition, directive processes work in conjunction with *goal evaluations* conducted by the regulatory process to identify and prioritize goal options within and across behavior episodes.

The term *personal goal* is used to represent this motivational component to emphasize the fact that the goals directing an individual's activity are *always* within the person (although the single word "goal" is also used as a convenient abbreviation). Personal goals are often constructed from context information—for example, people will typically adopt many of the goals shared by other individuals or institutions in their context (especially if they have not been exposed to alternative possibilities), and are usually quite willing to commit themselves to task goals assigned by legitimate authority figures (Locke & Latham, 1990a, 1990b). Nevertheless, culturally defined goals and goals assigned by teachers and employers can only have a motivational impact if they are adopted, in some form, as *personal* goals. This is particularly obvious when people resist contextual pressures to behave in a certain way (e.g., when students choose to pursue goals other than those specified by their teacher, or when workers defy the mandates of their employer); however, the same principle holds even when people are blatantly manipulated by environmental contingencies or powerful social and political forces: people will *always* behave to try to attain consequences *they* value within the limitations of what they are able to imagine and what they believe the current context affords. As Ford and Lerner (1992) explain:

> A goal cannot truly be imposed on people. They must adopt it as a personal goal for it to perform a directive function. They often do so because it becomes a subgoal for some other personally valued goal, that is, it either helps them produce some other result they want or helps them avoid some other result they do not want. For example, prisoners of war often perform personally distasteful tasks to avoid possible death or some severe feared punishment. (pp. 181-182)

2. Personal Agency Beliefs. As explained in Chapter 2, these cognitions serve a regulatory feedforward function—that is, they are both anticipatory and evaluative in character (in contrast to feedback information, which is focused on past and current events). *Capability beliefs* are evaluative expectancies about whether one has the personal capabilities needed to attain the goal specified by the directive process; *context beliefs* are evaluative expectancies about whether the person's context will facilitate or support the person's goal-attainment efforts. Together they provide the person with the information needed to decide whether to initiate, maintain, amplify, or inhibit some pattern of goal-directed activity.

Although this motivational component could simply be labeled "capability and context beliefs," the term *personal agency beliefs* (or PABs) is used to emphasize that it is the *patterning* of these two processes that determines whether a person will activate or inhibit behavior. For example, as explained in the first section of Chapter 5, positive capability beliefs may lead to robust persistence, tenacious perseverance, antagonistic protest, or philosophical acceptance depending on their relationship to the person's context beliefs. The PAB concept can also be used to represent motivational expectancies that do not explicitly refer to either the person's capabilities or the environment's responsiveness, but instead focus generally on the attainability of the desired outcome. This is similar to the strategy used by Skinner, Chapman, and Baltes (1988) in identifying a separate concept they call "control beliefs," and by Weisz and Stipek (1982) in defining their concept of "perceived control." It is also characteristic of the way in which the concept of *expectancy* is defined and operationalized in expectancy-value theories of motivation (e.g., Atkinson, 1964; Feather, 1982; Kuhl, 1984; McClelland, 1985; Vroom, 1964).

3. Emotional Arousal Processes. Emotions are motivational processes because they provide the person with evaluative information about problems and opportunities of potential personal relevance and help prepare the person to deal with these problems and opportunities. Thus, they are anticipatory in the sense of creating what Frjida (1988) calls a "state of action readiness" (p. 351). Because they also serve an arousal function, emotions are a key source of energy in motivational patterns (although not the only source of energy in the overall person system).

Because nonemotional affective states such as pain and fatigue also serve a regulatory and preparatory function, they constitute a fourth category of motivational processes. MST does not, however, confer "major component" status on these processes for two reasons: they primarily serve the biological subsystems of the person (e.g., by signalling potentially damaging deviations from biological steady state functioning), and they are usually linked to emotional processes that regulate psychological and behavioral functioning (e.g., physical discomfort may be linked with surprise, annoyance, fear, or discouragement). Indeed, as D. Ford (1987) notes: "emotions represent complex patterns of preparation for different kinds of behavior demands that augment and amplify or attenuate activity arousal patterns" (p. 501).

Occasionally concepts representing attention and consciousness arousal processes (e.g., reflective self-awareness, metacognition) are also characterized as motivational processes (e.g., McCombs, 1991a; Ridley, 1991). From the perspective of Motivational Systems Theory, however, this represents a confounding of the *capability* for energizing motivational (and some nonmotivational) components of the human system (e.g., by focusing a person's attention on the personal goals, emotions, and personal agency beliefs directing and regulating their behavior) and the motivational components per se. Although motivational patterns cannot be changed (constructed, modified, transformed) in the absence of attention and consciousness arousal (see Chapter 2), and such change is likely to be greatly facilitated by relatively intense investments of attentional energy—as implied by such concepts as metacognition and reflective self-awareness—this energizing capability is an instrumental skill that influences the present contents of consciousness rather than an evaluative process that represents anticipated future events and consequences.

Nonmotivational Components of the Living Systems Framework

The major difficulty with trying to construct boundaries between motivational and nonmotivational processes is that all system components must be related to each other in some fashion to maintain unitary person-in-context functioning. Consequently, many person and environment components that are not motivational in character nevertheless influence and are influenced by the motivational processes of goals, emotions, and personal agency beliefs in very significant ways. Distinguishing between motivational and nonmotivational processes therefore requires a precise set of defining criteria such as those identified in the preceding section. The rationale for excluding each of the other LSF-defined components of the person-in-context system from the domain of motivation is described next.

Environmental processes can clearly be excluded from the domain of motivation based on the criterion that motivation resides within the person. There are usually strong links between environmental and motivational processes, however, because goals, emotions, and personal agency beliefs are organized in behavior episodes and behavior episode schemata anchored, in part, by context information, and because the environment usually affords the attainment of certain goals and not others.

This combination of independence and interdependence between motivational and environmental processes is a crucial principle for both researchers and practitioners. Whether designing an experiment or an intervention, outside agents cannot directly "grab hold" of a person's thoughts and feelings and manipulate them as if they were changing the channel on a television set or feeding commands to a computer. They can try, however, to *influence* motivational processes through environmental "handles" or "action levers" (Katzell & Thompson, 1990) such as those used in effective parenting, teaching, counseling, and business management. Thus **motivation can be facilitated or constrained, but not imposed**—no one can be directly forced to care about something, to be optimistic or pessimistic about something, or to feel a particular emotion. On the other hand, it is usually possible to alter the *probability* that a person will adopt or learn a particular pattern of personal goals, emotions, and personal agency beliefs. Indeed, when a behavior pattern persists unchanged in the face of compelling contextual incentives, pressures, and supports designed to constrain or facilitate change in that pattern, it is often viewed as evidence of mental dullness (i.e., the person is not "getting the message") or even mental illness (i.e., the person does not appear to be "in touch with reality," as illustrated by compulsive, paranoid, or addictive behavior patterns).

A number of within-person processes serve primarily an instrumental rather than an evaluative function and are therefore excluded from the domain of motivation. *Control processes* and *transactional processes* are perhaps the most obvious of these because they are responsible for designing and executing the actions needed to make progress toward goal attainment. This encompasses the preparatory processes of cognitive planning and problem solving, as well as the present-oriented functions served by motor and communicative actions, ingestive and eliminative actions, and sensory-perceptual actions. *Means evalutions* conducted by the regulatory process also fit into this category because they support the control process and therefore serve an instrumental function at the person-in-context level of analysis (despite serving an evaluative function at the subsystem level).

Information processing and memory functions and *attention and consciousness arousal processes* are also excluded from the domain of motivation, even though they provide content and energy for the governing functions (including thoughts about personal goals and personal agency beliefs), because of their instrumental character. In other words, they help carry out the "orders" that are crafted by the team of motivational processes, but they do not contribute to the initial design of those orders (although they can contribute to the modification of those orders by feeding information back through the regulatory process). The same basic logic applies to *biological processes* and *activity arousal processes*, which are involved in energizing action, but not in an evaluative and future-oriented way (with the exception of certain nonemotional affects, as noted earlier). They, too, are more like the "troops" working to carry out the orders delivered to them by their "commanders" at "motivational headquarters."

Finally, *performance evaluations* conducted by the regulatory process are excluded from the domain of motivation, not because they are instrumental in character, but, rather, because they focus on the past and present rather than the future. Guided by selective attention processes, they try to determine "how things are going" but not what this means for the future. That is the job of personal agency beliefs.

The distinction between these feedback and feedforward processes is a crucial one, and one that is often not carefully made or fully appreciated. Motivationally, what matters is not success or failure per se, but rather how the person interprets and integrates that information into the goal, emotion, and personal agency belief components of their current BES. This assertion is clearly supported by evidence indicating that thoughts about *anticipated* consequences (i.e., personal agency beliefs) are more predictive of motivational outcomes such as choice, effort, and persistence than are thoughts about *perceived* consequences (i.e., performance evaluations) (Bandura, 1986). Indeed, it is common for people to discount successes or failures in a selective manner or to weight them in ways that tend to confirm their hopes or fears (Nisbett & Ross, 1980). Thus, although evaluations concerning performance accomplishments are the primary source of information used to construct and modify personal agency beliefs (Bandura, 1986), they do not themselves serve a motivational function.

A summary of the boundary-defining analysis just described is presented in Table 3.1.

Motivation Defined

The concept of motivation is inherently broad and multifaceted (Cofer & Appley, 1964; Pinder, 1984; Weiner, 1990). Consequently, it is often used in ambiguous or imprecise ways (deCharms, 1987; D. Ford, 1987). Nevertheless, if it is carefully defined and delimited, the concept of motivation provides a uniquely valuable way of describing the *integrated patterning* of a set of intimately related processes. Thus, based on the foregoing analysis, **the concept of motivation is defined in Motivational Systems Theory as the organized patterning of an individual's personal goals, emotions, and personal agency beliefs.** Symbolically this can be represented as a formula of three interacting components:

Motivation = Goals x Emotions x Personal Agency Beliefs

Thus motivation is an integrative construct representing the direction a person is going, the emotional energy and affective experience supporting or inhibiting movement in that direction, and the expectancies a person has about whether they can ultimately reach their destination. Motivation is *not* primarily one or another of these processes—it is the organized patterning of all three components functioning as an interdependent "triumvirate," influencing and

TABLE 3.1   Summary of LSF Processes Included in and Excluded From the MST Conceptualization of Motivation

In	*Out*
Directive Cognitions (**PERSONAL GOALS** and goal evaluations)	Environmental Processes
	Biological Processes
Regulatory Feedforward Cognitions (**PERSONAL AGENCY BELIEFS**, i.e., capability and context beliefs)	Information Processing and Memory Functions
	Attention and Consciousness Arousal Processes
	Activity Arousal Processes
Emotional Arousal Processes (**EMOTIONS**)	Control Cognitions (planning and problem-solving thoughts and means evaluations)
Nonemotional Affective States (e.g., pain and fatigue)	Transactional Processes (e.g., motor and communicative actions)
	Regulatory Feedback Cognitions (performance evaluations)

being influenced by the "instrumental troops" who receive their instructions from "motivational headquarters."

The Organized Patterning of Motivational Processes

Multiplication rather than addition signs are used in the formula representing the MST definition of motivation to convey the idea that the relationships among the components of human motivational patterns are often complex and nonlinear. For example, if one of the components is "missing" in a particular episode (i.e., no goal is activated, personal agency beliefs are highly negative, or emotions are inhibiting goal-directed activity), the person will not be motivated to initiate activity in that episode even if the other components are firmly in place. Moreover, if such activity is initiated but one or more components "drop out" of the equation (e.g., "I don't want to do this anymore"; "I'm not going to be able to do this"; "This is too boring/scary/frustrating/depressing/disgusting/embarrassing to continue"), the episode will be terminated prematurely, either because the goal has been evaluated as unattainable or because some other goal has taken precedence (the two ways in which behavior episodes may conclude unsuccessfully).

Consider, for example, the case of a middle-aged man who has been given "doctor's orders" to start a vigorous exercise program. If such a program is irrelevant to his personal goals (e.g., he is unconcerned about his health status or other people's reactions to his failure to start an exercise program), he will not act on his doctor's advice no matter how positive his emotions and expectancies about vigorous exercise might be. Alternatively, even if he has strong goals that are congruent with the doctor's advice, he may still do nothing if he lacks faith in his doctor (negative context beliefs), doubts his own ability to carry out those orders (negative capability beliefs), or fears that vigorous exercise will produce harmful consequences (inhibiting emotions). Similarly, a woman who is considering the purchase of a home computer will be unlikely to invest in a machine if she is skeptical about its practical utility (no relevant personal goals), feels anxious around computers (inhibiting emotions), doubts her computer capabilities (negative capability beliefs), or believes that computers are unreliable (negative context beliefs).

These examples also illustrate a basic principle for researchers and interventionists: **all three motivational components must be carefully monitored and facilitated to "motivate" someone successfully.** Each component is necessary, but none are sufficient for the activation of strong motivational patterns. Like the countries represented in the United Nations Security Council, each process has "veto" power over the others. In other words, strong motivational patterns require clear "aye" votes from all three components. Some activity is possible if there is confusion or uncertainty in one or two components (analogous to an abstention vote cast by a UN delegate who is conflicted or waiting for more information), but motivational patterns are usually weak or inconsistent under such conditions.

For example, consider the contrasting results one might expect from two different ways of organizing a class designed to teach computer novices how to use a word processing program. In a class organized primarily around the objective of covering a predetermined amount of information, motivational considerations are likely to begin and end with efforts to focus students' attention on the instructional goals of the class. The instructor would be primarily concerned with his own goals and actions (i.e., figuring out how to present the course material in a clear and efficient manner) rather than those of his students. Consequently, if students experienced motivational difficulties as a result of feeling confused or overwhelmed, the teacher would probably be unaware of these problems or dismiss them as "their problem, not mine."

In contrast, a teacher who organized the class primarily around motivational objectives (e.g., helping people become comfortable and confident with computers) would be "on the lookout" for negative emotions and weak personal agency beliefs and regard them as a failure of instruction. Thorough coverage of the course material might be sacrificed if a slower pace, more individualized instruction, or more time applying the learned material was required to maintain a motivationally positive computer BES. Such an instructor would emphasize the relative ease with which further learning could occur after the class ended given a solid motivational foundation, and would be acutely aware of the long-term obstacles to effective use of the computer created by a computer BES infused with anxiety, self-doubts, or antagonism. The broader purposes and payoffs for becoming computer literate would also be emphasized in an effort to help students overcome the potentially debilitating motivational consequences of a marginal or faltering level of cognitive and emotional commitment to the learning process.

This example also illustrates the fallacy of assuming that, because all behavior episodes and BES are anchored by personal goals (along with context information), goals must be *the* core elements in any given motivational pattern. Such a deduction is simplistic and fails to recognize the exquisite interdependence of the three basic motivational components. For example, people often fail to pursue goals that are important to them because they believe that these goals are unattainable (negative personal agency beliefs), or because less important goals that are more emotionally compelling have greater immediate salience (e.g., "feeling good" goals such as having fun or avoiding laborious effort). A lack of energy resources (e.g., due to fatigue or depression) may also lead to the inhibition or premature termination of potentially rewarding behavior episodes.

Moreover, because cognitive and emotional evaluations of current behavior episodes are the primary mechanisms underlying the formation of new goals, emotions and personal agency beliefs play a critical role in the development and elaboration of personal goals (Deci & Ryan, 1985; Pervin, 1991; Ryan & Stiller, 1991). This process can occur not only in instrumental episodes, but in observational and thought episodes as well. For example, a behavior episode directed by a curiosity goal ("try this," "watch this," or "think about this") may lead to the development of new goals around that previously unfamiliar experience if it stimulates interest, excitement, or a sense of personal competence.

Nevertheless, goals do play a leadership role in motivational patterns by defining their content and direction. If there is no goal in place, extant emotional energy will be expended aimlessly and unproductively, like a car idling in neutral. Similarly, capability and context beliefs about a particular kind of achievement will have no impact or significance if the person has no desire to achieve in that area. Thus goals, emotions, and personal agency beliefs depend on each other in ways that are so fundamental that the relevance, potency, and very existence of each process depends on the others. That is why motivation is defined in Motivational Systems Theory as the organized patterning of all three of these processes, and why motivation can serve as a useful concept—despite the inherent complexity of motivational patterns—if it is defined precisely in these terms.

Suggestions for Further Reading

Ford, M. E. (in press). A living systems approach to the integration of personality and intelligence. In R. J. Sternberg & P. Ruzgis (Eds.), *Intelligence and personality*. New York: Cambridge University Press.

Kleinginna, P. R., Jr., & Kleinginna, A. M. (1981). A categorized list of motivation definitions, with a suggestion for a consensual definition. *Motivation and Emotion, 5,* 263-291.

CHAPTER FOUR

Personal Goals

If you care enough about a result, you will almost certainly attain it.
William James

PERSONAL GOALS HAVE TWO BASIC PROPERTIES: they represent the consequences to be achieved (or avoided), and they direct the other components of the person to try to produce those consequences (or prevent them from occurring). These are the *content* and *process* aspects of personal goals. Table 4.1 provides an overview of the major concepts used in MST to describe the content of people's goals and the methods or styles they use to conceptualize goals at both the behavior episode and BES levels of analysis.

Goal Content

In MST the term *goal content* is used to describe the desired or undesired consequence represented by a particular goal. Questions such as "What do you want?", "What are you trying to accomplish?" and "Why did you do that?" require answers framed in terms of goal content.

Answering such questions with accuracy and precision is often a complex and challenging task (Pervin, 1991). Because people are capable of imagining many different kinds of consequences, the

TABLE 4.1 Overview of MST Goal Concepts

	PRIMARY LEVEL OF ANALYSIS	
	Within Episode	*Across Episode*
CONCEPTS PERTAINING TO GOAL CONTENT		
Single Goals	Taxonomy of Human Goals	
Multiple Goals	Goal Alignment (vs. Goal Conflict)	Goal Balance (vs. Goal Imbalance)
CONCEPTS PERTAINING TO HOW GOALS ARE CONCEPTUALIZED	Goal-Setting Processes	Goal Orientations

menu of possibilities in any given behavior episode may be quite large. In addition, people can (and often do) organize their behavior patterns around multiple goals simultaneously, so that a "correct" answer to such questions may not always be a complete answer. The specific content of a goal may also change during the course of a behavior episode in a dynamic and somewhat unpredictable fashion in response to feedback and feedforward information. Finally, a person's goals may not be cognitively represented in an easily communicated form. In fact some goals may operate outside the person's own awareness. For example, a strong but vaguely conceived goal may not be represented in a perceptible (e.g., verbal or imagistic) form. As noted in Chapter 2, this is a prerequisite for bringing information into consciousness (D. Ford, 1987).

Surprisingly, the fundamental problem of trying to specify the content of people's goals has received very little attention in recent years. This theoretical gap can be attributed to two major obstacles: the tendency to conceptualize goals as temporary, task-specific phenomena with little psychological meaning or enduring significance, and disillusionment with early efforts to construct broad taxonomies representing different kinds of goal content (e.g., McDougall, 1933; Murray, 1938). Because these taxonomies failed to distinguish clearly between behavior patterns and the desired consequences of these behavior patterns, they came to be seen as little more than tautological and arbitrary lists of little explanatory value (as noted in Chapter 1). Maslow (1943, 1970) and McClelland (1961, 1985) were able to overcome this problem to some extent, and consequently their motivational taxonomies have endured for a much longer period of time in textbooks, business seminars, and the like. Both Maslow and McClelland failed, however, to explicate the diversity of goals that may be involved in some of their most important motivational categories (e.g., Maslow's "Cognitive" and "Self-Actualization" needs; McClelland's "Motive for Success" and "Motive to Avoid Failure").

Perhaps in part as a consequence of these shortcomings, the most prominent theories in the contemporary motivational literature either fail to address goal content issues in a serious way (e.g., Bandura, 1986; Carver & Scheier, 1982, 1985; Csikszentmihalyi, 1990; Fishbein & Ajzen, 1975; Kuhl & Beckmann 1985, in press; Locke & Latham, 1990a, 1990b; Schunk, 1991a, 1991b; Seligman, 1975, 1991; Skinner, 1974; Vroom, 1964), or focus on just one or two "basic" human motives or needs such as understanding and mastering the environment, feeling free and in control of one's actions, or feeling competent and worthy (e.g., C. Ames & R. Ames, 1984a, 1984b; Brehm, 1972; Covington, 1984a, 1984b; deCharms, 1968, 1976; Deci & Ryan, 1985, 1991; Elliott & Dweck, 1988; Festinger, 1957; Nicholls, 1984a, 1984b; Weiner, 1986; White, 1959). Thus there is still a need for a general, comprehensive taxonomy of goal content that can serve as a useful heuristic device for researchers and practitioners who seek to understand the direction and organization of human behavior.

In MST the Ford and Nichols Taxonomy of Human Goals is used to satisfy this need (Ford & Nichols, 1987, 1991, 1992). This 24-category taxonomy was developed over the course of several years of research and clinical work with a variety of students, clients, and professionals. It builds on and extends the tradition of seeking some way to describe the basic content of the purposes, desires, and concerns that motivate human behavior, but avoids many of the problems that have plagued earlier efforts to construct such descriptions (e.g., conceptual confounding and tautological reasoning). This does not mean that the categories in this taxonomy represent "ultimate truths" about the nature of human motivation; any goal taxonomy will necessarily be limited by the fact that a person's thoughts about desired and undesired outcomes will generally be idiosyncratic, context-specific, and highly personal. Nevertheless, a standardized classification scheme can facilitate the process of making comparisons across individuals and social groups and can serve as a conceptual anchor in classifying goals within an individual's hierarchy of goals (Emmons, 1989). The Ford and Nichols taxonomy is thus offered as a potentially useful starting point for describing and classifying people's goals in a succinct, efficient, and comprehensive manner.

The Ford and Nichols Taxonomy of Human Goals is summarized in Table 4.2. Each goal is defined by a primary label and several additional words and phrases that help explicate the intended meaning of each goal label. Because there are an unlimited number of variations on these goals that people may conceive of at the behavior episode level of analysis, the categories in this taxonomy are intended to represent *classes* of goals at a relatively abstract or decontextualized level of analysis. Thus each goal category can be interpreted as a conceptual "prototype" representing a set of desired states or outcomes that are similar in meaning.

Before considering each of the categories of goal content represented in the taxonomy, it is important to understand several properties of the taxonomy as a whole. First, in contrast to the need theories of Maslow (1943, 1970) and Aldefer (1969, 1972), there is no implication in either the ordering or hierarchical arrangement of these categories that some goals are more important or more fundamental than others. Each category simply describes a particular kind of consequence that people may desire to achieve. Some goals may, on average, be more compelling than others (e.g., happiness, physical well-being, positive self-evaluations, belongingness) (Ford & Nichols, 1991), but that is an empirical question rather than a theoretical assumption. Such averages may not be particularly meaningful in any case because individual goal hierarchies are remarkably personal and variable (Ford & Nichols, 1992; Nichols, 1991; Winell, 1987).

It is also important to keep in mind the fact that behavior is often (perhaps usually) guided by multiple goals simultaneously. Indeed, behavior patterns in which multiple purposes are served by a common course of action are likely to yield unusually powerful motivational results (Atkinson & Birch, 1974; Pintrich & Garcia, 1991; Slavin, 1981; Wentzel, 1989, 1991a, 1991b). Accordingly, there is no assumption in the taxonomy that the activation of one goal will necessarily preclude the pursuit of other goals.

Related to this point is the possibility that investigators may be able to identify, either within or across individuals, "clusters" of goal content that represent complex combinations of the motivational "themes" listed in the taxonomy. For example, friendship goals may represent a merging of belongingness, resource acquisition, and resource provision concerns (Ford, Burt, & Bergin, 1984). The "Need for Achievement" defined by McClelland et al. (1953) may reflect a varying blend of mastery and superiority goals. Religious motivational patterns may also involve a rich combination of multiple goals—as well as considerable variation in the particular mix of goal content represented in these patterns.

Having outlined the basic nature and intent of the taxonomy as a whole, it is now possible to return to the task of defining each of the categories of goal content represented in the Ford and Nichols Taxonomy of Human Goals. At the highest level of abstraction, the taxonomy is divided into two types of goals: goals that represent desired consequences within individuals, and goals that represent desired consequences with respect to the relationship between people and their environments. These two categories are, by definition, exhaustive of all possible goals representing some outcome of person-in-context functioning.

There are three different kinds of within-person consequences that a person might desire: affective goals, cognitive goals, and "subjective organization" goals. Affective goals represent different kinds of feelings or emotions that a person might want to experience or avoid. Cognitive goals refer to different kinds of mental representations that people may want to construct or maintain. Subjective organization goals represent special or unusual states that people may seek to experience or avoid that involve a combination of different kinds of thoughts and feelings.

There are two broad categories of desired person-environment consequences in the taxonomy: social relationship goals and task goals. Within the former category, four goals represent the desire to maintain or promote the self (i.e., self-assertive goals), and four goals represent the desire to maintain or promote the well being of other people or the social groups of which one is a part (i.e., integrative goals). Task goals represent desired relationships between the individual and various objects in the environment (including people when they are being conceived of in impersonal terms).

Affective Goals

The first two goals listed under this heading reflect the well-established psychological principle that people are "intrinsically" motivated to seek and maintain an optimal level of arousal (Berlyne, 1971; Hebb, 1955; Malmo, 1959). *Entertainment* goals represent a desire to increase one's level of arousal by doing something that is stimulating, exciting, dangerous, or simply different from one's current activity (e.g., "There's nothing to *do* around here" or "Let's party!"). Thrill seekers, risk takers, adolescents, and people who are easily bored by daily routines are likely to be particularly interested

TABLE 4.2 The Ford and Nichols Taxonomy of Human Goals

DESIRED WITHIN-PERSON CONSEQUENCES

Affective Goals

Entertainment	Experiencing excitement or heightened arousal; Avoiding boredom or stressful inactivity
Tranquility	Feeling relaxed and at ease; Avoiding stressful overarousal
Happiness	Experiencing feelings of joy, satisfaction, or well-being; Avoiding feelings of emotional distress or dissatisfaction
Bodily Sensations	Experiencing pleasure associated with physical sensations, physical movement, or bodily contact; Avoiding unpleasant or uncomfortable bodily sensations
Physical Well-Being	Feeling healthy, energetic, or physically robust; Avoiding feelings of lethargy, weakness, or ill health

---

Cognitive Goals

Exploration	Satisfying one's curiosity about personally meaningful events; Avoiding a sense of being uninformed or not knowing what's going on
Understanding	Gaining knowledge or making sense out of something; Avoiding misconceptions, erroneous beliefs, or feelings of confusion
Intellectual Creativity	Engaging in activities involving original thinking or novel or interesting ideas; Avoiding mindless or familiar ways of thinking
Positive Self-Evaluations	Maintaining a sense of self-confidence, pride, or self-worth; Avoiding feelings of failure, guilt, or incompetence

---

Subjective Organization Goals

Unity	Experiencing a profound or spiritual sense of connectedness, harmony, or oneness with people, nature, or a greater power; Avoiding feelings of psychological disunity or disorganization
Transcendence	Experiencing optimal or extraordinary states of functioning; Avoiding feeling trapped within the boundaries of ordinary experience

---

in entertainment goals. In contrast, *tranquility* goals represent a desire to decrease one's level of arousal by resolving or avoiding problems, conflicts, unwanted obligations, or other stressful or disturbing circumstances (e.g., "I really don't want to deal with that right now" or "I just want to relax and get away from it all"). Graduate students in high-pressure programs, workers suffering from "burnout," parents of

TABLE 4.2 Continued

DESIRED PERSON-ENVIRONMENT CONSEQUENCES

Self-Assertive Social Relationship Goals

Individuality	Feeling unique, special, or different; Avoiding similarity or conformity with others
Self-Determination	Experiencing a sense of freedom to act or make choices; Avoiding the feeling of being pressured, constrained, or coerced
Superiority	Comparing favorably to others in terms of winning, status, or success; Avoiding unfavorable comparisons with others
Resource Acquisition	Obtaining approval, support, assistance, advice, or validation from others; Avoiding social disapproval or rejection

---

Integrative Social Relationship Goals

Belongingness	Building or maintaining attachments, friendships, intimacy, or a sense of community; Avoiding feelings of social isolation or separateness
Social Responsibility	Keeping interpersonal commitments, meeting social role obligations, and conforming to social and moral rules; Avoiding social transgressions and unethical or illegal conduct
Equity	Promoting fairness, justice, reciprocity, or equality; Avoiding unfair or unjust actions
Resource Provision	Giving approval, support, assistance, advice, or validation to others; Avoiding selfish or uncaring behavior

---

Task Goals

Mastery	Meeting a challenging standard of achievement or improvement; Avoiding incompetence, mediocrity, or decrements in performance
Task Creativity	Engaging in activities involving artistic expression or creativity; Avoiding tasks that do not provide opportunities for creative action
Management	Maintaining order, organization, or productivity in daily life tasks; Avoiding sloppiness, inefficiency, or disorganization
Material Gain	Increasing the amount of money or tangible goods one has; Avoiding the loss of money or material possessions
Safety	Being unharmed, physically secure, and free from risk; Avoiding threatening, depriving, or harmful circumstances

---

young children, and temperamentally anxious people are all likely to have strong tranquility goals.

Happiness goals represent a desire to experience, restore, or maintain the positive emotional states associated with effective functioning and good outcomes, and to avoid the negative emotional states associated with failure, incompetence, and bad outcomes (e.g., "I wish I could stop feeling so depressed" or "I'm going to start concentrating on my *own* happiness for a change"). Because happiness is both an intrinsically pleasurable experience and a signal that progress toward other goals is going well, it is at or near the top of most people's goal hierarchies.

Bodily sensation goals represent specific physical and sensory experiences that one would like to have or avoid (e.g., "I sure could go for a nice hot [shower/cup of coffee/sexual encounter] right now" or "I don't want to [eat those yukky vegetables/get my hair wet/go to the dentist], Mommy"). People who find a broad range of bodily sensation goals attractive and desirable are sometimes described as being "sensual"; in contrast, those who seek to avoid unpleasant or uncomfortable sensations with unusual frequency are often characterized as being "sensitive." In contrast to bodily sensation goals, which tend to be localized and transitory, *physical well-being* goals represent outcomes associated with more general body states of longer duration (e.g., "I need to get more exercise" or "I just want to feel well again, Doc"). Elderly people, people in ill health, hypochondriacs, and physical fitness enthusiasts are all likely to prioritize goals in this category.

Cognitive Goals

The first two categories in this part of the taxonomy refer to what is often called "the need to know." Two qualitatively different kinds of knowing are distinguished. *Exploration* goals reflect a desire to change the unknown into the known by acquiring new information of potential personal relevance (e.g., "Let's see what's in the news today" or "Don't keep me in the dark, just tell me what's going on"). Such goals are usually achieved simply by seeking out and attending to relevant information in the environment. In contrast, *understanding* goals reflect a desire to acquire knowledge in the deeper sense of constructing elaborated, intellectually satisfying representations of personally meaningful phenomena (e.g., "I wonder why he's behaving like that?" or "I'm confused—can you explain this to me?"). Thus the relatively superficial processes of observation and discovery, which are sufficient for pursuing exploration goals, must be supplemented by processes of reasoning, interpretation, or analysis to accomplish understanding goals. These latter goals are particularly attractive to scholars, philosophers, highly educated people, and people who prefer reading to watching television.

Progress toward understanding goals is usually evaluated against criteria such as truth, accuracy, validity, or persuasiveness. In contrast, *intellectual creativity* goals reflect a desire to engage in mental activities or construct mental products for which the primary criteria are novelty, cleverness, or a subjective sense of elegance (e.g., "I'd like to come up with something that's really different this time" or "Tonight I'm going to make up the best story you've ever heard"). Creative writers, musicians, humorists, and people who enjoy "brain teasers" are among those most likely to be attracted to intellectual creativity goals.

Positive self-evaluation goals reflect a desire to view one's self as being competent, worthy, or virtuous (e.g., "I'm really not such a bad person" or "I could do it if I really wanted to"). This category of goals is highlighted in a number of contemporary motivation theories (e.g., Covington, 1984a, 1984b; Deci & Ryan, 1985; Harter, 1990; Tesser, 1986), and for good reason—like the affective goal of happiness, the desire to maintain a fundamentally positive self-image is a strong and pervasive goal for most people.

Subjective Organization Goals

Some consequences that people seek to experience or avoid involve a complex combination of cognitive and affective states. The label "subjective organization" is intended to convey the particularly rich character of these desired within-person experiences.

Unity goals represent a desire to maintain an overall sense of coherence and psychological integration or to experience a profoundly meaningful sense of connectedness, harmony, or oneness with God or one's physical or social surroundings (e.g., "I could look at the stars for hours" or "I've got to hold myself together—I feel like I'm falling apart"). In contrast, *transcendence* goals represent a desire to go beyond the ordinary thoughts and feelings of everyday life and "transcend" to some sort of "high" or "peak experience" (e.g. "Nothing can match the wonderful feeling I get when I go [sailing/running/shopping]" or "Let's make this a day we'll never forget"). Maslow (1971) used the term "transcenders" to describe a subset of self-actualized people who are particularly likely to have peak experiences and to think about life in terms of idealized states and outcomes (see also Privette, 1983). The exquisitely powerful and satisfying state of "flow," as described by Csikszentmihalyi (1990) in his theory of optimal experience, also exemplifies a kind of transcendent state to which one might aspire.

Social Relationship Goals

In social relationships people try to accomplish two fundamental kinds of goals: maintenance or promotion of the self, and maintenance or promotion of other people or the social groups of which one is a part. These are manifestations of what Koestler (1967, 1978) calls the *self-assertive* and *integrative* tendencies of hierarchically organized living systems. Although these tendencies sometimes come into conflict with one another in specific situations, it is possible (and quite common) for people to have strong goals and impressive accomplishments with regard to both integration and self-assertion (Bakan, 1966; M. Ford, 1981; Spence & Helmreich, 1978; Wiggins & Holzmuller, 1978). This illustrates the human capacity for organizing behavior patterns that enable them to accomplish multiple goals simultaneously.

The eight goals listed under the categories of self-assertion and integration are matched sets defined by four issues of critical importance to the functioning of living systems. Specifically, individuality and belongingness goals represent concerns about one's *identity* as an individual in social settings; self-determination and social responsibility goals focus on the issue of behavioral *control*; superiority and equity goals center on the issue of *social comparison*; and resource acquisition and resource provision goals deal with *social exchange* processes.

Individuality goals represent a desire to maintain or enhance one's identity as a separate person by developing or expressing beliefs, values, self-concepts, behavior patterns, or stylistic characteristics that are uniquely personal or different from those of other relevant people (e.g., "I don't want to be like them—I want to be my own person" or "I'll do it my way"). Nonconformists, creative individuals, and people with very strong and definite values or belief systems are especially likely to be concerned with individuality goals.

Belongingness goals, on the other hand, reflect a desire to create, maintain, or enhance the integrity of the social units of which one is a part (e.g., "Let's get our [family/whole department/old gang] together for a [reunion/party/few laughs]" or "Let's try to work this out—our relationship is too important to let it end like this"). A person can experience a sense of belonging with (i.e., feel a part of) any number of social groups, including families, friendships, clubs, communities, ethnic groups, political parties, athletic teams, and so forth. Because these groups provide a context for social exchange processes (i.e., resource provision and resource acquisition), belongingness goals are often associated with not only an altruistic desire to help and support significant others, but also with a self-enhancing desire to obtain social validation and approval (Ford, Burt, & Bergin, 1984). Nevertheless, belongingness goals per se are *integrative* concerns focused on the preservation or promotion of a group's existence or functioning. Such concerns are a central and pervasive part of most people's goal hierarchies.

Self-determination goals reflect the human desire for freedom, independence, and choice in contexts that threaten to restrict or undermine these conditions (e.g., "I want to do it myself" or "Don't tell me what to do!"). Because motivational patterns tend to be more robust and enduring when people believe they have options and the power to choose among those options, this goal is at the core of several of the most prominent theories in the contemporary literature, namely, reactance theory (Brehm, 1966, 1972; Brehm & Brehm, 1981), personal causation theory (deCharms, 1968, 1976, 1984), and self-determination theory (Deci, 1980; Deci & Ryan, 1985, 1987, 1991). It is clear, however, that the strength of this goal varies across people and contexts (Burger, 1989). For example, two-year-olds, teenagers, and Type A individuals are notorious for their unusually strong self-determination goals.

Social responsibility goals represent a desire to avoid social and ethical transgressions and to facilitate smooth social functioning by behaving in accordance with social rules, expectations, and obligations (e.g., "I have to go now—I promised my parents I'd [cut the grass/babysit my kid sister/be home by midnight]" or "I can't do that—that would be [cheating/stealing/breaking the rules]"). Wanting to be socially responsible implies that some form of social control has been accepted as legitimate and necessary. Such acceptance is generally more likely to occur in the context of self-determination, however. In other words, people are more likely to act in a socially responsible manner when social constraints are seen as personally chosen or collaboratively defined rather than externally imposed (Deci & Ryan, 1985). People who take rules and commitments seriously and who value qualities such as reliability, trustworthiness, and integrity are especially likely to give social responsibility goals high priority.

Superiority goals represent a desire to be better or higher than other people on some personally relevant dimension such as academic or occupational achievement, income or material possessions, territorial coverage, athletic performance, popularity, beauty, moral virtue, and so forth (e.g., "I want to [win/be #1/be better than anyone else in the class]" or "I'll show you who's boss around here"). Because people who are dissimilar in their developmental status, life circumstances, or social roles are unlikely to provide a meaningful basis for comparison, superiority goals are primarily relevant to relationships with peers (e.g., siblings, neighbors, classmates, athletic opponents, job-market competitors, etc.). Highly competitive individuals, people who practice one-upmanship, and people who view social relationships in terms of conquests and victories are among those who find superiority goals particularly attractive and compelling.

Equity goals also focus on social comparison concerns, but in this case the desired consequence is *similarity* among people on some relevant dimension (e.g., "Everybody should get exactly the same [amount/opportunity/treatment]" or "That's not fair!"). Like superiority, equity is a particularly salient issue in relationships with peers (e.g., friends, spouses, coworkers, or juries); however, it is also an important concern of parents, employers, elected officials, and others in positions of authority who must be attentive to group members' demands for fair and unbiased treatment (Adams, 1963, 1965). Equity goals are prominent among people who are bothered by social injustice, unequal resource distribution, and the victimization of helpless or disadvantaged individuals.

Resource acquisition goals represent a desire to obtain valued emotional, informational, or material resources from parents, friends, teachers, counselors, clergy, government agencies, and the like (e.g., "Please tell me you love me" or "I could really use your help right now"). *Resource provision* goals, on the other hand, reflect a desire to enhance other people's welfare by offering them resources such as advice, instruction, emotional support, cognitive validation, task assistance, or material aid ("Here, let me give you a hand" or "I feel so sorry for those people—is there anything I can do to help?"). Resource acquisition and resource provision concerns are usually embedded in social relationships involving reciprocal social exchange processes (e.g., friendship or spousal relationships) or in asymmetrical social roles in which one person is responsible for providing resources to another (e.g., parent-child or teacher-student relationships). These goals are sometimes pursued, however, in situations that involve neither belongingness nor social responsibility goals. This is particularly likely for people who tend to be emotionally needy or insecure (with regard to resource acquisition goals) and for people who tend to be unusually caring and altruistic (with regard to resource provision goals).

Task Goals

Mastery goals represent a desire to improve one's performance on a task or to reach or maintain a challenging standard of achievement (e.g., "I know I can do better if I keep trying" or "I did it!") (C. Ames & R. Ames, 1984a, 1984b; Dweck, 1986; Elliott & Dweck, 1988). Mastery goals differ from superiority goals in that goal attainment is defined in personal terms (e.g., in terms of one's past or possible future performances) rather than in terms of comparisons with others (except when such comparisons provide one with a standard for measuring personal progress, as in the case of athletic records or other exemplars of good performance). Perfectionists, people who are dissatisfied with mediocrity, and people who view incompetence as an opportunity for self-improvement are particularly likely to activate mastery goals in the context of personally relevant tasks.

Analogous to the distinction between understanding and intellectual creativity goals, mastery and *task creativity* goals differ in that the latter are typically evaluated on subjective criteria such as artistry or originality rather than in terms of objective standards of excellence or improvement (e.g., "I wonder what I could make out of these materials?" or " Let's see what happens if I put this here"). Artists, architects, and young children are among those most likely to be fascinated by tasks that afford the attainment of task creativity goals.

Whereas mastery goals are associated with high (or increasing) levels of performance on personally challenging tasks, *management* goals represent a desire to maintain organization, efficiency, or productivity with respect to the relatively mundane tasks of everyday living (e.g., "I've [listed/scheduled/planned out] everything that needs to be done" or "I hate it when people are [slow/messy/incompetent]"). People who value efficiency, order, neatness, and punctuality, and who dislike deviations from desired, expected, or planned outcomes are particularly likely to give management goals high priority.

Material gain goals represent a desire to obtain money or valued material possessions such as clothing, jewelry, toys, furniture, electronic equipment, automobiles, real estate, and so forth (e.g., "Keep the praise, just give me the raise" or "I've just *got* to have that [car/dress/necklace/computer]"). People who are living beyond their means, ambitious people who want to "move up" in the world, and (by definition) materialistic people are among those most likely to be preoccupied with material gain goals.

Finally, *safety* goals reflect a desire to protect one's self from physical harm or to avoid circumstances that may be risky or damaging to one's health (e.g., "I'm not getting in the car with you after all you've had to drink" or "Make sure all the doors are locked before you come to bed"). Although safety goals are a prominent part of most people's goal hierarchies, they are especially salient concerns for cautious people, people who have a low tolerance for health risks, and people who take a pragmatic approach to hazards and dangers (i.e., "Better safe than sorry").

Conclusion

As the preceding descriptions illustrate, goal content can be usefully classified into a finite number of categories. However, it is important to keep in mind that the personalized and contextualized nature of goals produces an infinite number of variations on any particular goal theme. Consequently, to represent the idiosyncratic features of an individual's goal content in a truly precise way, it is necessary to use an idiographic approach such as those involving the assessment of a person's "core goals" (Nichols, 1990, 1991), "current concerns" (Klinger, 1975, 1977, 1987), "personal strivings" (Emmons, 1986, 1989), "personal projects" (Little, 1983, 1989), "life tasks" (Cantor & Fleeson, 1991; Cantor & Kihlstrom, 1987; Cantor & Langston, 1989), or "possible selves" (Cantor, Markus, Niedenthal, & Nurius, 1986; Markus & Nurius, 1986; Markus & Ruvolo, 1989).

The taxonomy can facilitate even these kinds of assessments, however, by serving as a prompt for helping people identify goal themes that are not easily brought into consciousness or put into verbal form (Nichols, 1991). For example, the taxonomy might serve as a heuristic tool for initiating a discussion between a career counselor and a high school or college student, for helping a teacher gain insight about what is likely to motivate his or her students, or simply as a device for promoting self-understanding. The taxonomy also provides a useful mechanism for making comparisons of goal content across individuals and social groups. For instance, it might be used as a conceptual anchor for analyzing conflicts or potential conflicts in marital, family, or other long-term relationships or as a tool to help evaluate the qualifications of job applicants for positions that require certain kinds of goal profiles (e.g., the prioritization of resource provision goals in the helping professions; an emphasis on social responsibility and management goals in clerical or administrative positions; concern about safety goals for drivers, inspectors, and the like). Finally, because effective communication requires a shared set of concepts and concept labels, the taxonomy may be helpful in facilitating discussion and collaboration among scholars and professionals interested in describing the content of human motivational patterns in particular individuals or groups of people or in identifying the kinds of goals afforded by a particular work or social context.

Goal Hierarchies

A recurring theme in MST is that behavior is often organized to serve multiple purposes simultaneously, both within and across behavior episodes. This implies that different kinds of goal content must be coordinated and prioritized in some coherent way if effective functioning is to be maintained. The term *goal hierarchy* is used to refer to such organization.

Within-Episode Goal Hierarchies

At the level of a specific behavior episode, goal hierarchies consist of organized sequences of embedded subgoals that serve as targets or markers of progress toward the overall goal (or goals) of the episode. For example, a baseball player preparing for a game might engage in an elaborate sequence of resting, healing, eating, stretching, practicing, and mental preparation activities that serve the larger purpose of playing well. Similarly, a politician seeking reelection may construct a campaign strategy requiring the attainment of a diversity of subgoals involving different policies, media, and constituencies.

When the attainment of the ultimate goal (or goals) directing a behavior episode requires substantial time and effort (e.g., writing a book, painting a house, running a marathon, earning a college degree), motivation is generally enhanced by focusing one's attention on subgoals that are more proximal in time and less daunting or intimidating in terms of the effort and capabilities required for goal attainment (Bandura & Schunk, 1981; Morgan, 1985; Schunk, 1990b, 1991b). As Bandura and Schunk (1981) explain:

Self-motivation can be best created and sustained by attainable subgoals that lead to future larger ones. Proximal subgoals provide immediate incentives and guides for performance, whereas distal goals are too far removed in time to effectively mobilize effort or to direct what one does in the here and now. Focus on the distant future makes it easy to temporize and to slacken efforts in the present. (p. 587)

Similarly, people who are experiencing anxiety or pressure to perform well (e.g., on stage, on an important test, or in an athletic competition) can facilitate the organization of effective behavior patterns by focusing their attention on "controllable short-term goals" rather than more distal goals over which they have less direct influence (Barden & Ford, 1990, 1991). This motivational technique is effective because the negative consequences of performance anxiety, such as forgetting important information or choking under pressure, are more a function of cognitive-attentional "worry" than emotionality per se (Baumeister, 1984; Morris, Davis, & Hutchings, 1981; Tobias, 1979). In other words, when people concentrate on motivationally inhibiting aspects of a situation (e.g., imagined deficits in personal capabilities or the possibility of undesired consequences occurring), they are less able to focus their attention on what they need to do to continue to make progress toward their goal. In contrast, by making an effort to attend only to the immediate actions (or subgoals) that need to be accomplished in the here and now, even highly anxious people can reduce worry, stay on task, and perform at or near their maximum potential (Barden & Ford, 1990, 1991).

Assuming that one is capable of accomplishing the proximal subgoals that have become the interim criteria for success, and the environment is responsive to the person's goal attainment efforts, feedback information indicating that "things are going well" will begin to flow into the system. This information helps sustain and nurture motivation by triggering emotions associated with the repetition and continuation of successful behavior episodes (i.e., satisfaction and excitement) and by facilitating the development and maintenance of positive personal agency beliefs (Bandura, 1986; Bandura & Schunk, 1981; D. Ford, 1987; Schunk, 1990b, 1991b; Winell, 1987).

In sum, one of the key principles of MST is that **motivation in behavior episodes that are challenging, stressful, or laborious can be enhanced by focusing one's attention on short-term goals that are clearly within the boundaries of one's current capabilities and environmental opportunities.**

One must be careful not to carry this principle to extremes, however. In situations where the "distal" goals directing an episode are actually well within reach, it may be counterproductive to focus one's attention on proximal subgoals (Harackiewicz & Sansone, 1991; Manderlink & Harackiewicz, 1984; Powers, 1973). Under such circumstances it may be hard to construe the interim steps to goal attainment as important goals in their own right, either because they are trivially easy to accomplish or because they do not signify meaningful progress toward the overall goal of the episode (as in the case of efforts to define educational goals in terms of overly concrete "behavioral objectives"). Focusing attention on highly proximal subgoals may also have the unintended effect of disrupting a well-organized behavior pattern, as illustrated by a golfer who thinks about specific muscle movements while swinging a club or a speaker who concentrates on the words she wants to say rather than on the meaning she is trying to convey.

Even in cases where motivation is facilitated by focusing on proximal subgoals, it is important not to lose sight of the ultimate goals being served by the attainment of these subgoals. Otherwise a person can get rather far "off track" in terms of the correspondence between his or her actions and long-term goals (Winell, 1987). Thus **effective functioning requires a strategic emphasis on attainable short-term goals combined with a periodic review of the long-term goals that give meaning and organization to one's short-term pursuits** (Bandura, 1986; Barden & Ford, 1991; Winell, 1987). Harackiewicz and Sansone (1991) make a similar point in their discussion of goals and intrinsic motivation:

> People generally begin an activity with some idea about what they are trying to do or accomplish. . . . Within the context of these general goals that characterize the "purpose" of task engagement, [people] may pursue more specific goals or "targets." . . . Target goals guide an individual's behavior, and purpose goals suggest the reasons for the behavior. Both kinds of goals may influence how a person approaches and experiences an activity, how well they perform, and how much they enjoy the activity. (p. 21)

Alignment of Multiple Goals Within Behavior Episodes

As noted earlier, a particularly important principle with regard to goal hierarchies at the behavior episode level of analysis is the fact that behavior patterns can and often do serve multiple purposes simultaneously (D. Ford, 1987; Pervin, 1991). In other words, a single course of action may lead to a variety of desired outcomes. The motivational significance of this principle lies not so much in the increased efficiency that such behavior patterns afford, but, rather, in the increased motivational power that results when a person has more than one reason for engaging in a course of action (e.g., D. Bergin, 1987). As Winell (1987) explains, "when a behavior serves multiple purposes, motivation is high and the system runs smoothly" (p. 269). Thus a basic proposition of MST is that **the most motivating activities and experiences in life will be those that involve the simultaneous pursuit and attainment of many different kinds of goals.**

For example, an expert pool player might spend several hours each day at the local pool hall because: (a) the competition is fun and exciting (entertainment), (b) it's an easy way to earn some money (material gain), (c) the game itself offers a continuous challenge (mastery), (d) he enjoys teaching other people the game (resource provision), (e) it's where his friends hang out (belongingness), and, (f) overall, these achievements make him feel happy and good about himself (happiness and positive self-evaluations). Similarly, an expert shopper might spend a great deal of time in malls and department stores because: (a) it enables her to make necessary purchases and to acquire attractive, fashionable clothing and accessories for herself and her family (management, material gain), (b) finding quality goods or bargain prices is a compelling challenge (mastery), (c) she enjoys buying gifts that will be especially pleasing to friends and family members (resource provision), and (d) it gives her a sense of relaxation, well being, and freedom from everyday chores and responsibilities (tranquility, happiness, self-determination).

If it is indeed the case that activities and experiences will tend to be particularly attractive or compelling when they afford the attainment of multiple goals simultaneously, then it seems clear that parents, teachers, employers, counselors, and other interventionists should be continually asking themselves, "How can I design or modify this context so that it offers more opportunities for attaining different kinds of goals?" For example, the extraordinary success of certain kinds of cooperative learning arrangements (i.e., those that combine group rewards with individual accountability) in promoting academic achievement and social competence appears to be attributable to the synergistic merging of social relationship goals with the more typical menu of cognitive and task goals afforded by traditional classroom arrangements (C. Ames & R. Ames, 1984a, 1984b; Johnson & Johnson, 1975; Johnson, Maruyama, Johnson, Nelson, & Skon, 1982; Slavin, 1981, 1984, 1987, 1989). In other words, by providing clear incentives for doing well as a group and by making students accountable to other students (i.e., because the group cannot attain its goals without each group member learning the material or contributing to the completion of a task), teachers can link peer pressure and friendship concerns with academic goals in mutually facilitative patterns (i.e., social responsibility, belongingness, resource provision, and resource acquisition goals can be aligned with the teachers' instructional objectives). The importance of peer norms and expectations in facilitating and constraining student achievement has also been emphasized by Maehr and Fyans (1989) in their work on school cultures.

Another way to facilitate cognitive and skill development in education-related behavior episodes is to redesign the learning activities themselves (Bandura, 1986; Brophy, 1987; Csikszentmihalyi, 1990; Malone & Lepper, 1987). For example, by placing information-giving and behavioral rehearsal activities into game-like contexts, educators may be able to make the learning process enjoyable and/or personally challenging for some students who would otherwise show little interest in these activities (i.e., instructionally relevant goals can be aligned with the students' entertainment, mastery, or superiority goals) (D. Bergin, 1989). Similar motivational enhancements may be obtained by embedding learning activities into role playing or simulation contexts that stimulate students' interest and curiosity (i.e., entertainment and exploration goals can be aligned with learning and skill-development goals). Also, by offering students options or opportunities to make choices about personally relevant aspects of a learning activity (e.g., the order or pace of instruction), self-determination goals can be aligned with instructionally relevant goals (Deci & Ryan, 1985; Deci, Vallerand, Pelletier, & Ryan, 1991).

The principle of goal alignment is also of critical importance in work contexts that require committed, effortful activity. Indeed, most of the preceding examples are as applicable to the workplace as they are to the classroom. For example, Japan's economic success may be largely attributable to the culture's tendency to align social relationship and task goals in motivational patterns that mirror those that tend to emerge in cooperative learning arrangements (Walton, 1986). Similarly, the remarkable effectiveness of self-managed teams in boosting work productivity in companies as diverse as Corning, 3M, Texas Instruments, General Mills, Federal Express, Chaparral Steel, and Aetna Life & Casualty (Dumaine, 1990) illustrates how both job involvement and organizational commitment can be significantly increased by aligning task goals with opportunities for self-determination (personal empowerment), intellectual creativity (inventing improved ways of doing business), and belongingness (being part of an interdependent group with a common set of goals). As Maehr and Braskamp (1986) conclude in their analysis of work motivation:

One does not simply select "motivated people" to have a motivated work force; one must also take into account the work and the organizational climate. The organization must provide opportunities for workers to effectively pursue personal incentives that are salient to them. (pp. 121-122)

Another benefit that can result from designing social contexts and tasks that afford the attainment of multiple goals might be called *motivational insurance*. For example, by providing opportunities for self-determination or peer interaction, it may be possible to facilitate meaningful engagement in low-achieving students who generally focus more on fun and friendships than on learning and self-improvement (Wentzel, 1989). Similarly, by organizing tasks so that they require teamwork and accountability to the group, students and workers who might be unenthusiastic about the substance of a task (e.g., memorizing geographical facts, dealing with dissatisfied customers) will nevertheless have other reasons to commit themselves to good performance on the task (e.g., fulfilling one's responsibilities to others, avoiding social disapproval from peers or coworkers). In short, although *high* achievement may require motivational patterns strengthened by the union of multiple goals (Wentzel, 1989, 1991a, 1991b), one may be able to insure at least *adequate* levels of performance by designing classroom and work contexts so that everyone can find at least one good reason to invest themselves in contextually appropriate activities (Pintrich & Garcia, 1991).

Designing contexts so that they afford the attainment of multiple goals is not always an easy task. It may require considerable creativity and a willingness to break out of old habits and routines. The more complicated and often more difficult problem, however, lies in trying to organize contexts so that they facilitate goal *alignment* rather than goal *conflict* (Wentzel, 1989, 1991b). As Dodge, Asher, and Parkhurst (1989) point out, "often, environmental and personal constraints prevent the accomplishment of multiple goals. Priorities must be evaluated and compromises must be reached. Even important goals must be sacrificed occasionally" (p. 122).

The extensive literature on intrinsic motivation and external rewards illustrates how goal conflicts can arise from well-intentioned efforts to enhance motivation. Specifically, numerous researchers have demonstrated that giving people rewards for engaging in an activity can sometimes *decrease* their enjoyment of that activity or their desire to continue their involvement with that activity (e.g., Amabile, DeJong, & Lepper, 1976; Danner & Lonky, 1981; Deci, 1975,

1980; Deci & Ryan, 1985; Lepper & Greene, 1978; Loveland & Olley, 1979; Morgan, 1984). This undermining effect appears to be most likely to occur when one of three different kinds of goal conflicts is created:

1. The reward is seen as an attempt to control a person's behavior (Deci, 1975, 1980; Deci & Ryan, 1985), thus introducing a conflict between the goals that initiated the behavior pattern and the person's self-determination goals (e.g., "You're just saying those nice things so I'll do what you want").

2. The reward distracts the person's attention from his or her original goals for engaging in the activity, thereby reducing rather than increasing the salience of those goals (e.g., "Now that my allowance depends on my grades, all I really care about is what's going to be on the test").

3. The reward alters the psychological meaning of the task in a way that causes the person to devalue the original goals for engaging in the activity (e.g., "This must not be worth doing for its own sake if they have to promise me a reward to do it").

Similar effects have been observed for other kinds of manipulations capable of creating unintended goal conflicts (e.g., goal-setting procedures) (Harackiewicz & Sansone, 1991).

The ubiquity of this undermining phenomenon has led some to conclude that "extrinsic" motivation (i.e., a motivational pattern directed by goals such as material gain or resource acquisition) is bad and should be avoided whenever possible. Although this may be sound advice when motivation is already at a high level (i.e., "If it ain't broke, don't fix it"), it is clearly an overgeneralization (Harackiewicz & Sansone, 1991; Miller & Hom, 1990; Morgan, 1984). Motivational decrements with respect to a particular activity or experience will only result if the reward produces an unintended goal conflict. For example, when a person has no goals (or has avoidance goals) for engaging in an activity, rewards can help facilitate motivation by providing the person with a reason to act (Loveland & Olley, 1979; Miller & Hom, 1990; Pintrich & Garcia, 1991). Similarly, if a reward is given in an "informational" way rather than in a "controlling" manner (i.e., it serves to enhance personal agency beliefs rather than raise concerns about self-determination), the reward is likely to strengthen rather than undermine the existing motivational pattern (Deci & Ryan, 1985; Morgan, 1984). In many cases it may even be possible to align existing goals with the desired outcome represented by the reward, thereby creating an even more potent motivational pattern (Atkinson, 1964; Locke, Bryan, & Kendall, 1968; Pintrich, 1989; Pintrich & Garcia, 1991; Wentzel, 1991a, 1991b). Indeed, a corollary of the multiple goals hypothesis proposed earlier is that **highly motivating activities and experiences will often be directed by goal hierarchies with both intrinsic and extrinsic properties** (e.g., an interesting and well-paying job, an enjoyable and useful social relationship).

Because the concepts of "intrinsic" and "extrinsic" motivation have historically been defined and operationalized as mutually exclusive oppositional forces (e.g., Csikszentmihalyi, 1978; Deci, 1975; Harter, 1981a; Lepper, 1981), and because there is no apparent consensus regarding what categories of goal content are intrinsic and extrinsic (Bandura, 1986; Csikszentmihalyi, 1990; Deci & Ryan, 1985; Malone & Lepper, 1987), these concepts are not highlighted in MST. Instead there is just "motivation"—or more precisely, there are motivational patterns that may vary in terms of goal content and the extent to which multiple goals are aligned in conflictual or mutually facilitative ways. Until greater consensus is reached regarding the prototypical properties of "intrinsic" and "extrinsic" motivational patterns, more precise communication and understanding can be obtained by detailing the specific goal content and relationships among multiple goals involved in the diversity of motivational phenomena represented by these labels.

Across-Episode Goal Hierarchies

The concept of goal hierarchy is also useful for representing the organization of an individual's personal goals at the BES or "personality" level of analysis. Indeed, one of the most promising recent developments in the field of personality psychology is the use of goal assessments to represent the core features of personality (e.g., Emmons, 1989; Ford & Nichols, 1991, 1992; Markus & Ruvolo, 1989; Nichols, 1991; Winell, 1987). This is congruent with the LSF conception of personality outlined in Chapter 2, in which stable, recurring BES that are psychologically anchored by salient personal goals are seen as the fundamental components of personality. Goal hierarchies have also been characterized as central features of personality in several other contemporary theories (e.g., Cantor & Kihlstrom, 1987; Lazarus, 1991a).

The importance of theoretical, empirical, and applied work on the organization of multiple goals at this broader level of analysis becomes even more apparent when it is understood that goal hierarchies are the organizing elements of the so-called "self-system" (i.e., the self-concepts and self-referent processes that define the content and dynamics of a person's behavior and personality), which has become such a prominent topic of study in contemporary psychology (e.g., Connell &

Wellborn, 1990; Harter, 1983; Markus, Cross, & Wurf, 1990; McCombs & Marzano, 1990; Raynor & McFarlin, 1986). As Csikszentmihalyi (1990) explains, "more than anything else, the self represents the hierarchy of goals that we have built up, bit by bit, over the years" (p. 34). If Weiner (1990) is correct in concluding that "the self is on the verge of dominating motivation" (p. 621), then efforts to conceptualize and assess across-episode goal hierarchies are clearly at the cutting edge of motivation theory and research (see also Maehr, 1989).

Recent efforts to study broad patterns of goal content have led to the development of several new procedures for representing goal hierarchies at the BES level of analysis. For example, Ford and Nichols (1987, 1991, 1992) have constructed the *Assessment of Personal Goals* (APG) to measure the general strength of each of the 24 goals in their Taxonomy of Human Goals. The APG is a self-administered paper-and-pencil instrument composed of 24 five-item scales. A diversity of item content is included in each scale in an effort to ensure that, in each case, the overall estimate of goal strength is representative of the broadest possible range of contexts. Goal hierarchies can then be represented in terms of a profile of scores which highlights goals that are particularly likely or unlikely to be of concern to the individual in contexts that afford the attainment of that goal.

More generally, the APG illustrates how the LSF concepts of behavior episode and behavior episode schemata can be used to help address the problem of assessing motivational components and patterns. The basic theoretical assumption is that the best way to index the general salience or strength of a goal, emotion, or personal agency belief (or combination thereof) is to first determine the probability that the motivational component or pattern in question will be activated within each of several specific, theoretically relevant behavior episodes, and then aggregate across these measurements (much like a person might abstract a BES from a set of related behavior episodes) (Nesselroade & Ford, 1987). Consequently, in the APG, items are presented in behavior episode form rather than in a more traditional propositional or trait label format. For example, one of the belonging-ness items presents the following hypothetical scenario: "A friend of yours is moving across the country to take a new job. Would it be important to you to stay in close touch with this friend by mail or phone?" In each such item respondents are asked to rate how likely they would be to desire a particular outcome or to be bothered by a failure to attain that outcome. Response options include "No, definitely not," "Probably not, but perhaps under some circumstances," "Hard to say, it depends on the circumstances," "Probably, but not necessarily in all circumstances," or "Yes, definitely" (in-between responses are also permitted, resulting in a nine-point rating scale).

Because the goal hierarchy representations provided by the APG are described in terms of standardized categories (i.e., those included in the Taxonomy of Human Goals), they are particularly useful when groups of people are being assessed (i.e., when data must be aggregated across individuals) or when comparisons across individuals need to be made. For example, the APG can facilitate the efforts of marriage and relationship counselors who need some way of comparing the goal priorities of different clients. It can also provide useful information to an employer who wants to compare a particular goal profile with that of some normative or exemplary group. Idiographic methods of assessing goal content are generally preferable in research designs and applied settings involving the individual case, however, because such procedures can use the self-constructed labels or mental images of the individual being assessed to describe the person's interests and concerns, thus yielding a more precise representation of their hierarchy of personal goals.

For example, Nichols (1991) has developed a companion measure to the APG, called the *Assessment of Core Goals* (ACG), in which an idiographic process is used to accomplish essentially the same purpose as the APG, namely, the identification and verbal labeling of broad, pervasive goals that may often function outside of awareness. The ACG is a carefully organized sequence of structured exercises through which an individual can move in incremental fashion toward a highly specific and personalized definition of his or her most central and powerful sources of motivation. This process involves four steps. In Step 1 participants recall and list past experiences that were exceptionally satisfying or enjoyable. Because strong positive affect signals the attainment of important personal goals (D. Ford, 1987; Nichols, 1990), it is assumed that core goals were probably involved in most of these experiences. The Ford and Nichols Taxonomy of Human Goals is used in this step as a prompt to help ensure that a broad range of experiences is considered in generating the list. In Step 2 participants more carefully examine up to 15 of these experiences and try to identify for each one the moment of peak satisfaction and the specific event that triggered that feeling. This step is designed to help the person focus on the specific behavior episode in which the core goal was actually attained. In Step 3 participants search for common underlying themes with regard to the goals being satisfied by these 15 experiences and begin the process of trying to construct accurate verbal representations of these themes. This is accomplished by grouping together experiences that seem to have produced the same or a similar ultimate result. This convergence of different experiences that satisfy the same underlying goal is essential to the identification of fundamentally important goals that guide behavior across many different contexts. Finally, in Step 4, participants work to refine and test their initial goal representations until they have defined their unique set of core goals with the greatest clarity and precision possible. Clinical evidence collected thus far indicates that most people define between one and five core goals through this process (Nichols, 1990, 1991).

The ACG's selective focus on "core" goals is based on the clinical observation that people generally have a small set of personal goals that are so important to them that a large portion of their strong feelings of satisfaction and frustration can be traced to these central organizing concerns. Indeed, some ACG respondents have reported having trouble thinking of any highly satisfying experiences that did not satisfy at least one of their core goals. In other cases the connections between core goals and satisfying and dissatisfying life experiences are harder to establish either because the difficulty with the process of identifying and labeling core goals, or because the goal hierarchy being assessed has many context-specific goals that are not clearly linked to more fundamental terminal goals. In this respect it is useful to think of core goals as being analogous to factors in a factor analysis—usually a small number of them are responsible for a large proportion of "variance" in the person's important life experiences, but in some instances a less interpretable "factor solution" will emerge.

Another measure that tries to abstract broad patterns of goal content from idiographic descriptions of specific behavior episode experiences is Winell's AIMS (Adult Intentional and Motivational Systems) Interview (Wadsworth [Winell] & Ford, 1983; Winell, 1987). This measure, which is also available in a self-administered paper-and-pencil format as part of the *Personal Goals Inventory* (PGI), yields a matrix representation of a person's short-, medium-, and long-term goals in six life domains: work and school, family, social life, leisure activities, personal growth and maintenance, and material/environmental concerns (i.e., the AIMS Chart). Attributes of these goals (e.g., importance, opportunity, difficulty, clarity) are then assessed using the second part of the PGI, called the Goal Descriptions Scales.

Emmons' (1986, 1989) "personal striving" approach to motivation and personality provides yet another way to represent goal hierarchies using idiographic descriptions of goal content. "Personal strivings," states Emmons (1989), "refer to the typical types of goals that a person hopes to accomplish in different situations. . . . A personal striving . . . unites what may be phenotypically different goals or actions around a common quality or theme" (p. 92). Personal strivings can be thought of as personalized and contextualized versions of the abstract goal categories represented in the Ford and Nichols Taxonomy of Human Goals, as illustrated by these examples of personal strivings provided by Emmons (1989): "set aside time for 'emotional rest' each day" (tranquility), "make a good impression" (resource acquisition), "show that I am superior to others" (superiority), "make life easier for my parents" (resource provision), and "have as much fun as possible" (entertainment). The *Personal Striving Assessment Packet* (Emmons, 1986) provides the tools needed to represent the nature of and relationships among a diversity of goals represented in this form, which Emmons (1989) characterizes as "the level of analysis that conveys an optimal amount of information about an individual" (p. 121).

Strategies for assessing goal hierarchies at somewhat more context-specific levels of analysis have also been developed in recent years, as illustrated by Klinger's (1977, 1987) work on "current concerns," Little's (1983, 1989) research on "personal projects," Cantor's focus on "life tasks" (Cantor & Fleeson, 1991; Cantor & Kihlstrom, 1987; Cantor & Langston, 1989), and Markus' work on "possible selves" (Markus & Nurius, 1986; Markus & Ruvolo, 1989). These efforts further illustrate the importance and heuristic value of trying to represent broad patterns of goal content in ways that reveal the priorities, conflicts, and instrumental-terminal relationships among multiple goals.

In sum, finding simple ways to express the complex organization of the goals that direct people's behavior over time and across contexts is a challenging task, but one that may yield tremendous practical benefits for counselors and other helping professionals in education, business, and private practice (Ford & Nichols, 1991).

Balancing of Multiple Goals Across Behavior Episodes

Analogous to the problem of aligning multiple goals within episodes, people must find ways to balance their goal-seeking efforts across episodes if they are to maintain effective overall functioning. For example, people who fail to balance strong self-assertive concerns with meaningful integrative goals are likely to be rejected by others for being uncaring, self-centered, domineering, or overly needy (Bakan, 1966;

Koestler, 1967). Conversely, people who fail to balance powerful integrative concerns with self-assertive priorities are likely to suffer behavioral and mental health problems associated with low self-esteem and a loss of personal identity (e.g., cult participation, eating disorders, suicide, etc.) (Koestler, 1967).

This does not mean that people need to have strong goals in every life domain or every category in the Taxonomy of Human Goals to function effectively. Indeed, if people regard too many goals as essential or crucial in importance, they are likely to suffer from considerable anxiety and frustration as a result of being unable to balance their many, often competing priorities (Ford & Nichols, 1992). Moreover, people may sometimes be able to reach extraordinary levels of accomplishment by focusing a great deal of their attention and effort on one particular goal. Nevertheless, as Dodge et al. (1989) point out, "the unrelenting pursuit of a single central goal is a risky business" (p. 124) that can lead to powerful feelings of emptiness and regret, even when the goal is attained. Thus, although it is no doubt the case that, as Winell (1987) states, "many patterns of goal-seeking are probably equally satisfying and successful" (p. 270), it is probably safe to say that single-minded patterns of goal seeking are very likely to produce negative consequences in the long run if they produce a highly unbalanced goal hierarchy (i.e., if they are accompanied by a gross neglect of other important life goals).

In addition to balance in terms of different kinds of goal content, it is important that goals be coordinated along a temporal dimension as well. Short-term goals that provide a focus for current activity must be linked to long-term goals that define the purpose and meaning of that activity (Barden & Ford, 1990, 1991; Harackiewicz & Sansone, 1991). As Csikszentmihalyi (1990) explains, "it is . . . necessary to have an overall context of goals for the events of everyday life to make sense" (p. 213). The prototypical characteristics of a well balanced, effectively functioning goal hierarchy with regard to temporal integration have been concisely summarized by Winell (1987):

> We would generally expect to see in an effective goal hierarchy some definite long-range values that give the person strong direction, a sense of coherence and meaning, and a basis for evaluating one's overall success in life. Intermediate goals would provide concrete objectives for organizing behavior, and immediate goal achievement would provide feedback to the system in the interest of larger objectives. Positive affect would also accompany these evaluative processes. Thus we would see . . . congruence among the levels of the hierarchy (from ultimate values to behavior episodes), producing efficiency and an overall sense

of harmony. . . . People would be focused on the future but would also
be able to experience the joy of the moment. (pp. 270-273)

Goal-Setting Processes

In many situations parents, teachers, employers, and researchers
can safely assume that a person has a particular goal "in mind" (e.g.,
when a task goal has been "assigned" by a legitimate authority
figure, or when a person has already stated the general nature of their
intentions). In such situations the concern often shifts from the
content of the person's directive thoughts to the *method* or *style* they
use to conceptualize the goal. At the behavior episode level, the
cognitive methods or strategies used to represent a goal are called
goal-setting processes. At the BES/personality level of analysis, one
can assess more general styles of goal pursuit, called *goal orientations*.
These can also function as goal-setting processes in specific behavior
episodes.

The extensive literature on goal-setting processes illustrates how the
informed use of goal-setting strategies and techniques can greatly
facilitate effective functioning (Bandura, 1986; Kanfer & Kanfer,
1991; Latham & Yukl, 1975; Lee, Locke, & Latham, 1989; Locke &
Latham, 1984, 1990a, 1990b; Locke, Latham, & Erez, 1988; Locke,
Shaw, Saari, & Latham, 1981; Mento, Steel, & Karren, 1987; Schunk,
1990b, 1991b; Tubbs, 1986). Locke and Latham (1990b) provide the
following summary:

> Nearly 400 (mostly experimental) studies have shown that specific,
> difficult goals lead to better performance than specific, easy goals, vague
> goals such as "do your best," or no goals. These results are based on
> studies conducted in the U.S. and seven other countries. The studies
> have used more than 40,000 subjects, 88 different tasks, time spans
> ranging from one minute to three years, and many different perfor-
> mance criteria, including behavior change, quantity and quality out-
> comes, and costs. The findings emerge at the level of the individual,
> group and organization. (p. 240)

Although the different methods people might use to conceptualize
a goal are usually operationalized in these studies in terms of experimental manipulations rather than through direct cognitive assessment, it has been empirically demonstrated that such manipulations
often do have a strong effect on personal goals (Garland & Adkinson,

1987). This is presumably because "assigned" goals are usually communicated to subjects by legitimate authority figures in contexts where it makes sense to pursue the goal (Locke & Latham, 1990b).

This remarkably robust set of findings illustrates that, under certain circumstances, personal goals can do much more for a person or organization than simply "point them in the right direction." If conceived of in sufficiently concrete terms, they can also define a precise "target" that the individual or group can try to "hit" or approach with their goal-seeking efforts (Harackiewicz & Sansone, 1991). Moreover, if the target is set at an optimally challenging level of difficulty—that is, a level that is "hard" but attainable, both in fact (implying adequate ability and a responsive environment) and belief (implying adequate capability and context beliefs)—progress toward higher levels of achievement and competence is likely to be maximized (Csikszentmihalyi, 1975; Deci & Ryan, 1985; Schunk, 1990b; White, 1959). Indeed, some have attributed Japan's economic success to their clever use of goal-setting techniques that emphasize "Kaizen"—constant improvement toward explicitly defined goals that are more challenging than current levels of achievement or productivity, but also well within reach if effort and commitment are maintained (Imai, 1986).

Consistent with the LSF emphasis on feedback and feedforward processes as regulators of goal-directed activity, numerous studies have demonstrated that goal-setting procedures will only have an enduring effect if (a) feedback information is provided that enables people to evaluate their ongoing progress and identify discrepancies between current and desired consequences (Bandura & Cervone, 1983; Becker, 1978; Erez, 1977; Strang, Lawrence, & Fowler, 1978), and (b) capability beliefs for attaining the desired consequences are positive and resilient in the face of potentially discouraging feedback information (Bandura & Cervone, 1986; Locke et al., 1984; Schunk, 1990b, 1991b; Wood & Bandura, 1989). In addition, consistent with the MST formula for effective functioning, individuals must have the actual skills needed to reach their goals and an environment that is reasonably responsive to their goal-attainment efforts (Locke & Latham, 1990b). The impact of goal-setting procedures can also be enhanced by aligning the goal being set (usually a task goal) with a material gain goal (e.g., through monetary incentives), a social responsibility or resource acquisition goal (e.g., by having individuals publicly commit themselves to the task goal), or some other personally relevant desired consequence (Hollenbeck, Williams, & Klein, 1989; Locke & Latham, 1990b; Locke et al., 1988; Shalley, 1991).

Goal Orientations

Ford and Nichols (1987) have outlined several dimensions along which people may vary in their general orientation to goal setting. *Active-reactive* refers to the extent to which goal-directed activity is initiated by the person or by ongoing events. Because an active goal orientation emphasizes self-direction, planfulness, and an anticipatory approach to goal setting, it tends to be associated with a greater sense of coherence and meaning (because goals are more likely to reflect stable personality patterns than varying situational opportunities), as well as a higher level of behavioral effectiveness (Covey, 1990; Csikszentmihalyi, 1990; M. Ford, 1982; Maehr & Braskamp, 1986). A reactive goal orientation may also yield positive outcomes in some contexts (e.g., those which call for spontaneity or openness to change), but generally only if it is embedded within a broader pattern of active goal setting and goal seeking.

Approach-avoidance refers to whether a person tends to conceptualize goals in terms of positive consequences to be achieved or negative consequences to be avoided (e.g., seeking to improve one's health versus avoiding illness; seeking approval versus avoiding disapproval). This difference in goal orientation can produce very different motivational patterns and consequences even when the same goal content is involved (Raynor & McFarlin, 1986). For example, one might expect to see rather dramatic differences between a casual drug user who wants to experience pleasant bodily sensations and an addict who is trying to avoid the unpleasant sensations associated with drug withdrawal. Similarly, McClelland (1961, 1985) found it useful to differentiate between people's "Motive for Success" and their "Motive to Avoid Failure" in his efforts to predict patterns of achievement-related behavior.

Maintenance-change refers to whether a person generally manifests a stability-maintaining orientation or a change-seeking, self-improvement orientation to goal setting and goal seeking. This is similar to Maslow's (1971) distinction between a *deficiency* and *being* motivational orientation; however, because a being orientation focuses primarily on personal growth in terms of within-person desired consequences, his concept of a *unified* orientation (i.e., an orientation in which "D" and "B" values are fused) may be more closely associated with behavioral change and improvement.

One can also combine the three preceding goal-orientation dimensions to define an even broader pattern, which Winell (1987) labels *coping* versus *thriving* (i.e., a reactive, avoidant, stability-maintaining orientation versus an active, positive, improvement-oriented pattern). Winell's (1987) argument for more emphasis on a thriving orientation in both research and clinical work is congruent with the MST emphasis on facilitating achievement and competence, and is supported by evidence linking aspects of a thriving orientation with indices of mental and physical health. For example, Kobasa's (1979) study of highly stressed executives with favorable and unfavorable health outcomes revealed that the primary factor differentiating these two groups was psychological "hardiness," a concept representing a motivational pattern characterized by a thriving goal orientation and robust personal agency beliefs.

Another goal orientation dimension that has generated considerable interest in the motivational literature is Kuhl's (1981, 1984, 1985; Kuhl & Beckmann, in press) distinction between a *state orientation*, in which people think about their goals in ways that tend to prevent progress toward a preferred state from occurring (e.g., by ruminating about causes and feelings or engaging in wishful thinking), and an *action orientation*, in which people think about their goals in ways that facilitate change toward a preferred state (e.g., by focusing on what action could be taken to solve a problem or reduce feelings of distress). Wicklund (1986) uses the terms *static* and *dynamic orientation* to describe a conceptually similar dimension.

Dweck and her colleagues (Dweck, 1986; Dweck & Leggett, 1988; Elliott & Dweck, 1988) have explicated a goal-orientation dimension that incorporates both the approach-avoidance dimension described earlier and Kuhl's emphasis on unproductive versus productive ways of thinking about desired consequences. Specifically, these researchers distinguish between a *helpless orientation*, in which the goal is to avoid negative social or self-evaluations of one's competence, and a *mastery orientation*, in which the goal is either to increase one's level of competence or to attain positive competence evaluations. A helpless goal orientation, because it generally implies negative PABs for good performance, is associated with a tendency to avoid challenging tasks and circumstances and to give up easily in the face of obstacles and failures. In contrast, a mastery goal orientation, because it implies positive PABs for current or future achievement, is associated with a tendency to seek out new challenges and to persist with renewed effort when problems and difficulties are encountered. The potentially far-reaching consequences of these different motivational patterns are documented and discussed in a number of recent publications (e.g., Dweck, 1986; Dweck & Leggett, 1988; Elliott & Dweck, 1988).

Nicholls (1984a, 1984b, 1990) has offered a related distinction that helps clarify two different mastery-oriented styles of goal seeking that Dweck and her colleagues distinguish in terms of whether people tend to have "entity" or "incremental" theories of intelligence. An *ego-involved* goal orientation is one in which a person is primarily interested in demonstrating ability in the sense of doing better than other people (i.e., superiority is the primary concern). This orientation is particularly characteristic of people who believe that ability is something you either have or you don't (i.e., an entity theory of intelligence). In contrast, a *task-involved* goal orientation is one in which a person is primarily interested in demonstrating ability in the sense of improving one's knowledge or mastery of a task (i.e., understanding or mastery is the primary concern). This orientation is particularly common among people who believe that ability levels can be changed (i.e., an incremental theory of intelligence).

C. Ames and R. Ames (1984a, 1984b) have also written extensively about the importance of this distinction, using the terms *ability-evaluative* and *task mastery* to describe these two goal orientations; however, they also emphasize the need to define a third motivational pattern that may be facilitated in achievement-related contexts, namely, a *moral responsibility* orientation in which cognitive and task goals are aligned with integrative goals such as resource provision and social responsibility. These have proven to be very useful distinctions in identifying and clarifying various patterns of achievement motivation. For example, C. Ames and R. Ames (1984a, 1984b) have linked these three motivational patterns to the literature on competitive, individualistic, and cooperative goal structures (respectively) and have persuasively argued (C. Ames, 1987) that:

> there is little, if any, viable evidence that a competitive goal structure in the classroom is associated with outcomes that are indicative of positive self-worth, continuing motivation, or quality of task engagement. (p. 142)

There is still a need for more research, however, both in the classroom and in the workplace, focusing on the possibility of aligning the goals prototypically associated with these different motivational arrangements. For example, in their extensive review of the literature on goal structures and achievement, Johnson et al. (1982) found that the positive effects of cooperative goal structures were not diminished with the addition of intergroup competition. Similarly, Wentzel (1989, 1991a, 1991b) has demonstrated in her research on multiple goals in the classroom that high-achieving students are distinguished from average- and low-achieving students by their greater efforts to achieve *all three* kinds of goals (i.e., evaluation, mastery, and social responsibility). Thus **achievement and competence are greatly facilitated by efforts to enhance goal alignment,** both in terms of the goals afforded by the context and the goal coordination skills of the individual (Wentzel, 1991b).

Wishes, Current Concerns, and Intentions

With respect to other motivational processes, personal goals typically do not operate in an uncompromising, dictatorial manner. Instead, they are closely linked with a variety of evaluative processes (i.e., goal evaluations, personal agency beliefs, and emotions) that help determine whether a particular goal should be activated, and if so, what priority it should have relative to other goals. Consequently, goals can vary dramatically in terms of the extent to which they are actually serving their function of directing and organizing ongoing behavior patterns. At one end of the continuum are goals that fail to gain priority because they are associated with strong inhibiting emotions (e.g., fear or guilt), or are evaluated as highly unrealistic or so discrepant from one's current state that meaningful progress toward the goal is impossible, at least under present circumstances. These are often called *wishes* (Heckhausen & Kuhl, 1985; James, 1892) or fantasies (Pervin, 1983). Such goals are unlikely to direct instrumental episodes, but they may direct episodes in which action is inhibited (i.e., observational or thinking episodes). Indeed, wishes and fantasies may be important mechanisms for maintaining hope and experiencing some degree of satisfaction in circumstances where action is inadvisable or infeasible.

Further along the continuum are goals that have "passed" a set of general evaluative "tests" (e.g., goal-importance and emotional-salience tests), and are now influencing the rest of the system through their selective organizing function (i.e., the goals have directed the instrumental "troops" to "stand by" for possible action). Klinger (1975) has labeled such goals *current concerns*. He also uses the term *commitment* to describe the enhanced priority that results from the evaluative affirmation of these goals. Because current concerns are not directly tied to specific behavior episodes, however, the term *general commitment* is used in MST to describe that outcome.

Finally, at the other end of the continuum are goals that are highly prioritized and currently directing or ready to direct system activity. These are called *intentions*. An intention can be thought of as a current concern that has been prioritized by cognitive and emotional regulatory processing and infused with emotional energy. In other words, it has passed not only a set of general evaluative tests, but also a set of specific tests pertaining directly to one's current circumstances (Pervin, 1991). As a result of passing these additional tests, "the coast is clear" for the person's instrumental processes to begin engaging in activity designed to achieve the goal. The person has made a *specific commitment* to achieving the goal in the current behavior episode.

It is important to note that the number and kind of evaluative tests that a goal must pass before it can become an intention may vary tremendously. At one extreme are people who agonize so much about whether to turn a goal into an intention that they become unable to make a commitment to any course of action (i.e., they suffer "paralysis through analysis"). Alternatively, in the case of impulsive behavior, activity may flow directly from the conceptualization of a goal without any evaluative tests being conducted beyond those already embedded in the BES anchored by that goal. Indeed, a major goal of socialization is to help people learn how to evaluate their goals in a conscious, realistic manner. By doing so they will be more likely to behave with "good intentions" in specific behavior episodes (i.e., to activate goals that are situationally appropriate and socially desirable) and to pursue important goals in a timely manner. Similarly, many educational and counseling interventions are designed to help people evaluate the goal choices they have made or are considering making in their personal and professional lives.

A variety of different criteria may be used by the psychological evaluators in "motivational headquarters" to determine which goals should be prioritized in the context of a specific behavior episode. In MST terms, these criteria generally focus on one or more of the following properties of behavior episodes:

1. *goal relevance* (i.e., what goals are meaningful or appropriate in a particular context);
2. *goal importance* (i.e., to what extent are the relevant goals in a particular context personally significant to the individual);
3. *goal attainability* (i.e., personal agency beliefs); and
4. *emotional salience* of the actions and consequences associated with pursuing and achieving the goal.

Heckhausen and Kuhl (1985) use the acronym "OTIUM" to describe essentially these same criteria. The "O" and "T" in OTIUM refer to whether the current context affords the *opportunity* and *time* needed to achieve the goal. The "I" stands for the *importance* of the goal being evaluated (e.g., is the goal a passionately desired outcome, or just a passing fancy?). The "U" stands for a feeling of *urgency*, such as that associated with an impending deadline or an opportunity that may soon disappear. This criterion represents the emotional component of the evaluative team, as it is associated with anxiety, excitement, and other anticipatory emotions (e.g., sexual arousal). Finally, the "M" refers to whether the person believes that the *means* needed to attain the goal are available (i.e., whether the person has the capabilities and responsive environment required for goal attainment). Thus like the MST criteria of goal relevance, goal importance, goal attainability, and emotional salience, the OTIUM criteria represent all three component processes of motivational patterns as well as the context in which they are embedded.

For example, a doctor treating a critically ill patient may decide not to proceed with efforts to save the person's life because: (a) the goal is no longer relevant—it's too late to do anything for the patient (no time), or the patient has left the hospital (no opportunity); (b) the goal of saving the person's life is diminished in value relative to other goals by the irreversible nature of the illness (reduced goal importance); (c) other patients have more immediately compelling problems (low urgency or emotional salience); or (d) the needed equipment, materials, or expertise are not available (no means/negative PABs). Similarly, a college student may put off writing a term paper because: (a) the instructor has not yet decided whether to make the paper a required assignment, (b) the student has an opportunity to pursue a high-priority entertainment or belongingness goal, (c) the paper isn't due for another week, or (d) the student lacks some crucial information or resource (e.g., instructions on how to write the paper, essential library materials, a functioning word processor).

Because the influence of goals on behavior is a function of the extent to which they are prioritized by cognitive and emotional regulatory processing (Pervin, 1991), the MST distinctions between wishes, current concerns, and intentions are important ones for researchers studying the impact of goals on a person's functioning. For example, the links between general indices of goal content and behavioral outcomes are typically subtle and complex (M. Ford, 1984, 1986; Markus & Ruvolo, 1989; Nichols, 1990; Pervin, 1989). Similarly tenuous relationships between cognition and behavior are typically found in studies of global attitudes and values (Ajzen & Fishbein, 1977, 1980; Fishbein & Ajzen, 1975). In contrast, studies of intentions provide evidence demonstrating that goals are strong and reliable predictors of what a person actually tries to do in a specific situation, especially if attentional energy is being devoted to a particular intention (Ajzen, 1985; Ajzen & Fishbein, 1980; Atkinson & Birch, 1970; Kuhl, 1985; Locke & Latham, 1984, 1990a; Tubbs & Ekeberg, 1991). As Csikszentmihalyi (1990) succinctly puts it, intentions are "the force that keeps information in consciousness ordered" (p. 27).

Yet it is precisely because intentions are more closely tied to the opportunities and constraints of current or impending behavior episodes that it is useful to have a conceptually "purer" way of thinking about goal content that can reflect not only those desired consequences that are currently being attended to, but also those that have been "put on the shelf," "lost in the shuffle," or not yet conceptualized in concrete, practical terms. For example, studies of "wishes" may be particularly informative in clinical and counseling settings involving confused or distressed people who are having difficulty formulating realistic goals or translating their goals into action. In contrast, studies focusing on current concerns—personal goals that are more realistic than wishes but not as closely tied to the opportunities and constraints of specific behavior episodes as intentions— might be of particular value in terms of understanding the links between goal hierarchies and broader patterns of achievement and competence (Emmons, 1989; Little, 1983; Wentzel, 1989; Winell, 1987).

The Role of Consciousness

As is the case with all cognitive processes, personal goals can and often do function outside awareness (Nisbett & Wilson, 1977; Pervin, 1983; Shevrin & Dickman, 1980). This is possible because goals are organized in behavior episode schemata that can guide behavior even when only a part of the activated BES is represented in consciousness. Such BES often include the prepackaged results of a diversity of goal evaluations, many of which need not be repeated each time the goal is considered (e.g., the importance of the goal and whether the means for achieving it are available). This capability for automating major BES components can greatly enhance the efficiency of goal-directed activity, especially in contexts characterized by stability and predictability. Indeed, focusing attention on the goals being served by a well-organized behavior pattern can sometimes disrupt performance, as when skilled athletes, test takers, and dating partners "choke" under the pressure of thinking about the importance of achieving their desired consequences or avoiding the "disastrous" consequences of failure (Baumeister, 1984). On the other hand, it is difficult to function effectively in complex, variable environments or to alter current steady state patterns without paying at least some attention to the goals directing those episodes.

In short, although some goals are easy to access and keep "in mind," it is quite possible (and probably very common) for people to organize their behavior around the idea of a desired or undesired consequence without being fully aware of what they are trying to do. In some instances they may even be mistaken about their "true intentions." Like the "hidden" mechanical components under the hood of a car, however, goals must be *available* to consciousness if they are to maintain their capacity to direct behavior in an efficient and effective manner. Helping people bring their goals into consciousness by putting them into some perceptible form (e.g., words or images) is the primary function of goal assessments and a major task of counselors and other helping professionals (Ford & Nichols, 1991, 1992).

Goals and Standards for Goal Attainment

The intimate relationship between directive and regulatory processes is illustrated by the problem of distinguishing between the thoughts that direct and organize an episode (personal goals) and those that are used as criteria for conducting performance evaluations. These latter thoughts are typically called *standards for goal attainment, performance standards,* or *achievement standards* (recall that in MST the concept of achievement is used to represent the attainment of any personally or socially valued goal in a particular context). Such standards are usually derived from one of two sources: contextual information (e.g., factual points of reference or normative guides to behavior) or the goals themselves (e.g., in the form of imagined possibilities) (Frey & Ruble, 1990; Higgins, Strauman, & Klein, 1986). In other words, standards tend to emerge from one or both of the two anchoring components of behavior episodes. Thus in some cases the person's goal representations will have the standards to be used to evaluate goal attainment embedded within them (which is how the concept of a "clear" or "specific" goal is usually operationalized) (Schunk, 1990b, 1991b), and in other cases this responsibility is delegated to the instrumental "troops" who are transacting with the environment. The former alternative is more likely to occur in highly organized contexts or in familiar episodes for which the person has a well-organized BES; the latter alternative is more common in unfamiliar situations or situations for which the "rules of the game" are open or not yet clear.

For example, a student might begin a class with the goal of earning a good grade without knowing precisely what "good" means in that particular context (i.e., because grading practices vary and the difficulty of the course is not yet known). After seeing the distribution of scores from the midterm exam for the course and hearing the instructor explain how those scores are likely to be translated into final grades, however, the student's desired outcome is likely to be elaborated to include a specific achievement standard. In other words, the standard is now embedded in the goal—the standard and the goal are "fused" (Ford & Lerner, 1992) into one inseparable unit.

Of course, the process of integrating standards for goal attainment into the goals they serve is a dynamic, continuous process rather than an all-or-none affair. For example, a business manager with a "be profitable" goal that includes a clear specification of the desired level of profit may routinely modify that goal based on changes in current economic conditions. An athlete with a very specific task goal (e.g., run a mile in under 4 minutes) may revise that goal upward or downward if he encounters unexpected success or suffers a performance-related injury. A prosecutor with a clear idea of how she wants a justice goal to be accomplished may alter that goal if problems or opportunities arise (e.g., unexpected testimony or a plea-bargaining offer). A parent with a strong desire to clean up a room full of toys may decide to "satisfice" (i.e., accept a less-than-optimal achievement standard) as it becomes clearer how much effort is required to achieve that goal.

The distinction between goals and standards becomes increasingly important as the directive process becomes less involved in the process of defining standards for goal attainment. For example, when people are asked to describe the goals that directed their behavior in episodes involving fun, relaxation, or being with friends, they often say that they had no goals. What they invariably mean, however, is that they had no concrete *standards* for goal attainment— whatever happened was fine with them as long as they were "having a good time" or "being with people they liked." Indeed, it is evident that a key source of pleasure in such episodes is being able to escape from the performance standards that pervade everyday life (D. Bergin, 1989)—the person can just "go with the flow," "take things as they come," and not worry about failure or incompetence (i.e., because success is almost guaranteed when the standards for goal attainment are so flexible). Conversely, many common motivational problems can be traced to goals that have been infused with standards for goal attainment that are too high or too rigid for the contexts in which they are being applied. Terms such as "perfectionistic" and "up-tight" are often used to describe such problems, as illustrated by people who constantly worry about the quality of their work, the adequacy of their emotional states, the appropriateness of their social behavior or physical appearance, or the status of their inter-personal relationships.

Inflexible standards for goal attainment are not always attribut-able to cognitive rigidity, however. Often such standards are an intrinsic part of the task or social context, as is often the case in competitive situations or other highly evaluative contexts in which there are clear "winners" and "losers." Predictably, the results are similar to cases in which it is the person defining the standard: unless capabilities are solid and personal agency beliefs are robust, it is difficult to avoid some degree of motivational debilitation. For ex-ample, in the education and business literatures virtually all of the contexts that are commonly associated with anxiety are contexts in which "right" and "wrong" ways of functioning are unusually clear and definite (e.g., test anxiety, math anxiety, computer anxiety, public speaking anxiety, etc.). Thus both **people and contexts with uncompromising standards are likely to be in a motivationally precarious position.**

The earlier use of the phrase "go with the flow" is quite similar to the more formal concept of *flow* introduced by Csikzentmihalyi (1975, 1978, 1990; Csikzentmihalyi & Csikzentmihalyi, 1988) to de-scribe the pattern of activity and enjoyment people experience in behavior episodes in which specific standards for goal attainment are permitted to emerge as a consequence of interaction with the environ-ment. Such episodes are goal-directed but unconstrained by the expec-tations and preconceptions that typically accompany "fixed" stan-dards for goal attainment. This enables people to "discover" the standards that are appropriate for them given the pattern of interests and skills they bring to the situation and the variety of transactional opportunities afforded by the task or social environment. The major advantage cited by Csikszentmihalyi of approaching situations without preconceived standards is much like that described in the previous paragraph—assuming that some general goal is activated and the context is organized to facilitate pursuit of that goal (e.g., by minimizing distractions and providing informative feedback), success, as well as the enjoyment and satisfaction that accompany success, are an almost inevitable consequence of engaging in the task or activity at hand. Csikszentmihalyi also emphasizes, however, another benefit of "flow" experiences, namely, the fact that creative processes and products are most likely to emerge when there are many different ways of engaging in an activity and no predetermined notion of what the optimal result might look like. As Ford and Nichols (1987) note, "the particular desired outcome of creative activity is usually not known in advance. Consequently, creativity goals must be specified or clarified as the activity progresses" (p. 302).

The connections between goals and regulatory processes are further explicated in Chapter 5, which focuses on the unique and joint contributions of emotions and personal agency beliefs to motivational patterns and behavioral regulation.

Suggestions for Further Reading

Ames, C., & Ames, R. (Eds.) (1989). *Research on motivation in education, Vol. 3: Goals and cognitions.* San Diego, CA: Academic Press.

Csikszentmihalyi, M. (1990). *Flow: The psychology of optimal experience.* New York: Harper & Row.

Elliott, E. S., & Dweck, C. S. (1988). Goals: An approach to motivation and achievement. *Journal of Personality and Social Psychology, 54,* 5-12.

Kuhl, J., & Beckmann, J. (Eds.) (1985). *Action control: From cognition to behavior.* Berlin: Springer-Verlag.

Locke, E. A., & Latham, G. P. (Eds.) (1990a). *A theory of goal setting and task performance.* Englewood Cliffs, NJ: Prentice-Hall.

Locke, E. A., & Latham, G. P. (1990b). Work motivation and satisfaction: Light at the end of the tunnel. *Psychological Science, 1,* 240-246.

Maehr, M. L., & Pintrich, P. (Eds.) (1991). *Advances in motivation and achievement, Vol. 7: Goals and self-regulatory processes.* Greenwich, CT: JAI Press.

Pervin, L. A. (Ed.) (1989). *Goal concepts in personality and social psychology.* Hillsdale, NJ: Lawrence Erlbaum.

Winell, M. (1987). Personal goals: The key to self-direction in adulthood. In M. E. Ford & D. H. Ford (Eds.), *Humans as self-constructing living systems: Putting the framework to work* (pp. 261-287). Hillsdale, NJ: Lawrence Erlbaum.

CHAPTER FIVE

Personal Agency Beliefs and Emotional Arousal Processes

You cannot stop the birds of worry from flying over your head. But you can stop them from building a nest in your head.

Proverb

Personal Agency Beliefs

EARLIER (IN CHAPTER 3) a heuristic scheme for classifying the processes contributing to effective functioning was introduced:

Achievement/Competence = Motivation x Skill x Responsive Environment

(Note that, for communicative ease, the "biology" component is not portrayed in this or subsequent representations of this formula; however, the reader should keep in mind that the motivation and skill components rest on a foundation of biological functioning.) One particularly useful property of this scheme that can now be explained is its ability to show how personal agency beliefs help integrate motivational patterns with the rest of the system. Essentially, *capability beliefs* are evaluations of whether one has the personal *skill* needed to function effectively, and *context beliefs* are evaluations of whether one has the *responsive environment* needed to support effective functioning. This can be represented as follows:

Achievement/Competence = Motivation (Goals x Emotions x
Capability Beliefs x Context Beliefs)

x Skill   x Responsive Environment

Thus PABs contribute to the decisions made in "motivational headquarters" by determining whether the instrumental "troops" have the ability and opportunity to achieve a desired result.

This formulation makes it clear that it is not enough to have a goal in mind and the objective skills and circumstances needed to attain it. People must also *believe* that they have the capabilities and opportunities needed to achieve their goal. Indeed, such beliefs are often more fundamental than the actual skills and circumstances they represent in the sense that they can motivate people to create opportunities and acquire capabilities they do not yet possess (Bandura, 1986; Gurin & Brim, 1984; Harter, 1981b; Maehr & Braskamp, 1986; Phillips & Zimmerman, 1990; Schunk, 1990b; Seligman, 1991). Consequently, as Kolligian and Sternberg (1990) point out: "at all points in the life cycle it is one's construal of reality, rather than reality itself, that most accurately predicts self-concepts, goals, academic performance, and overall mental health" (p. ix).

The fact that people will generally fail to capitalize on real and potential skills and opportunities if they lack a sense of personal agency should not be interpreted to mean that positive capability and context beliefs are *sufficient* for desired outcomes to occur. Ultimately people must still have relevant skills and a responsive environment. Indeed, qualities such as confidence, hope, and optimism may seem rather weak in the face of major skill deficits, chronic environmental stressors, and other formidable obstacles to goal attainment. They may also be of relatively little concern in situations requiring only modest skills or a minimal level of environmental responsiveness. Thus the "power of positive thinking" is of greatest relevance when it can "open the door" to possibilities and pathways that are neither impossible nor trivially easy to negotiate. In other words, **personal agency beliefs play a particularly crucial role in situations that are of the greatest developmental significance—those involving challenging but attainable goals.** Consequently, they are often key targets of intervention for parents, teachers, counselors, and others interested in promoting effective functioning.

Goals and Personal Agency Beliefs

Personal agency beliefs are evaluative thoughts involving a comparison between a desired consequence (i.e., some goal) and an anticipated consequence (i.e., what the person expects to happen if they pursue that goal). Consequently, personal agency beliefs pertaining to a particular goal have no meaning or functional significance if that goal is dormant or of no value to the individual. For example, if a young woman is uncertain about her ability to raise a child (capability belief) and anticipates that she would have to give up her career to do so (context belief), but has no interest in being a mother (personal goal), those beliefs will be of little significance in her life. It is only when a relevant goal is activated or being considered (e.g., the woman changes her mind or becomes pregnant) that such personal agency beliefs can have some motivational impact. Similarly, if someone feels completely incapable of picking up a snake (capability belief) and expects that this action could result in a fatal bite (context belief), but rarely ever thinks about the consequences of interacting with a snake (personal goal), his or her negative PABs will not have a meaningful impact on the person's everyday life (in contrast to a snake phobic, who may worry about the possibility of encountering a snake in a wide range of behavior episodes).

On the other hand, personal agency beliefs can have a tremendous impact on the *development and elaboration* of BES anchored around a particular goal. For example, if the woman in the preceding example became pregnant and was therefore forced to anticipate the consequences of motherhood, her decision about whether to have an abortion might be heavily influenced by her capability and context beliefs. Similarly, if a snake were to be seen slithering under a house that a person was planning to buy, that might alter the person's decision making and future life in a rather dramatic fashion. Still it is important to keep in mind that, in terms of current steady state functioning, **personal agency beliefs only matter if there is some goal in place.**

This principle has been noted by several theorists (e.g., Bandura, 1986; Phares, 1976) and is reinforced by the recent addition of a goal assessment to Harter's (1982) Perceived Competence Scale. The links between goals and personal agency beliefs, have apparently not been emphasized with sufficient strength and clarity, however, as evidenced by the fact that most investigators do not include goal importance as a factor in their research designs. Failure to take this variable into account has detracted from the interpretability of research on personal agency beliefs. For example, many instances in which assessments of learned helplessness, self-efficacy, locus of control, and the like have failed to predict theoretically expected consequences may be attributable to subjects' lack of concern about the content being assessed. Indeed, in feedback interviews focusing on the interpretation of people's scores on the *Assessment of Personal Agency Beliefs* (APAB), a 24-item measure of capability and context beliefs based on the Ford and Nichols Taxonomy of Human Goals, Ford and Chase (1991) found that low PAB scores for goals rated as "never" or "seldom important" were rarely accompanied by expressions of anxiety, worry, despair, or any of the other emotions normally associated with negative personal agency beliefs. In fact, these scores were generally dismissed by respondents as being essentially irrelevant—they merely reflected the person's lack of interest in those domains. Consequently, researchers and practitioners should adopt a cautious stance when trying to interpret PAB information that is not accompanied by evidence verifying that these beliefs reflect significant personal concerns.

Linking PAB and goal assessments can also help reveal when personal agency beliefs are likely to have their greatest motivational impact. For example, in a longitudinal study of 250 junior high school students, Meece, Wigfield, and Eccles (1990) found that the best predictor of math grades was students' expectancies for future math success (i.e., their personal agency beliefs). They also discovered, however, that the best predictor of students' intentions to continue with math coursework was the *importance* of math to the student. This suggests that the first priority of educators trying to facilitate long-term gains in mathematics achievement should be to persuade students of the personal relevance and value of math skills for their everyday lives and imagined futures. In other words, negative emotions and personal agency beliefs cannot emerge as major motivational barriers until students have accepted the premise that mathematics achievement is important. As Lee, Ichikawa, and Stevenson (1987) explain in their analysis of the differences in mathematics achievement in Chinese, Japanese, and American children:

> Mathematics is not emphasized in American elementary schools and the mathematics curriculum is not difficult. . . . Moreover, American children believe they are doing well in mathematics and their mothers express satisfaction with the children's academic performance. As a

consequence, the motivation of American children to apply themselves diligently to the study of mathematics does not appear to be as high as that of children in countries such as Taiwan and Japan, and American parents perceive less need to assist their children in mathematics or to seek changes in mathematics instruction than do Chinese and Japanese parents. . . . The problem in American elementary schools seems to be that of convincing both teachers and parents that mathematics and science . . . merit the children's close attention. (pp. 176, 178)

The shifting of the motivational burden from goals to personal agency beliefs after goal commitments have been made is also apparent in Miura's (1987) research on computer interest and use in junior high school students. In this study current and future goals related to computer use were strong predictors of anticipated future involvement with computers but relatively weak predictors of current computer use outside the classroom. On this latter criterion, self-efficacy for computer use was a much more informative predictor.

Another important consideration in understanding the links between goals and personal agency beliefs has to do with the *temporal proximity* of the goals being evaluated. Specifically, it appears that the demotivating impact of uncertainty about personal capabilities and environmental responsiveness may be reduced by focusing attention on "controllable short-term goals" (Barden & Ford, 1990, 1991)—that is, proximal subgoals that seem to be clearly attainable with a manageable degree of effort. Adopting such goals implies, virtually by definition, the activation of a BES with positive capability and context beliefs and a high probability of generating encouraging feedback information (Bandura, 1986; Bandura & Schunk, 1981). Under these circumstances it is usually possible to maintain a reasonably high level of motivation even when ultimate outcomes remain doubtful. This is especially likely if one can combine a confident, practical approach to the present ("I'm going to concentrate on what I can do right now and give it my best shot") with a philosophical view of the future ("Hopefully, everything will turn out for the best"). That is the approach connoted by the Japanese word "nintendo," which video game aficionados will not be surprised to learn means "work hard, but in the end it is in heaven's hands" (see also Azuma, 1984; Weisz, Rothbaum, & Blackburn, 1984).

Capability Beliefs

The concept of capability beliefs in Motivational Systems Theory is similar to Bandura's (1977b, 1982) concept of *self-efficacy* expectations.

For two reasons, however, the MST conceptualization of this motivational process affords greater theoretical scope and precision. First, because "skill" is defined in the MST formula for effective functioning as the entire set of nonmotivational psychological processes, capability beliefs can reflect confidence or doubts about any of a number of personal strengths or weaknesses: perceptual, motor, or communicative skills; memory or information-processing capabilities; self-control or self-regulatory skills; capabilities for dealing with stressful circumstances; or one's capacity for selective or sustained attentional or activity arousal. Thus it is explicitly recognized in MST that when people say they are unable to do something, they may be referring to different kinds of skill deficits in different circumstances—deficits that may vary in terms of how stable or alterable they are in the face of some experimental or therapeutic intervention. For example, it may be easier to put aside negative capability beliefs pertaining to arousal functions (e.g., one's ability to approach a feared object) than to overcome self-doubts about motor skills (e.g., accomplishing a difficult athletic feat) (Kirsch, 1982).

Bandura's failure to clarify the different kinds of skills that may be involved in self-efficacy judgments is one reason his theory has generated a fair amount of confusion and controversy in recent years (e.g., Corcoran, 1991; Kirsch, 1986). Bandura's (1977b) original definition of self-efficacy as "the conviction that one can successfully execute the behavior required to produce [particular] outcomes" (p. 193) was precise (because it focused specifically on transactional capabilities), but narrow. In contrast, his more recent definitions (Bandura, 1986), in which he has emphasized that "skills" involve the organization and orchestration of multiple cognitive, social, and motor capabilities, and that "self-efficacy is concerned with generative capabilities, not with component acts" (p. 397), are more comprehensive in scope. They are also, however, less precise in meaning because, in contrast to the LSF, there is no explicit model of functional capabilities and their organization in social cognitive theory, only a vague conception of "triadic reciprocality" among cognition, action, and the environment.

A second reason to prefer the MST formulation of capability beliefs is that the concept of self-efficacy has usually been restricted to beliefs about task goals in context-specific behavior episodes. Although this relatively narrow use of the self-efficacy concept may reflect tradition more than theoretical necessity, the word "task" does appear in some definitional statements (e.g., "self-efficacy is concerned with people's beliefs in their capabilities to mobilize the motivation, cognitive resources, and courses of action needed to exercise control over task demands" [Bandura, 1990, p. 316]). In contrast, capability beliefs may pertain to any kind of goal (e.g., affective goals, social relationship goals) and any level of abstraction, including highly abstracted BES (Ford & Chase, 1991).

Researchers and practitioners would be well advised, however, to heed the warnings of Bandura (1990) and others (e.g., Lefcourt, 1981; Phares, 1976) regarding the dangers of assuming that predictive precision can be obtained from generalized measures of personal agency beliefs (e.g., general self-esteem and locus of control measures). For example, in summing up the predictive power of global measures of internal versus external locus of control, Phares (1976) concluded that "I-E may do a good job of predicting people's behavior in general, but miss rather badly in any specific situation. Whether we can tolerate such misses depends on our purposes" (p. 46). Thus one must balance the conflicting goals of predictive generality and predictive precision by applying the following principle: assess capability and context beliefs at a level of generality that is as context-specific as possible given the breadth of the phenomena under investigation. If the phenomena of interest are, in fact, broad in content and manifested in a diverse array of contexts, then a relatively global assessment may be quite appropriate. Generalized assessments constructed from multiple context-specific assessments may be particularly effective in minimizing the resulting loss of predictive precision (e.g., Ford & Nichols, 1992; Nichols, 1991).

The concept of capability beliefs is also similar to Gurin and Brim's (1984) concept of *personal efficacy*; Skinner et al.'s (1988) and Chapman, Skinner, and Baltes' (1990) concept of *agency beliefs* (also called *capacity beliefs* by Skinner, Wellborn, and Connell [1990]); and the concept of *perceived competence* as used by Deci (1980), Harter (1982), and Weisz and Stipek (1982). In fact, the MST concept of capability beliefs was originally called perceived competence (M. Ford, 1985; Ford & Thompson, 1985) until an astute student pointed out the conceptual imprecision involved in restricting the term perceived competence to qualities of the *person* when the term competence was being used to refer to patterns of effective *person-environment* interaction. (Note also that, following the definitional logic outlined in Chapter 2, the term "perceived" was replaced by "beliefs" to avoid the problem of referring to cognitions as perceptions.) This personally compelling demonstration of the tendency of people to think of competence as a personal attribute rather than as a joint product of a motivated, capable person and a responsive environment (Sternberg, 1990) suggested that it would not be wise to substitute the term "competence beliefs" for "personal agency beliefs," even though it would be theoretically appropriate and parsimonious to do so.

Another problem with the concept of perceived competence is that it has become increasingly associated with evaluations of perceived ability *in comparison to other people* (e.g., Harter, 1982; Phillips & Zimmerman, 1990). Because such evaluations depend on both the person's capabilities *and* the environment's responsiveness (i.e., in terms of how tough the competition is), they are difficult to interpret. Indeed, as noted earlier, the problem of unconfounding such evaluations is the core of Dweck's (1986) distinction between incremental and entity theories of intelligence (Dweck, 1986), Nicholls' (1984a, 1984b) contrast between task- and ego-involved goal orientations, and C. Ames and R. Ames' (1984a, 1984b) distinction between task mastery and ability-evaluative motivational patterns. The concept of capability beliefs seems less likely to invite such confounding.

Context Beliefs

Just as the meaning of a capability belief depends on the specific skills required for a particular kind of achievement, the precise meaning of a *context belief* depends on the particular environmental components relevant to that achievement. For example, an avid golfer with compelling goals, positive emotions, and strong capability beliefs might nevertheless decide to cancel a long-awaited match if he anticipates: (a) unplayable weather conditions (unresponsive natural environment (e.g., "It looks like we may get some lightning"); (c) equipment failure (unresponsive designed environment (e.g., "I'm afraid I can't play until I get these clubs regripped"); (c) negative spousal reactions (unresponsive human environment, e.g., "I'd like to play but my wife won't let me"); or (d) restrictive policies regarding who can play (unresponsive sociocultural environment (e.g., "I think there's a tournament this week, so we probably won't be able to play"). In each case the environment is perceived as untrustworthy or uncooperative, and initiation of the golfing episode is inhibited.

Another way to understand the variety of meanings that may be represented in a context belief is to consider the different functional elements that are needed to have an optimally responsive environment. First, **the environment must be congruent with an individual's "agenda" of personal goals**. This means that it must afford the attainment of personally valued outcomes (Maehr & Braskamp, 1986). It also implies, however, that the context must not be experienced as overly controlling in terms of the way it defines the "menu" of possible goals. Motivation is usually diminished when people experience a lack of "ownership" or personal commitment to the goals they are pursuing, or when they feel that they have no choice about what goals to pursue or how to pursue them (Deci & Ryan, 1985). Contexts may also be viewed as unresponsive if they are overly demanding, that is, if the agenda of "goal requirements" defined by the context is regarded as unreasonable in terms of time, effort, difficulty, or obstacles to goal attainment.

Second, **the environment must be congruent with the person's biological, transactional, and cognitive capabilities.** For example, a context may be so dark, crowded, noisy, or physically unsafe that desired outcomes are virtually impossible to accomplish; or, the environment may be unresponsive in the sense that it fails to provide information about goals, standards, rules, procedures, or contingencies in a clear, consistent, or meaningful way. This kind of unresponsiveness is characteristic of many ineffective parents, teachers, administrators, and managers.

Third, **the environment must have the material and informational resources needed to facilitate goal attainment.** For example, people must have access to needed tools, equipment, transportation, supplies, and other materials. Desired goods and services must also be available and affordable. In addition, people must be able to obtain sound advice, instruction, training, and guidance when they are unable to continue making progress toward their goals on their own.

Finally, **the environment must provide an emotional climate that supports and facilitates effective functioning.** Concepts such as warmth, social support, and trust focus on this facet of environmental responsiveness. Such variables have been linked with enhanced motivation, learning, and performance in a diversity of contexts, including home, school, work, and clinical settings (e.g., Baumrind, 1978; C. Bergin, 1987; Brophy, 1987; Cohen & Wills, 1985; Erickson, 1963; Karimi, 1988; Zand, 1972).

The MST formulation of context beliefs is similar to but broader than a variety of related concepts, including *system responsiveness* (Gurin & Brim, 1984), *perceived contingency* (Weisz & Stipek, 1982), and *behavior-outcome expectancy* (Bandura, 1982). Each of these concepts emphasizes the core idea of contingency between a person's actions and the context's response. In addition, Skinner et al. (1988; Chapman et al., 1990) characterize their concept of *means-ends beliefs* (also called *strategy beliefs* by Skinner et al., 1990) as fitting into this family of concepts; however, their formulation appears to fit better under the LSF rubric of means evaluations because it focuses more on the general efficacy of various means to goal attainment than on the environment's responsiveness to a particular person's goal attainment efforts.

Context beliefs are also sometimes referred to as *perceptions of control* (e.g., Connell, 1985; M. Ford, 1985; Ford & Thompson, 1985). As noted earlier in this chapter, however, the same or similar terms are also used to refer to personal agency beliefs in general (e.g., Burger, 1989; Chapman et al., 1990; Skinner et al., 1988; Skinner et al., 1990; Weisz & Stipek, 1982). The conceptually ambiguous status of the term "perceived control" (Weisz & Cameron, 1985) decreases its utility and makes it unsuitable for inclusion in MST.

Another source of conceptual confusion in this literature is the confounding of personal agency beliefs with the sources of information that may influence those beliefs—for example, feedback about past accomplishments (which may or may not influence feedforward processes) and, in particular, causal attributions. Because causal attributions are, by definition (Weiner, 1986), cognitive efforts to interpret the meaning of *past* outcomes rather than expectations about the attainability of *future* outcomes, they are not motivational processes per se (as a number of motivation scholars have noted, e.g., Mook, 1987; Petri, 1991). It is clear that causal attributions can sometimes influence motivational patterns in powerful ways by altering expectations about whether one is capable of producing future outcomes (e.g., Lee et al., 1987; Schunk, 1982, 1983, 1984), by leading people to anticipate a responsive or unresponsive context (e.g., Dodge, 1980; Dodge & Frame, 1982; Dodge & Somberg, 1987), or by triggering different kinds of emotion patterns (e.g., Weiner, 1979, 1980, 1986). Causal attributions often have little or no influence on motivation and achievement, however, either because: (a) the attributions have little relevance to the individual's personal goals, (b) they are not particularly informative with regard to either the person's capabilities or the context's responsiveness, or (c) they are informative but unimpressive compared to preexisting beliefs based on many behavior episodes. Consistent with this view, Covington and Omelich (1979), in a test of the presumed causal role of causal attributions in motivational patterns, concluded that causal attributions are more likely to serve as self-serving excuses than as anticipatory motivators of achievement efforts.

Along these lines, there appears to be a general and accelerating shift taking place in the motivational literature away from causal attributions to the more directly influential processes of capability and context beliefs. This is illustrated by the decreasing emphasis placed on attributional processes in recent motivational formulations (e.g., Abramson, Metalsky, & Alloy, 1989; Bandura, 1986; Dweck & Leggett, 1988; Markus, Cross, & Wurf, 1990; McCombs & Marzano, 1990; Schunk, 1991b), and the general decline in the amount and scope of research being conducted primarily within the attributional paradigm (e.g., C. Ames & R. Ames, 1985, 1989; R. Ames & C. Ames, 1984; Maehr & Ames, 1989; Maehr & Kleiber, 1987; Maehr & Pintrich, 1991; Schunk, 1990a; Sorrentino & Higgins, 1986; Sternberg & Kolligian, 1990).

Personal Agency Belief Patterns

Although Motivational Systems Theory is not unique in emphasizing the joint contributions of capability and context beliefs to effective functioning (e.g., Bandura, 1982; Deci & Ryan, 1985; Gurin & Brim, 1984; Weisz & Stipek, 1982), there is a tendency for theories focusing on personal agency beliefs to generate research primarily on one process or the other, thereby obscuring the degree to which they jointly contribute to effective functioning and the mechanisms by which they do so. For example, the attributional reformulation of learned helplessness theory (Abramson, Seligman, & Teasdale, 1978) resulted in part from a recognition that capability beliefs needed to be more explicitly incorporated into the theory. The locus of control literature is filled with results that are anomalous or hard to interpret because capability beliefs were neglected or context beliefs were assessed in a way that confounded capability and context beliefs (Gregory, 1981; Phares, 1976). Most of the research generated from Bandura's (1977b) self-efficacy theory has focused on capability beliefs despite the fact that he has stated (Bandura, 1982) that "in any given instance behavior would be best predicted by considering both self-efficacy and outcome beliefs" (p. 140).

MST addresses the need to develop theoretically sound and pragmatically useful ways of representing the patterning of capability and context beliefs by offering a taxonomy designed to capture the essential qualities of 10 conceptually distinguishable personal agency belief patterns. This 3 X 3 heuristic scheme is summarized in Table 5.1, along with brief definitions of each of the concept labels used to summarize these 10 patterns.

A *Robust* pattern of personal agency beliefs is the most motivationally powerful pattern (Bandura, 1982; Deci & Ryan, 1985; Seligman, 1991; Snyder et al., 1991). That is because people with strong capability

TABLE 5.1 The MST Taxonomy of Personal Agency Belief Patterns

| | | CAPABILITY BELIEFS | | |
		Strong	*Moderate or Variable*	*Weak*
C O N T E X T B E L I E F S	**Positive**	**R** Robust Pattern	**M** Modest Pattern	**F** Fragile Pattern
	Neutral or Variable	**T** Tenacious Pattern	**V** Vulnerable Pattern	**S** Self-Doubting Pattern
	Negative	**A1 or A2** Accepting or Antagonistic Pattern	**D** Discouraged Pattern	**H** Hopeless Pattern

Definitions (adapted from *Webster's Seventh New Collegiate Dictionary*):

R Pattern	Robust—"strong and firm in purpose or outlook"
M Pattern	Modest—"placing a moderate estimate on one's abilities"
F Pattern	Fragile—"intact but easily broken or damaged"
T Pattern	Tenacious—"suggests strength in dealing with challenges and obstacles"
V Pattern	Vulnerable—"functioning adequately but may be at risk under conditions of stress"
S Pattern	Self-doubting—"having a lack of faith in one's chances for success"
A1 Pattern	Accepting—"to endure difficulties quietly and with courage"
A2 Pattern	Antagonistic—"tending toward actively expressed annoyance or hostility"
D Pattern	Discouraged—"being deprived of but potentially maintaining some confidence or hope"
H Pattern	Hopeless—"having no expectation of success"

beliefs and positive context beliefs maintain the expectation that their goals will ultimately be achieved even in the face of obstacles, difficulties, and failures. Negative outcomes are seen as temporary, unrepresentative, and, therefore, rather uninformative with regard to future possibilities (e.g., "I'm not going to let a few [mistakes/setbacks/rejections] get me down—I know good things are going to start happening soon" or "I can do anything if I put my mind to it").

A *Tenacious* PAB pattern is also high in motivational potency because it, too, leads to effortful persistence in challenging or stressful circumstances. The major difference between the R pattern and T pattern is that in the latter pattern some degree of environmental unresponsiveness is viewed as predictable and unsurprising. This expectation enables people to prepare in advance, both behaviorally and psychologically, for anticipated obstacles and difficulties (e.g., "These people are tough, but so am I" or "It's not going to be easy, but I can reach my goal if I keep at it and don't let the [criticism/hassles/losses] get to me").

The *Modest* PAB pattern is also generally a "green light" pattern with regard to efforts to attain desired outcomes; however, the character of this pattern is rather different from that of the Tenacious pattern in that the self is regarded as somewhat more fallible and the context is seen as a source of strength rather than a potential obstacle to goal attainment. These expectations are ideal for learning and skill-development contexts, situations involving cooperation among people with different kinds of expertise, and other situations requiring a healthy respect for one's limitations and deficiencies (e.g., "I can do pretty well if I'm realistic and stay within my capabilities" or "I can get by with a little help from my friends").

The *Vulnerable* PAB pattern is characterized by uncertainty or vacillation between favorable and unfavorable expectations for goal attainment. The "mixed" motivational messages resulting from this pattern are unlikely to be negative enough to inhibit progress toward important goals; however, they may trigger symptoms of anxiety and worry and contribute to a cautious approach to goal setting and goal seeking (e.g., "Sometimes I think I'll do just fine, but other times I fear the worst" or "I usually try to avoid [taking tests/getting up in front of people/going to formal parties] because I never know what to expect").

The *Antagonistic* and *Accepting* PAB patterns are both characterized by a general sense of self-adequacy combined with a significant degree of distrust or hostility toward the environment. People manifesting these patterns generally blame some aspect of the context rather than themselves for problems and failures (Brehm & Brehm, 1981; Chesney & Rosenman, 1985; Dodge, 1980). This enables them to maintain some degree of motivation even in highly unresponsive circumstances, either by triggering heightened arousal and high-amplitude behavior (e.g., "I'm not quitting until I make this @*!?$# thing work!" or "I'll show that [teacher/driver/jerk] who's boss around here!"), or by triggering psychological coping processes designed to minimize the adverse impact of the problematic context (e.g., "I know I can't stop it, but at least I can predict when it's going to happen" or "All I can do is accept it and try not to think about it") (Weisz & Cameron, 1985; Weisz, Rothbaum, & Blackburn, 1984).

In contrast to the A1 and A2 patterns, Fragile personal agency beliefs are characterized by a general belief in the context's adequacy combined with a significant degree of self-deprecation and self-devaluation. People manifesting this pattern generally blame themselves rather than the context for problems and failures (Bandura, 1982; Dweck & Leggett, 1988; Kolligian, 1990). Consequently, such people are like fragile flowers that need a great deal of water and sunshine to continue growing—as long as the weather is good (i.e., good outcomes are occurring), functioning is not significantly impaired. Even a small amount of adversity may be sufficient, however, to trigger demotivating thoughts and emotions or efforts to seek assistance from others (e.g., "I've just been lucky—I'm really not very [smart/attractive/competent]" or "You're going to have to help me—there's no way I can do this on my own").

People manifesting a Self-doubting pattern of personal agency beliefs resemble those with Fragile PABs in that they too have a fundamental lack of confidence in their personal capabilities; however, motivation is more seriously impaired in this case because the context is less likely to be seen as a reliable source of help and support. In such cases it may be extraordinarily difficult to sustain efforts to pursue even highly desired outcomes (e.g., "I just know I'm going to blow this" or "The only thing that will save me now is a miracle").

The Discouraged PAB pattern is also a highly demotivating pattern, although in this case the primary source of any remaining hope for good outcomes is the self rather than the context. Thus, at least initially, Discouraged people are less likely to focus on their personal deficiencies than on the impossibility of making progress in the current context. Trying to increase people's capabilities and experiences of success—a primary remedy for Self-doubting individuals—is therefore less relevant for Discouraged people than efforts to change the context in some significant way (e.g., "I just can't seem to get this thing to work—I might as well get rid of it" or "This is awful—now what in the world am I going to do?"). When goals are very important and the emotions associated with this pattern are strong (e.g., a mixture of rage and dread), Discouragement can escalate to Desperation, as described, for example, in Benight's (1992) "Competent-Incompetent Desperation Shift" (CIDS) theory of sudden cardiac death.

Finally, there is the Hopeless pattern of personal agency beliefs. This is the most motivationally debilitating pattern because neither the self nor the context are seen as having any potential to improve current or anticipated negative events (Abramson, Metalsky, & Alloy, 1989; Seligman, 1975; Pattillo, 1990). Consequently, good outcomes are seen as impossible; bad outcomes are seen as inevitable; and no course of action can be imagined that would change these expectations (e.g., "It's nice to think about, but there's no way it could ever happen" or "It's no use—I give up"). This pattern has been linked empirically not only with depression, but also with premature death (Pattillo, 1990; Seligman, 1975).

Although it is easy to think of the 10 PAB patterns just described in trait-like terms, such interpretations should be avoided in all but the most extreme cases (i.e., those involving extraordinarily pervasive BES). PAB patterns are not necessarily stable or consistent qualities of people. They represent, rather, thoughts about personal and environmental resources that may vary across situations and change over time in significant ways. For example, it is probably commonplace for people to vacillate between two or more PAB patterns within the same behavior episode. Moreover, even highly ingrained patterns are likely to be influenced by significant changes in personal capabilities, environmental responsiveness, or habits of selective attention to positive and negative features of the self and context. Thus parents, teachers, counselors, and others seeking to alter problematic PAB patterns should proceed with the belief that they probably can have a positive impact if they remain sufficiently determined and persistent (i.e., a Tenacious PAB pattern might serve them particularly well).

It is also important to understand that no single PAB pattern is best for all circumstances. Different PAB patterns will be adaptive in different kinds of behavior episodes. In fact, all 10 patterns can facilitate effective functioning in circumstances where personal agency beliefs are well matched with possible futures. For example, a Self-doubting pattern would be much more adaptive than a Robust pattern of thinking for a compulsive gambler or a teenager who thinks she can get away with shoplifting, unsafe sex, or drinking and driving. Similarly, the anger and determination that accompanies Antagonistic thinking may be just what is needed to overcome seemingly intractable obstacles to goal attainment (e.g., "I'm mad as hell, and I'm not going to take it anymore!"). Even a Hopeless pattern can be adaptive, at least temporarily, in circumstances where the desired outcomes are in fact unattainable (e.g., spending time with a deceased family member; excelling at a sport that is far beyond one's physical capabilities).

In most circumstances, however, effective functioning is facilitated by maintaining a Robust, Tenacious, or Modest pattern of personal agency beliefs, depending on the circumstances, and trying to ignore thoughts representing the other patterns (Barden & Ford, 1990, 1991; Beck & Freeman, 1990; Seligman, 1991). The Robust pattern is the strongest overall pattern, and is, therefore, particularly adaptive in "now or never" situations where effective independent performance is essential (e.g., taking a test, giving a speech, interacting with a client, playing a sport, performing in a concert, etc.). In such situations it is usually desirable to escalate trust and self-confidence to their maximum level so that there is no doubt or confusion about what BES to activate and no preoccupying anger or worry to distract one from smooth execution of learned routines (Bandura, 1986; Barden & Ford, 1990, 1991). In contrast, Modest thinking is particularly appropriate in situations where one is *preparing* for future performance situations (e.g., studying for a test, training for a musical or athletic performance) (Bandura, 1986), or when interdependent action among people with different skills is required. Finally, Tenacious thinking is particularly well suited for circumstances in which one must "grind it out" or "stick with it" in a persistent and determined manner despite difficult challenges and obstacles to goal attainment.

As one might expect given the central role of personal agency beliefs in contemporary motivational theorizing, a number of scholars have outlined motivational patterns that are congruent with those described in Table 5.1. These descriptions, which generally focus on the particularly distinctive cases represented in the corners of Table 5.1 (i.e., the R, A1, A2, F, and H patterns), are summarized in Table 5.2.

Emotional Arousal Processes

Emotions are motivational components that are themselves complexly organized patterns of several processes. As noted in Chapter 2, emotional arousal patterns consist of three integrated subcomponents: an *affective (neural-psychological) component* (i.e., the general subjective feeling part of the emotion); a *physiological component* (i.e., a supporting pattern of biological processing); and a *transactional component* (i.e., expressive gestures that influence relevant aspects of the context). Emotions thus wed regulatory and energizing processes into a powerful unit that can be flexibly linked to almost any event or behavior

TABLE 5.2 Concepts Associated With the Most Distinctive Patterns Represented in the MST Taxonomy of Personal Agency Belief Patterns

---

ROBUST (R) Pattern (Strong Capability/Positive Context Beliefs)
Intrinsic Motivational Pattern (Deci, 1980)
Internal Locus of Control (Rotter, 1966)
Positive Self-Efficacy/Positive Outcome Expectancy Pattern (leading to assured, opportune action) (Bandura, 1982)
Learned Optimism (Seligman, 1991)
Hope (Snyder et al., 1991)

ANTAGONISTIC (A1) Pattern (Strong Capability/Negative Context Beliefs)
Extrinsic Motivational Pattern (leading to active efforts to regain a sense of self-determination) (Deci, 1980)
Powerful Others Locus of Control (leading to resistance, protest, or active change of context) (Levenson, 1981)
Positive Self-Efficacy/Negative Outcome Expectancy Pattern (leading to social activism, protest, grievance, or milieu change) (Bandura, 1982)
Reactance Pattern (Brehm, 1972)

ACCEPTING (A2) Pattern (Strong Capability/Negative Context Beliefs)
Extrinsic Motivational Pattern (leading to cognitive adaptation to one's loss of self-determination) (Deci, 1980)
Powerful Others Locus of Control (leading to cognitive adaptation to these controlling circumstances) (Levenson, 1981)
Secondary Control (accepting and accommodating to reality using cognitive strategies designed to reduce the impact of an unresponsive environment—i.e., predictive, illusory, vicarious, interpretive, and selective attention control) (Weisz & Cameron, 1985; Weisz, Rothbaum, & Blackburn, 1984)

FRAGILE (F) Pattern (Weak Capability/Positive Context Beliefs)
Negative Self-Efficacy/Positive Outcome Expectancy Pattern (leading to self-devaluation and despondency) (Bandura, 1982)
Personal Helplessness (Abramson, Seligman, & Teasdale, 1978)
Perceived Incompetence (Phillips, 1984)
Perceived Fraudulence (Kolligian, 1990)

HOPELESS (H) Pattern (Weak Capability/Negative Context Beliefs)
Amotivational Pattern (Deci, 1980)
Chance Locus of Control (Levenson, 1981)
Negative Self-Efficacy/Negative Outcome Expectancy Pattern (leading to resignation and apathy) (Bandura, 1982)
Universal Helplessness (Abramson, Seligman, & Teasdale, 1978)

---

episode characteristic—especially those that involve the cognitive-evaluative components of the episode (e.g., personal agency beliefs) and the anchoring components of goals and contexts.

Goals and Emotional Arousal Processes

The subjective experience of an emotion reveals the degree of success, failure, or problems a person is experiencing—or anticipates experiencing—in the pursuit of currently active personal goals. Therefore, as with personal agency beliefs, emotions that are not anchored to a goal that is currently directing or influencing the individual's activity (i.e., an intention or a current concern) will generally have little behavioral meaning or personal significance (Campos & Barrett, 1984; Pervin, 1991). In other words, although strong emotions can arise as a consequence of conditions such as illness or neurological dysfunction, emotional patterns are most likely to be activated when some problem, degree of progress, or opportunity arises in the course of anticipating or pursuing a goal, and the person evaluates it as such (Lazarus, 1991a, 1991b, 1991c). Lazarus and Folkman (1984) use the term *primary appraisal* to describe this evaluative process. Frijda (1988) calls it *the law of concern*: "Emotions arise in response to events that are important to the individual's goals, motives, or concerns" (p. 351). More specifically, Frijda (1988) states:

> Events that satisfy the individual's goals, or promise to do so, yield positive emotions; events that harm or threaten the individual's concerns lead to negative emotions . . . emotions are [also] elicited by novel or unexpected events [that may be of interest or concern to the individual]. (p. 349)

As noted in Chapter 3, emotions, once activated, may contribute to the development and elaboration of new goals around previously uninteresting or unfamiliar things, activities, or people. Facilitating that process, however, is usually very difficult when there is no goal (or an avoidance goal) in place. Indeed, one of the most useful skills that a parent or teacher can develop is the ability to link existing goals of the child to experiences that the child might otherwise never engage in (e.g., eating new foods, learning to use the toilet, participating in extracurricular activities, taking on challenging academic work). For example, offering an uninvolved student or poor eater some privilege or reward that communicates pride or admiration for "a job well done" at school or at the dinner table can infuse a previously meaningless or unpleasant event with activating emotions and facilitate the development of goals other than those that originally directed the child's behavior (e.g., "I never knew school could be so fun" or "Hey Mikey—he likes it!"). Similarly, by organizing the social environment in relationship to the students' goals in ways that evoke emotions such as pride, guilt, and acceptance, previously uncompelling academic or work goals can be infused with new meaning and commitment.

The close link between goals and emotions is also of great practical significance for those who are trying to understand the concerns of a troubled child or a disturbed client. Although emotions do not provide direct information about what a person is trying to accomplish or avoid, as Fridja (1988) explains, they "point to the presence of some concern" (p. 351) by influencing selective attention, recall, event interpretation, learning, decision making, and problem solving in predictable ways (D. Ford, 1987; Hoffman, 1986; Masters, Barden, & Ford, 1979). Thus, concludes Frijda (1988): "emotions form the prime material in the exploration of an individual's concerns" (p. 352). This is increasingly true to the extent that the individual is unable to bring his or her thoughts about desired and undesired consequences into consciousness (e.g., by putting them into words, as in talk therapy, or pictorial images, as in art or dream therapy).

The problem of bringing information into consciousness pinpoints a primary reason that emotions are so important in understanding the content and organization of motivational patterns. Unlike cognitive motivational processes, emotions, once activated, *cannot* be kept out of consciousness. In other words, although one may be able to ignore to some extent the perceptions and evaluative thoughts that trigger a particular emotion pattern and perhaps suppress certain motoric (or even physiological) components of an emotion pattern (e.g., an angry facial expression), the psychological consequence of emotional activation is an *immediate conscious experience* with a positive or negative valence. Thus, with few exceptions, emotions are always "valid" in the sense that they signal the presence of, and concern about, a particular set of conditions in current or anticipated behavior episodes (e.g., anger is activated by conditions evaluated as thwarting of obstructive to goal attainment; pleasure signals real or anticipated progress toward desired outcomes). The perception or evaluation of these conditions may be inaccurate or maladaptive, but the emotions that flow from the way a person construes a situation will almost always "make sense" within those parameters. Emotions, therefore, can provide clues about other properties of behavior episodes. For example, if one understands that anxiety and fear prototypically occur in conditions interpreted as having the potential to cause psychological or physical harm, it becomes possible to explore the goals underlying this emotional response and to examine the conditions being interpreted as personally threatening or damaging. One can apply this same strategy to the analysis of dreams and other thinking episodes because the subjective experience of an emotion can be counted on to be an accurate indicator of the thought patterns organizing those episodes.

Thus learning how to interpret a person's emotional life in terms of the goals and contexts that organize those feelings and give them meaning is a particularly important skill for psychotherapists who must deal with "unconscious" goals (i.e., desired and feared outcomes that are difficult to verbalize or are suppressed from consciousness as a defensive strategy). It is also an important skill for child psychologists and other professionals who work with young children because the ability to verbalize goals pertaining to affective states and social relationships is a relatively late developmental achievement (Shantz, 1983).

It is important not to overestimate the potential informativeness of emotional responses, however. There are many other sources of variance in emotional displays besides the person's current concerns—for example, the individual's idiosyncratic style of emotional expression, the possible decoupling of the expressive and affective components of an emotional response, the extent to which the emotional experience is altered by contextual influences and emotional self-control strategies, and deviant biological states (D. Ford, 1987; Izard, 1991; Thompson, 1991). In addition, emotions, once activated, tend to take on a life of their own (Frijda, 1988), so that they may persist in some form (e.g., a mood state) even after the goal is attained or some other goal takes precedence. As Lazarus (1991a) puts it, "when provoked, an emotion is its own system that has its own special rules of operation" (p. 822). Emotions may also wane in magnitude even when a goal remains strong and active if the conditions eliciting the emotion are not perceptually or cognitively salient. Indeed, every emotional state will eventually dissipate unless it is reactivated in some way (e.g., through cognitive rumination), just as a flywheel on a machine will slowly stop unless periodically given another push (D. Ford, 1987). Nevertheless, because one of the components of each emotion pattern is directly accessible to outside observers (i.e., the transactional component), and because another component (i.e., the affective component) is always manifest in consciousness, emotions provide a uniquely valuable way of probing into motivational patterns when it is difficult for people to communicate to others the substance of the goals and personal agency beliefs organizing those patterns.

Cognitive Evaluations and Emotional Arousal Processes

As one might expect in a complexly organized system, emotions can be triggered in several different ways. Because emotion patterns include a physiological component, they can be activated or influenced by certain kinds of *biochemical processes and agents* (e.g., hormonal activity, antidepressant drugs) (D. Ford, 1987; Murray, 1978). Because they also include a transactional component, emotions can sometimes be initiated, at least in a weak form, by engaging in the *motor activity* characteristic of a particular emotion (e.g., forcing a smile or other emotion-specific facial expression) (Ekman, Levenson, & Friesen, 1983; Laird, 1974; Zuckerman, Klorman, Larrance, & Spiegel, 1981). In addition, emotions can be triggered by *direct perception* (i.e., without intervening cognitive activity) in circumstances that convey information matching the conditions for which the emotional pattern evolved as a fixed action pattern (e.g., interest in moderately novel surroundings, fear of strangers). That is the way most emotional experiences are initiated in very young children (D. Ford, 1987; Hoffman, 1986; Schellenbach, 1987).

In older children and adults, however, emotions are more commonly activated by *cognitive evaluations* pertaining to current or potential concerns in real or imagined circumstances (D. Ford, 1987; Frijda, 1988; Hoffman, 1986; Lazarus, 1991b; Lazarus & Folkman, 1984). Such evaluations may or may not require conscious cognitive processing (Lazarus, 1991a, 1991b). That is because much of the cognitive and emotional activity potentiated by the activation of a BES can occur outside awareness—especially if that activity involves habitual, well-learned patterns (e.g., social relationship patterns involving thoughts and feelings of affection, anxiety, or hostility). Consequently, affective reactions to objects, persons, and events are often experienced before conscious awareness of the evaluations triggering those reactions has occurred (Lazarus, 1982, 1984, 1991b; Zajonc, 1980, 1984). In fact, there is no guarantee that the person will ever be aware of why they experienced a particular emotion because humans can only be conscious of thoughts that they are able to put into perceptible form. Indeed, a major goal of counseling and psychotherapy is to help people identify or clarify the cognitive evaluative patterns that are responsible for strong and persistent emotion patterns.

Historically, cognitive and emotional regulatory processes have often been portrayed as "enemies" vying for control over the person's intentions and actions (Ford & Urban, 1963; Freud, 1923, 1933; Lazarus, 1991b, 1991c). Although that may be a useful way to think about their relationship in some kinds of behavior episodes (e.g., those involving unreasonable fears or irrational anger), it is generally more accurate to think of emotions and cognitive evaluations as a regulatory "team," with each "player" contributing to effective decision making in different and unique ways. Personal agency beliefs, because they are more likely to incorporate considerations about long-term consequences and the potential availability of alternative courses of action, are particularly useful for decisions about "big picture" matters, such as whether one should initiate or continue a complex, difficult, or time-consuming course of action (e.g., writing a book, developing a new product, accomplishing political change, becoming highly proficient at a sport or academic subject). The motivational significance of personal agency beliefs is particularly evident when such courses of action are highly consequential in terms of personal goals and life contexts (e.g., going to graduate school, taking a new job, having children, merging with another company, changing long-standing habits or life-style patterns).

Emotions, on the other hand, are better suited for short-term regulatory problems and opportunities. Indeed, emotions evolved to help people maintain or facilitate effective functioning in circumstances requiring the rapid and efficient mobilization and deployment of energy resources and transactional capabilities (D. Ford, 1987). As Frijda (1988) explains:

> The primary phenomenon of emotion, one may argue, is what can be called the "control precedence" of action readiness . . . . The action readiness of emotion tends to occupy center stage. It tends to override other concerns, other goals, and other actions. It tends to override considerations of appropriateness or long-term consequence . . . . The notion of control precedence captures in some sense the involuntary nature of emotional impulse or apathy, its characteristic of being an "urge," both in experience and in behavior. (p. 355)

Thus emotions are particularly useful when effective functioning requires immediate or vigorous action in the context of a concrete problem or opportunity such as escape from imminent harm, removal of an obstacle to goal attainment, or inhibition of a personally or socially damaging action. In other words, the primary function of emotions is to augment ongoing behavior patterns (D. Ford, 1987).

An understanding of the specialized regulatory functions of emotions and cognitive evaluations can provide interventionists (and ordinary people) with an empowering source of information about how to influence motivational patterns. For example, it has been well documented that concrete, vivid images have a much stronger impact on intentions and actions than do abstract verbal representations, even when these abstract representations logically convey much more information (Fiske & Taylor, 1984; Nisbett & Ross, 1980). That is why advertisers and political strategists, who are trying to influence short-term buying and voting decisions, emphasize emotionally evocative visual images and "sound bites" in their campaigns (Adams, 1990; Petty & Cacioppo, 1984). Experienced consumers and political activists also use emotionally arousing strategies to accomplish their objectives, having learned that, in most cases, the squeaky wheel does indeed get the oil.

Parents, teachers, and counselors can also use knowledge about the differences and relationships between cognitive and emotional regulation to help guide intervention decisions. For example, in situations where the goal is long-term learning and no immediate action is required, a relatively low-key presentation focusing on informational clarity may be the intervention of choice (e.g., a quiet lecture about rules and expectations, a matter-of-fact conversation pointing out enduring motivational strengths or weaknesses). In contrast, if the desired outcome is some immediate behavior change (e.g., keeping a child from behaving in an unsafe or hurtful manner, getting some required action from a bureaucrat or employee), a less ambitious but more emotionally compelling strategy focusing on the here-and-now may be needed. For example, one might resort to an emotional plea, a sincere expression of affection or concern, a stern warning, or any of a number of other emotionally laden tactics. In similar fashion, the effectiveness of goal-setting interventions can be increased by conceptualizing short-term goals in ways that promote a sense of emotional urgency (e. g., via deadlines), thus escalating current concerns to the status of intentions and creating a state of "action readiness."

The critical role that emotions can play in the success of some kinds of interventions is particularly well illustrated in problem domains involving intensely pleasurable or exciting activities and outcomes (e.g., sexual misbehavior, drug and alcohol abuse, gambling addictions, overeating, etc.). In such domains interventions that provide information unconnected to strong emotional content are notoriously ineffective (e.g., lectures, textbooks, pamphlets, etc.). In contrast, interventions that link irresponsible or self-destructive behavior to strong inhibiting emotions such as fear, guilt, or disgust, and that connect strong positive emotions to constructive alternative behaviors, are much more likely to have an enduring impact.

Constructing emotionally powerful interventions that are ethical, free from negative side effects, and effectively linked to relevant goals and contexts is a challenging task. When one is trying to alter behavior regulated by powerful emotions such as sexual passion or intense excitement, however, it is usually necessary to "fight fire with fire" by trying to infuse the emotion-laden BES guiding behavior in those circumstances with strong inhibiting emotions and emotionally compelling alternatives to irresponsible behavior. As Pervin (1991) explains:

> We must consider the power of the addiction in terms of the positive affect associated with it—the power of the craving or urge which dominates the attention of the person and compels action. In all cases that I have seen of this sort, at the point of breakdown in volition or enactment of the addiction the person reports a heightened state of arousal associated with some tension and considerable pleasurable affect—either actual at the time or anticipated in terms of the mental representation of the goal . . . the goal itself is associated with powerful positive affect— the high of the drug, the warmth of the alcohol, the fullness associated with eating, the orgasm associated with the pornographic movie or prostitute. This does not mean that the action will in all cases lead to that affective experience or that the person even expects it to, but rather that the experience is possible and that is enough. (p. 16)

Given the obvious salience of emotions in regulating immediate action, it is surprising how little attention has been given to emotional processes in contemporary motivational theorizing. This may reflect a belief that emotions have little long-term meaning or significance—a view that would seem to fit the characterization of emotions as short-term regulatory specialists, but which fails to recognize the salience of emotions as deeply rooted components of enduring BES. It may also reflect a belief that emotional influences are simply manifestations of personal agency beliefs—the primary processes of interest in many contemporary theories of motivation (e.g., Bandura, 1986; Covington, 1984b; deCharms, 1968; Deci & Ryan, 1985; Harter, 1990; Levenson, 1981; Seligman, 1991; Tesser & Campbell, 1985; Weiner, 1986). There is no simple correspondence between emotions and personal agency beliefs, however. For example, a Discouraged

PAB pattern may be associated with a complex mixture of emotions reflecting surprise, anger, depression, guilt, and resentment (cf. Benight, 1992). Thus such theories do not do justice to the unique role that emotions play in motivational patterns, nor do they adequately recognize the bidirectionality of influences between cognitive and emotional regulatory processes (Lazarus 1991a, 1991b) and between goals and emotions (Pervin, 1991).

In short, emotions are not simply motivational "add-ons" or "afterthoughts"—they are major influences in the initiation and shaping of goals and personal agency belief patterns that may seem relatively ephemeral or labile at the level of specific behavior episodes, but that in fact may be every bit as influential as cognitive processes in terms of enduring motivational patterns. Increasing recognition of this fact has led Hoffman (1986) to conclude that "it may not be an exaggeration to suggest that psychology is in the early stages of a paradigm shift in which affect no longer takes a back seat" (p. 244). Klinger (1985) makes this same assertion in even stronger terms:

> There is growing reason to believe that affective response forms the core of evaluation. . . . The most fundamental role of cognitions in evaluation, then, is to transform perceptual input into a form . . . capable of eliciting in the individual one or another kind of affective response. (p. 313)

Emotional Content and Associated Motivational Functions

Different kinds of emotional patterns evolved to help people deal with different kinds of pervasive, prototypical problems and opportunities of living. Emotions thus represent universal "themes" in human functioning and development (Lazarus, 1991a, 1991b). Based on a thorough review of the literature on emotional patterns, including other differential emotions theories (e.g., Cattell, 1957; Ekman, 1972; Izard, 1977, 1979, 1991; Plutchik, 1962, 1980; Tomkins, 1962, 1963), D. Ford (1987) has identified what appear to be 14 basic emotional patterns representing qualitatively distinct kinds of motivational influences. These patterns include eight kinds of instrumental emotions that evolved to help regulate behavior episodes in general and six kinds of social emotions that evolved to help facilitate the maintenance and operation of social relationships and social groups. Each pattern is described using a set of related emotion labels rather than a single word to emphasize the principle that basic emotion patterns may manifest themselves in somewhat different ways depending on the magnitude of the emotional response and the context in which it is activated.

The LSF emotion taxonomy is adopted as a component of Motivational Systems Theory, with credit also given to the diversity of emotion theorists who contributed to the development of that taxonomy.

Four Instrumental Emotions That Help Regulate the Initiation, Continuation, Repetition, and Termination of Behavior Episodes. Adaptive functioning requires the continuation and repetition of effective behavior episodes and the discontinuation of ineffective episodes. The emotion of *satisfaction-pleasure-joy* evolved to help motivate people to continue behavior episodes in which they are making progress toward their goals and to repeat behavior episodes in which they have successfully achieved their goals. This emotion pattern is therefore the primary emotion associated with achievement and competence (e.g., "This is going great" or "I did it!"). Conversely, the emotion of *downheartedness-discouragement-depression*, which facilitates the termination of unsuccessful behavior episodes, is the primary emotion associated with personal failure and incompetence. This emotion pattern evolved to help people avoid unproductive activity and unrealistic perseverance toward a goal (e.g., "This is going nowhere" or "I can't do it").

Because humans need information to maintain and improve their steady state patterns, the emotion of *curiosity-interest-excitement* evolved to encourage the collection, organization, and retention of new information. This emotion pattern promotes exploratory and investigatory behavior in contexts that involve novelty or variability within familiar boundaries (e.g., "What have we here?" or "Let's check this out"). Activation of this emotion is especially likely when the context is clearly relevant to one's personal goals (i.e., novel or variable circumstances that are deemed irrelevant by goal evaluation processes will not trigger this emotion). The emotion of *disinterest-boredom-apathy*, on the other hand, functions to delay or terminate behavior episodes involving irrelevant or highly familiar information. This emotion pattern helps people avoid wasting their time trying to collect, organize, or remember useless information or information they have already learned (e.g., "Who cares," "Why bother," or "We've been over this a million times").

Four Instrumental Emotions That Help Regulate Efforts to Cope With Potentially Disrupting or Damaging Circumstances. Behavior episodes often need to be revised while in progress due to the actual or potential impact of changing conditions on the person. The function of the *startle-surprise-astonishment* emotion pattern is to interrupt ongoing behavior episodes and reorient focal attention so that sudden, unexpected events can be evaluated for their potential personal significance (e.g., "What in the world was that?" or "What's going on here?"). *Annoyance-anger-rage* facilitates the surmounting or removal of obstacles to goal attainment. It is elicited by evaluations indicating that something or someone is obstructing or impeding progress toward a goal, and tends to produce high-amplitude behavior such as aggression, protest, social activism, or highly energized activity characterized by intense determination (e.g., "I'll show you!" or "@#$%&*&%$#@!!"). *Wariness-fear-terror* helps people avoid or proceed cautiously in circumstances involving real or potential threats to one's psychological or physical well-being. This emotion pattern is elicited by evaluations indicating that something or someone may cause damage, harm, or emotional suffering (e.g., "I'm worried about what might happen" or "Oh, no!"). Finally, *dislike-disgust-loathing* evolved to help people avoid contaminated environments that might produce illness, infection, or death. It is elicited by conditions evaluated as foul or noxious and is associated with the biological response of nausea (e.g., "That's disgusting!" or "Yuck!").

Three Social Emotions That Help Regulate Interpersonal Bonding. Social group living provides humans with obvious survival and reproductive advantages. *Sexual arousal-pleasure-excitement* evolved to facilitate the initiation and repetition of sexual encounters essential for the reproduction of the species. It is elicited by evaluations indicating that a sexually receptive partner is or may be available (e.g., "Your place or mine?" or "Oh, honey"). The emotion of *acceptance-affection-love* facilitates cooperative social functioning, the development of satisfying interpersonal relationships, and the sheltering and nourishing of helpless persons by supporting the process of interpersonal bonding and the development of mutual commitment and trust between people. It is the primary emotion associated with caring, sharing, friendship, and service to others (e.g., "We're all in this together" or "That's what friends are for"). Conversely, *loneliness-sorrow-grief* helps people cope with the loss of meaningful and cherished relationships by encouraging union and reunion with other significant people in their lives (e.g., "I need you—I can't deal with this on my own"). It also encourages people to restore or replace important social bonds that have been broken or seriously weakened (e.g., "Please come home—we miss you").

Three Social Emotions That Help Regulate Conformity to or Cooperation With Social Expectations and Patterns of Social Organization. When people operate as components of social systems, their functioning must be constrained in certain ways to facilitate the coherent functioning of the larger group. The emotion pattern of *embarrassment-shame/guilt-humiliation* encourages people to stay within the boundaries of organizing group constraints such as those defined by social norms, moral values, and rules of conduct, both formal and informal. It is the primary emotion supporting conformity, obedience, and socially responsible behavior (e.g., "I'll just *die* if anyone finds out about this!" or "I can't do that—I'd feel too guilty"). Conversely, *scorn-disdain-contempt* encourages people to reject others from a social group or relationship, or to influence those others to behave better when they have committed a social transgression or behaved in an unacceptable, offensive, or incompetent manner (e.g., "You don't belong here—leave" or "You know better than that—shape up or ship out!"). Finally, *resentment-jealousy-hostility* facilitates the use of coercive, corrective actions against people who are disrupting or not conforming to existing or desired social arrangements. This emotion helps people protect themselves against real or imagined threats to their social values, interests, and relationships (e.g., "Stay away from my things!" or "You apologize right now—or else!").

Next Steps

Comparisons between MST concepts and principles and those of other motivation theories were made throughout the last two chapters in an effort to highlight both the unique contributions of MST and its ability to function as an integrative framework. In Chapter 6 a more systematic effort is made to show how 31 other theories and categories of theories of motivation can be organized around the basic MST concepts of personal goals, personal agency beliefs, and emotional arousal processes. This is followed by a chapter that focuses on applied and developmental issues and a final chapter that summarizes the basic concepts and principles of Motivational Systems Theory.

Suggestions for Further Reading

Bandura, A. (1986). *Social foundations of thought and action: A social cognitive theory.* Englewood Cliffs, NJ: Prentice-Hall.

Deci, E. L., & Ryan, R. M. (1985). *Intrinsic motivation and self-determination in human behavior.* New York: Plenum.

Frijda, N. H. (1988). The laws of emotion. *American Psychologist, 43,* 349-358.

Hoffman, M. L. (1986). Affect, cognition, and motivation. In R. M. Sorrentino & E. T. Higgins (Eds.), *Handbook of motivation and cognition: Foundations of social behavior* (pp. 244-280). New York: Guilford.

Izard, C. E. (1991). *The psychology of emotions.* New York: Plenum.

Lazarus, R. S. (1991). *Emotion and adaptation.* New York: Oxford University Press.

Plutchik, R. (1980). *Emotion: A psychoevolutionary synthesis.* New York: Harper & Row.

Seligman, M. E. P. (1991). *Learned optimism.* New York: Alfred A. Knopf.

Sternberg, R. J., & Kolligian, J., Jr. (Eds.) (1990). *Competence considered.* New Haven, CT: Yale University Press.

Wood, R., & Bandura, A. (1989). Social cognitive theory of organizational management. *Academy of Management Review, 14,* 361-384.

CHAPTER SIX

Integration of Historical and Contemporary Theories of Motivation

It helps, I think, to consider ourselves on a very long journey: the main thing is to keep to the faith, to endure, to help each other when we stumble or tire, to weep and press on.

Mary Caroline Richards

Purpose of This Chapter

As NOTED IN CHAPTER 1, the present book was designed to provide scholars, professionals, instructors, and students with an alternative to the traditional "survey-of-theories" method of portraying the nature of human motivation. Specifically, an explicit effort was made in the preceding chapters to focus on the substance and significance of motivational processes and patterns and to avoid highlighting artificially constructed rivalries among "competing" theorists. Thus the strategy taken thus far has been to link theorists' names and concepts to a core set of ideas rather than to present each theory as if it represented a separate set of ideas. This addresses the concern expressed so eloquently by Staats (1991) in his call for integrative theorizing:

> Scientists, at first, only have a goal of finding new and different phenomena, not of finding relationships between them. Only over long periods

and with continuing efforts are the different pieces of knowledge gradually joined into a unified structure . . . .There are many common concepts and principles and findings in which commonality is not
recognized because they are described in different languages and are
parts of different theories. The theories may be in competition or the
separation may be accidental through the use of different subjects and
different methodologies and apparatuses, or through development in
different problem areas. The widespread, unrecognized commonality
magnifies psychology's diversity immeasurably, making the knowledge
in the discipline vastly more complicated and unrelated than it need
be . . . .The ability to see commonality, in principle, through thickets of
superficial difference is at the heart of creating unified science. (pp.
899-900, 905)

There are also limitations inherent in the use of an integrative
strategy, however. In particular, it is sometimes difficult to highlight
the internal consistency and unique contributions of different conceptual frameworks using such a strategy. Consequently, the present chapter provides readers with comprehensive coverage of the field of motivation using a device that preserves the integrity of different
motivational frameworks and yet further advances the goal of showing
how these frameworks can be organized around the core concepts of
MST. Specifically, Table 6.1 (at the end of the chapter, pp. 174-200)
summarizes the information and ideas represented in 32 different
theories and categories of theories of motivation (including Motivational Systems Theory) and links them to the MST concepts of personal
goals, personal agency beliefs, and emotional arousal processes.

Overview of Motivation Theory Summary Table

Most textbooks and review chapters on motivation limit coverage
to a relatively small subset of theories that have achieved a high level
of contemporary or historical popularity within a particular discipline or profession (e.g., business, education, social and personality
psychology). In contrast, Table 6.1 is intended to provide readers
with a comprehensive "map" of the entire range of motivation theories that have been developed over the years in a variety of fields
of study. These include not only all of the theories that are currently
prominent in the motivation literature, but also the "grand" psychological theories that dominated the field in the early part of the
century (e.g., psychoanalytic theory, drive theory, field theory), as
well as classic theories of work motivation (e.g., equity theory,

two-factor theory, expectancy theory). Among the contemporary motivational frameworks, Table 6.1 includes theories that are fading in influence but that still retain considerable popularity (e.g., operant learning theory, causal attribution theory, expectancy-value theories of achievement motivation); theories that appear to be growing in scope and influence (e.g., goal-setting theory, social cognitive theory, self-determination theory, "action" theories); and less widely cited theories that may be deserving of greater attention than they have received thus far (e.g., optimal experience theory, personal investment theory, idiographic theories of goal content).

With regard to substance, the theories covered in Table 6.1 include those organized primarily around goal concepts (e.g., need theories, goal orientation theories); theories focused mainly on arousal processes (e.g., optimal level theories, differential emotion theories); and theories anchored in concepts associated with personal agency beliefs (e.g., personal causation theory, learned helplessness theory). Very few theories provide detailed consideration of all three of these processes, yet many attempt to integrate concepts representing at least two of these motivational components. For example, most contemporary theories of motivation might be labeled "cognitive" theories in the sense that they emphasize concepts associated with both the goal and personal agency belief components of motivational patterns (e.g., self-determination theory, personal investment theory, social cognitive theory, goal-setting theory, action control theory, theory of reasoned action) (Pintrich, 1991).

Of course the brief summaries of each theory provided in this chapter and in Table 6.1 cannot (and are not intended to) provide readers with anything more than a general overview of the major concepts represented in each theory. Indeed, it would take several volumes to provide elaborated descriptions of each theory (e.g., Cofer and Appley's [1964] classic work, in which such descriptions are provided for theories representing fewer than half of the categories included in Table 6.1, is almost a thousand pages long). Nevertheless, by consulting the numerous references associated with each theory, readers can take this comprehensive "map" and fill in as much detail as needed for their particular purposes. Moreover, by starting with this organizing device, readers can avoid the common experience of being unable to connect the conceptual fragments they encounter in various source materials.

Identity Crisis Revisited

In Chapter 1 the term "identity crisis" was used to characterize the disunity evident in the field of motivational theorizing. The number and diversity of theories represented in Table 6.1 provides impressive evidence for the appropriateness of this description. Not only do different theories emphasize different motivational components, they rarely use the same concept labels to describe similar kinds of motivational phenomena and often vary in the way they use similar terms. For example, to represent the idea of whether a person believes he or she has the ability to accomplish some desired outcome, a scholar or professional may choose among a variety of rather dissimilar-sounding concept labels, including expectancy for success, learned optimism, perceived competence, self-efficacy, or capability belief. Although the use of multiple concept labels might be manageable if there was clear and precise agreement about either the equivalence of these terms or the common and distinctive features of each concept, such agreement is generally not apparent in the motivation literature. Similarly, the basic idea of "something a person wants" has been represented by a diversity of concept labels, including need, value, incentive, and goal. Although one could try to make subtle distinctions among these concepts (e.g., a "need" or "value" is often regarded as a more intrinsic or fundamental motivational influence than a "goal" or "incentive"), it is conceptually simpler and less theoretically divisive to use one general concept label (e.g., personal goal) that can be modified to represent variations in content, pervasiveness, or level of abstraction.

Another major factor that contributes to a sense of theoretical disorganization and divisiveness is the fact that many motivation theories are essentially "mini-theories" that are intentionally anchored around just one or two categories of goal content. For example, self-worth theories are based on people's strong desire to maintain positive self-evaluations. Optimal level theories focus primarily on the ubiquitous goals of entertainment (wanting to increase arousal) and tranquility (wanting to decrease arousal). Equity theory is restricted to the goal of maintaining equity (or avoiding inequity) in social exchange relationships. Effectance motivation theory deals primarily with the goals of exploration and mastery. Reactance theory, self-determination theory, and personal causation theory all emphasize self-determination and positive self-evaluation goals. Given that it obviously makes little sense to pit theories that address different content against each other, theoretical integration, not theoretical competition, should be emphasized.

Because the conceptual and terminological idiosyncrasies of different motivation theories are so salient, they tend to obscure the impressive degree of underlying convergence among these theories. Identifying such convergence is the key to resolving the identity crisis in the field of motivation. The columns in Table 6.1 provide the MST resolution to this problem.

In the remainder of this chapter each theory or category of theories is briefly summarized. Because notes of comparison and convergence often involve nonadjacent table entries, theories other than the one currently being summarized are referenced by number each time they are mentioned in the text. Citations to source material are omitted from the text because they are redundant with the references included in Table 6.1.

32 Theories and Categories of Theories of Motivation

1. Psychoanalytic Theory. Freud's theorizing about the powerful internal forces influencing human behavior set the stage for many early theories of human motivation. His emphasis on deep, pervasive drives and instincts—including not only those related to sex and aggression, but also ego- and superego-linked motives associated with competence and morality—helped stimulate early efforts to identify the content of and relationships among major directive influences. Moreover, the enduring influence of his focus on arousal reduction and pleasure seeking as fundamental motivational principles are evident in many historically prominent theories of motivation (e.g., drive theory [5], field theory [6], operant learning theory [11]). In addition, his emphasis on the motivational power of particular emotional states (e.g., anxiety and guilt) has provided those attempting to bring emotional processes back into the mainstream of motivational theorizing with a major source of historical strength and inspiration. Thus, although some of the details of Freud's theorizing appear to be little more than speculative storytelling, the core concepts can be easily identified in updated form even in some contemporary theories focused on the directive and arousal components of motivational patterns.

2. Instinct Theory/Hormic Psychology. McDougall's focus on instincts and the emotion-laden objects associated with those instincts is basically congruent with the emphasis in psychoanalytic theory [1] on the unseen and often unconscious forces within the individual that determine behavior; however, McDougall posited a much longer list of instincts (13 instincts plus a number of "minor" instincts) in an effort to account more specifically for the great variety of activity evident in human behavior patterns. Unfortunately, as noted in Chapter 1, each instinct category functioned more as a label than as an explanation for different kinds of behavior. Moreover, because there was no way to account for newly constructed behavior patterns (or qualitatively distinct variations on old behavior patterns) except by positing a new instinct, the list of instincts appeared to be capable of growing indefinitely. Nevertheless, several of the categories represented in this early motivational taxonomy are quite similar to those represented in the Ford and Nichols Taxonomy of Human Goals. Moreover, McDougall was one of the few early motivation theorists to emphasize the purposive character of human behavior—a contribution for which he should perhaps be given more credit (Pervin, 1983).

3. Need Theories. Like McDougall [2], Murray attempted to develop a comprehensive list representing the fundamental content of human motivational patterns. Although fewer of his 28 categories were described in explicitly behavioral terms (i.e., they did not appear to be quite so tautological), Murray's list of needs did not really resolve the problems associated with McDougall's taxonomy and ultimately met the same fate. The concept of "need," which Murray helped popularize, remains, however, a widely used concept in contemporary motivational theorizing.

Maslow developed a much shorter list of general need categories that introduced the intuitively compelling idea that needs are ordered hierarchically in such a way that higher-order, "growth" needs (e.g., self-actualization) can only be attained after lower-level, "deficiency" needs (e.g., physiological and safety needs) have been adequately addressed. This helps explain why Maslow's theory continues to be featured (occasionally in combination with Aldefer's even more concise taxonomy of existence, relatedness, and growth needs) in motivational textbooks and seminars, even though there is little empirical support for the assumption that needs are hierarchically organized and inadequate of conceptual clarity with regard to the content of the higher-order needs in his taxonomy. Its remarkable endurance is also attributable, however, to the fact that, until very recently (Ford & Nichols, 1987, 1991), no one else has made a serious and comprehensive effort to identify the general categories of goal content that seem to pervade human activity—a truly puzzling theoretical gap when one considers the fact that what a person is trying to accomplish is the heart of any motivational pattern!

4. Two-Factor Theory. Another theory that bears a striking resemblance to the ideas developed by Maslow and Aldefer [3] is Herzberg's two-factor theory. This theory attempts to distinguish "hygiene factors" (i.e., elements of the job context associated with survival and stability maintenance goals, such as pay and job security) from "motivator factors" (i.e., job elements associated with personal growth and development such as autonomy and creativity). Moreover, it attempts to differentially link these two sets of factors with job satisfaction and dissatisfaction: whereas motivator factors are seen as the key to job satisfaction, hygiene factors are hypothesized to be the primary determinants of job dissatisfaction. This intriguing idea has helped two-factor theory maintain its status (despite modest empirical support) as one of a handful of prominent work motivation theories (Pinder, 1984).

5. *Drive Theory.* The emergence of drive theory as the dominant theory of motivation in the middle part of the century was a particularly unfortunate event in the history of motivational theorizing. Although it helped elevate motivation to the center stage of psychological science, its eventual demise seemed to be associated with the rejection of motivation as a worthy topic for psychological study—a conceptual dismissal that may still not be fully reversed. Drive theory's effort to conceptualize motivation in terms of internal states of arousal was not only incompatible with the behavioristic stream of influence that followed, it was also incongruent with the cognitive "revolution" whose seeds were planted in the 1950s and 1960s (a revolution that may have been facilitated by Tolman, the one major theorist who insisted on adding cognitive concepts to the basic drive theory paradigm).

The awkwardness of trying to explain behavior without accepting the motivational significance of people's thought processes is illustrated by the introduction and elaboration of the drive theory concept of a "fractional anticipatory goal response." This concept was invented to try to explain how behavior can be future-oriented in the absence of any conception about the future. Interestingly, this was also a major issue in the early development of control system models of human functioning [31]. It was not until motivational scholars fully accepted the idea that cognitive representations of desired and expected futures could direct and regulate current behavior that theories of motivation were able to account for the variability, flexibility, and creativity in human behavior patterns.

6. *Field Theory.* With its emphasis on concepts such as need, tension, and frustration, field theory bears more than a superficial resemblance to drive theory [5]. Field theory, however, appears to be better summarized as a kind of bridge between drive theory and expectancy-value theories of motivation [12, 13, 14, 15, 16]. Along

with Tolman [5], Lewin was the first to emphasize the importance of expectancies in motivational patterns (Lewin used the term "potency" to refer to this concept). Moreover, Lewin was the first to address problems involving goal setting and the management of goal conflicts using, at least in part, a cognitive perspective. In short, Lewin probably deserves more credit for his role in the history of motivational theorizing than he typically receives.

7. Actualization Theory. The work of Rogers exemplifies another important stream of influence in the history of motivational theorizing. Actualization theory not only focused attention on motives associated with personal growth and development, it also helped lay a foundation for the emergence of "self" theories by emphasizing the strong and pervasive human need for positive social and self-evaluations [8, 22, 25]. Indeed, Rogers' concept of a "fully functioning individual" appears to be somewhat analogous to the currently popular concept of "flow" as defined in optimal experience theory [24].

Maslow's (1971) compelling distinction between "deficiency" and "being" motivational orientations also contributed significantly to this stream of motivational theorizing. Indeed, this distinction, along with his concept of a "unified" orientation involving the integration of these two approaches to dealing with life's problems and opportunities, offers considerable promise in terms of stimulating further theoretical developments, both in terms of the goal-orientation literature (cf. Winell, 1987) and in terms of understanding the problem of coordinating and aligning multiple goals.

8. Cognitive Dissonance Theory. If one were to combine drive theory's [5] concept of arousal reduction with Lewin's [6] focus on goal conflicts and Roger's [7] emphasis on personal growth and self-evaluation needs, one might come up with something like cognitive dissonance theory. Specifically, this theory posits that, due to underlying needs for understanding and positive regard, people will be motivated to reduce the tension associated with conflicting personal beliefs, attitudes, or actions. This basic idea generated a great deal of research over a period of several years and can still be recognized in several more recently generated theories (e.g., causal attribution theory [20]; self-worth theory [22]). Nevertheless, because of its relatively narrow focus, and because people often disattend to cognitive conflicts rather than try to resolve them, cognitive dissonance theory is no longer a significant part of the contemporary scene.

9. Optimal Level Theories. At about this same time a qualitatively distinct family of theories emerged that helped accelerate a move away from conceptions of motivation centered around arousal reduction mechanisms. Although diverse in terms of specific concepts and principles, a general underlying theme evident in these theories is the idea that people are intrinsically motivated to seek out an optimal level of stimulation or incongruity that may involve arousal reduction *or* an increase in arousal, depending on the person and circumstances involved. This has proved to be a popular and useful idea, and it continues to be a highly influential principle in contemporary motivational theorizing, as illustrated by its application to problems such as shyness, risk taking, and stress.

10. Equity Theory. Consistent with a growing trend toward specialized theorizing organized around one or two powerful motivational principles, equity theory emerged in the field of work motivation during the 1960s and continues to be cited as one of a handful of major theories in that field. Although it has been applied to a diversity of circumstances, equity theory gained prominence primarily by serving as a tool for understanding the ubiquitous problem of how employees will react motivationally to different kinds of compensation situations. Specifically, the theory proposes that equity is an important, perhaps even overriding, concern in many such situations—at least for some people (Huseman, Hatfield, & Miles, 1987). General empirical support for this premise has helped the theory maintain prominence despite its relatively narrow focus.

11. Operant Learning Theory. Because this theory eschews concepts referring to cognitive and affective experience, it is questionable whether it should even be classified as a theory of motivation. From the perspective of Motivational Systems Theory, it is probably better described as a theory about contextual factors that may facilitate or constrain motivation. Nevertheless, because motivation can only be defined within operant learning theory in terms of contextual influences, and because this theory is traditionally included in motivational textbooks and review articles, it is represented in Table 6.1, albeit somewhat awkwardly and without much elaboration.

Given its blatant rejection of motivational concepts that had gained such widespread acceptance over a period of many years, it is rather amazing that Skinner's views could become so popular and influential in such a short period of time. The field was apparently ready to reject what many had come to regard as vague, "unscientific" explanations of motivation and behavior based on phenomena that could not be directly observed (e.g., instincts, needs, and drives). Skinner's relatively simple and empirically compelling experiments demonstrating how behavior patterns could be "shaped" and "controlled" (i.e., facilitated and constrained) using his procedures also impressed many motivation researchers.

Interestingly, Skinner's core principle of "selection by consequences" is quite congruent with MST and other theories that emphasize how feedback processes can influence the selective activation and prioritization of personal goals and the means used to attain those goals (D. Ford, 1987). Indeed, selection by consequences is a fundamental mechanism by which incremental change in behavior patterns occurs (see Chapter 2). Nevertheless, because operant learning theory fails to consider the role of goals, emotions, and personal agency beliefs in shaping such change, it is more accurately described as a historically important influence on motivational theorizing than as a major contemporary theory of human motivation.

12. Social Learning Theory. If one were to accept some of the fundamental ideas of operant learning theory [11] without prohibiting the use of concepts representing internal psychological phenomena, one might end up with something like Rotter's social learning theory, which links behavioristic concepts such as reinforcement and reinforcement history to an analysis of the person's needs and expectancies within and across different sets of circumstances. Although it is no longer a prominent conceptual framework, it is notable because it was in the context of this theory that Rotter introduced the "locus of control" concept to psychological scholars and practitioners. Research on this widely studied topic greatly facilitated interest in concepts associated with personal agency beliefs—indeed, it was the first theory to conceptualize expectancies for goal attainment explicitly in PAB terms. It was also an important theory because it helped initiate the development of what are collectively called expectancy-value theories of motivation [e.g., 13, 14, 15, 16].

13. Expectancy-Value Theories of Achievement Motivation. Despite being strongly at odds with behavioristic assumptions about human motivation, McClelland's theory of achievement motivation gained a prominent place among motivation theories during the 1950s and 1960s. Although its impact has faded over the years, it continues to influence theory and research in the field, perhaps most directly through the "dynamics of action" elaborations of this framework.

Several properties of McClelland's ideas and research program contributed to the emergence of his theory as an influential position. First and perhaps foremost, McClelland was the first to address in a focused and systematic way the problem of understanding motivation in the context of achievement-related tasks (e.g., at school and in the workplace). He did so using a novel methodological approach (projective testing) that was intriguing to many psychologists, or at least to those who were comfortable with the assumption that achievement-related motives (needs, values, expectancies, hopes, fears) are largely unconscious forces that can only be revealed using such methods. Even for those less comfortable with this approach, many were attracted to McClelland's technique of combining assessments of multiple motivational factors into equations designed to predict broad patterns of achievement-related behavior. Moreover, because McClelland was the first (and still one of the few) theorists to represent motivation in terms of the patterning of factors representing all three major motivational components, he was deservedly seen as offering an unusually comprehensive framework for understanding human motivation. (He also explicitly noted that achievement depends on having the ability and opportunity to act on one's motives, consistent with the MST formula for effective functioning.) Finally, McClelland was instrumental in making expectancy-value conceptions part of the motivational establishment.

14. Expectancy Theories of Work Motivation. At about the same time that McClelland, Atkinson, et al. were formulating and elaborating their ideas in the field of achievement motivation, expectancy-value theories began to emerge in the field of work motivation, led by Vroom's foundational effort in 1964. Often called VIE (value-instrumentality-expectancy) theory, this approach to work motivation remains an influential part of the contemporary scene. The distinction between the concepts of expectancy and instrumentality is a particularly interesting part of this family of theories in that it appears to foreshadow the emergence of later efforts to distinguish between capability and context beliefs. Also contributing to the enduring impact of this approach is its inclusion of multiple motivational and nonmotivational influences on behavior and its avoidance of the language of unconscious motive systems. On the other hand, the lack of emphasis on emotional influences helped establish an almost exclusively cognitive approach to motivation that contributed to the isolation of emotion theory and research noted in Chapter 1.

15. Theory of Action Control. A much more recent expectancy-value framework that incorporates and expands upon the constructs of the dynamics of action [13] and VIE [14] approaches is the theory of action control proposed by Kuhl and his colleagues. This framework, which appears to be growing in scope and popularity, accepts the basic orientation and ideas of other expectancy-value theories, but also explicates the specific self-regulatory, goal-evaluation, and goal-orientation processes involved in the initiation and maintenance of behavioral intentions. The distinction between state and action goal orientations (Kuhl & Beckmann, in press), and the detailed specification of the goal evaluation processes involved in moving "from wishes to action" (Heckhausen & Kuhl, 1985), are particularly notable contributions of this motivational framework (see Chapter 4). Klinger (1985) puts it well, however, when he identifies emotion as the "missing link" in this way of thinking, characterizing it as "an action theory still lost in thought" (p. 311).

16. Theory of Reasoned Action. Another version of action theory that has been particularly influential in the fields of work motivation and health psychology is the theory of reasoned action developed by Ajzen and Fishbein. As in the theory of action control [15], a major focus of this theory is on understanding how people move from relatively global, abstract thoughts about desired and expected outcomes (attitudes and beliefs) to specific, concrete thoughts about desired and expected outcomes (intentions and expectations), with a strong emphasis on action as the primary dependent variable of interest. Although emotional arousal processes are not given much consideration in this theory either (as one might expect given its title), the theory of reasoned action probably deserves more credit and attention from motivation scholars in education and personality and social psychology than it has received thus far. Its highlighting of behavioral intentions and expectations as the most direct predictors of a person's actions is highly congruent with the emphasis found in other contemporary motivation theories focused on goal-setting processes and personal agency beliefs (e.g., [24, 27, 28]).

17. Differential Emotion Theories. The growing independence of cognitive and emotional perspectives on human motivation during the 1960s and 1970s is evidenced not only by the increasingly cognitive focus of mainstream motivational theorizing, but also by the separate emergence of a number of taxonomies and theories designed to identify and distinguish among the different emotion patterns involved in the regulation and energizing of human behavior. Differential emotion theories are sometimes juxtaposed with cognitive theories of motivation (e.g., in review articles and motivation textbooks); however, it was not until D. Ford (1987) developed his Living Systems Framework, with its own expanded differential emotion theory component (see Chapter 5), that a systematic attempt was made to show how this approach could be integrated with cognitive-motivational approaches. Continuing to bring the knowledge being generated under the leadership of differential emotion theorists into the mainstream of motivational theory and research is clearly one of the major priorities for motivational scholars in the 1990s (Izard, 1991; Weiner, 1990).

18. Causal Attribution Theory of Motivation and Emotion. Because causal attributions are not motivational processes per se (see Chapter 5), many of the ideas in this theory are not directly motivational in character or substance. Moreover, there is little evidence to support the theory's basic premise that most people have a strong, pervasive need to analyze and understand the causal factors underlying their experience. Indeed, Sorrentino and Short's (1986) criticism of such assumptions is particularly applicable to this theory:

> We wish to draw the attention of many cognitive theorists . . . to the fact that there are many people who simply are not interested in finding out information about themselves or the world, who do not conduct causal searches, who could not care less about socially comparing themselves with others, and who "don't give a hoot" for resolving discrepancies or inconsistencies about the self. (pp. 379-380)

Nevertheless, the use of the word "motivation" in the theory's title, as well as its inclusion in this table, can be justified on the grounds that causal attributions can, under certain circumstances, have a direct and important influence on a person's goals, emotions, and personal agency beliefs (see Chapter 5).

Given the apparent decline in the use of causal attribution theory to guide motivational research, it appears that this theory's future impact will be felt primarily through its influence on other contemporary frameworks (e.g., learned helplessness theory [21] and self-efficacy theory [27]). Because recent elaborations of causal attribution theory have focused on the emotional consequences of attributional patterns, it may also contribute to the eventual integration of cognitive and emotional perspectives on motivation. The use of the phrase "motivation and emotion" in the title of the theory, however, clearly conveys a major barrier to true integration!

19. Reactance Theory. Perhaps it is only coincidental that in the politically tumultuous decade between the mid-1960s and mid-1970s, several frameworks emerged in which an attempt was made to explain how people react motivationally to events that threaten their sense of personal freedom and control. One such theory is reactance theory, which focuses on the high-amplitude emotional and behavioral responses (e.g., anger, aggression, defiance) that often result when people believe that their goal-attainment efforts have been (or are likely to be) thwarted, or when they believe that desirable options have been taken away from them. Although this motivational mini-theory also appears to be fading in influence, it continues to offer valuable insights about a particular kind of motivational pattern that is not fully captured in any other theory.

20. Personal Causation Theory. This theory, which was developed and tested by deCharms in the context of students' experience in schools, was also built on the idea that people have a strong desire to maintain a sense of personal autonomy and control—that is, they like to feel like they are the "origin" of their behavioral choices. Compared to reactance theory [19], however, deCharms did not place as much direct emphasis on the potential for anger, aggression, and the like in circumstances that made students feel like a "pawn." He stressed, rather, the likelihood that students would become motivationally disengaged from their academic work and seek other contexts in which to exercise their personal agency under such circumstances. Although this theory is no longer widely cited, it is not because his ideas have been judged inadequate or uninformative; rather, it is largely because deCharms' ideas and applications are incorporated within Deci and Ryan's broader and more empirically visible self-determination framework and research program [25].

21. Learned Helplessness/Hopelessness/Optimism Theory. As the extended label used here implies, this theory has undergone several transformations since it was originally introduced in the early 1970s. The original theory of learned helplessness focused almost exclusively on beliefs about behavior-outcome noncontingency (i.e., beliefs about environmental unresponsiveness, called context beliefs in MST) and their affective consequences. Because Seligman was among the first (along with Rotter [12]) to detail the nature and consequences of this demotivating pattern, and because Seligman was able to write about the implications of his theory in unusually compelling terms (Seligman, 1975), even this early version of the theory generated a great deal of excitement and research activity. It soon became evident, however, that to account for the diversity of ways that people respond to noncontingent events, it would be necessary to elaborate the theory by taking into account, at least indirectly, factors associated with personal goals and capability beliefs.

For example, because people often (mistakenly) believe that they are directly or indirectly responsible for noncontingent positive events (Weisz & Cameron, 1985), and because the outcomes of such events are often more important to a person than beliefs about why they occurred, the hypothesized motivational consequences of learned helplessness are generally not evident in the context of positive events (although over time such noncontingency can result in a Fragile pattern of personal agency beliefs, as explained in Chapter 5). Even in the context of noncontingent negative events, helplessness/hopelessness is strongly influenced by the extent to which such events seem arbitrary and unpredictable (Levenson, 1981; Weisz & Cameron, 1985), and by the importance of those events with respect to the individual's current concerns. Moreover, the impact of perceived noncontingency appears to depend greatly on the extent to which pessimistic thinking becomes incorporated into a person's BES repertoire as an enduring and pervasive element. Specifically, it appears that internal, stable, and global causal interpretations for negative events ("It's my fault/I'll never be able to succeed at this/I can't do anything right") are particularly likely to lead to feelings of depression and hopelessness. The openness of proponents of the learned helplessness/hopelessness/optimism framework to such phenomena and their ability to capitalize on such findings has helped them stay at the forefront of contemporary motivational theorizing.

22. *Self-Worth Theories.* This family of theories is anchored by the premise that people are highly motivated to maintain a fundamental sense of personal value or worth, especially in the face of competition, failure, and negative social feedback. While similar in some respects to other theories that emphasize the human desire for personal agency (e.g., [19, 20, 21, 23, 24, 25]), self-worth theories place relatively little weight on the person-environment goal of self-determination, and instead highlight the within-person goal of maintaining positive self-evaluations—a difference in focus also manifested in the shift toward self-evaluative causal interpretations in learned helplessness theory. Perhaps the most unique feature of self-worth theories, however, is that they offer interesting ways to explain a diversity of seemingly self- defeating or even self-destructive behavior patterns (e.g., not

trying to attain valued goals, avoiding seemingly reasonable challenges, setting unrealistic goals). Thus, despite their somewhat narrow focus, self-worth theories are likely to continue to generate research interest and activity for many years to come.

23. *Effectance Motivation Theories.* The 1959 publication of White's classic article, "Motivation Reconsidered: The Concept of Competence" was a major event in the history of motivational theorizing, not only because it contributed to a growing disenchantment with arousal-reduction approaches to motivation, but also because it provided the foundation for other theories focused on personal agency beliefs and the intrinsic human desire for personal agency. It also helped popularize the concept of "optimal challenge" (i.e., a goal whose attainment requires a significant but reasonable investment of personal effort, and is therefore particularly meaningful in terms of personal efficacy and feelings of pleasure). Twenty years later Harter proposed an updated version of White's theory and began to emphasize the differentiation and proliferation of domains of competence across the life span. Because Harter has carefully distinguished between domain-specific personal agency beliefs and those pertaining to general self-worth, and has included assessments of both kinds of motivational content in much of her research, she has also made significant contributions to the development of self-worth theories [22].

24. *Optimal Experience Theory.* The core concepts in this theory are very similar to those emphasized in effectance motivation theories [23]: optimal challenge, sense of personal control and effectiveness, and feelings of enjoyment and pleasure (versus boredom and anxiety). Csikszentmihalyi has contributed several new theoretical elements, however, that sharpen and enhance the practical utility of this perspective. First, he has added goal-setting concepts to this basic framework of ideas, emphasizing the role of clear and definite personal goals and flexible standards for goal attainment in optimal experience (see Chapter 4). Second, Csikszentmihalyi has highlighted the role of attention and consciousness in maintaining and altering motivational patterns (i.e., the key to optimal experience is controlling the contents of consciousness). In addition, his concept of "flow" has provided the field of motivation with a more sophisticated way of thinking about motivational patterns that have the characteristics he associates with optimal experience, namely, an overall subjective experience of focused attention, sense of control, personal meaning, and pleasure. Indeed, this focus on the patterning of goals, emotions,

and personal agency beliefs is one of the most unique and valuable features of optimal experience theory.

25. Self-Determination Theory. This dynamic, multifaceted theory combines a number of useful and productive ideas found in theories that highlight personal agency beliefs and the desire for human agency. The idea that people have an innate need to maintain a sense of self-determination is also a core principle of reactance theory [19] and personal causation theory [20]. The related idea that people have a strong need to maintain a sense of personal competence is a basic premise of self-worth theories [22]. The concept of optimal challenge is prominent in effectance motivation theories [23] and optimal experience theory [24]. Beliefs about internal versus external locus of causality are represented in a similar form in social learning theory [12], causal attribution theory [18], and learned helplessness theory [21].

Although the integration of these various concepts is itself a notable achievement, Deci and Ryan have also contributed a heuristically powerful set of ideas focused on the motivational impact of different kinds of experiences and the more enduring motivational patterns that may result from such experiences. Specifically, they distinguish among: (a) experiences that tend to facilitate a sense of effectance and self-determination (i.e., *informational* experiences that promote an *autonomous* or "intrinsic" motivational orientation—the major focus of effectance motivation theories [23] and optimal experience theory [24]); (b) experiences that undermine a sense of self-determination and tend to facilitate compliance or defiance (i.e., *controlling* experiences that promote a *control* or "extrinsic" motivational orientation—the major concern of reactance theory [19] and personal causation theory [20]); and (c) experiences that signify a lack of competence and tend to reduce both intrinsic and extrinsic motivation (i.e., *amotivational* experiences that promote an *impersonal* motivational orientation— the major concern of learned helplessness [21] and self-worth [22] theories). The coherence and broad applicability of these ideas have helped elevate self-determination theory to a position of prominence among contemporary theories of human motivation.

26. Theory of Personal Investment. As illustrated by several of the preceding summaries, a common strategy in contemporary motivational theorizing is to begin with what is presumed to be a fundamental human need or desire (e.g., self-determination, self-worth, mastery, understanding) and then attempt to explicate the nature and consequences of different motivational patterns anchored around that goal.

In contrast, personal investment theory takes a rather different approach, one that merits much more attention and appreciation than it has received thus far. In this approach the focus is not on the degree to which people are motivated or demotivated with respect to some particular need or desire, but rather on how motivational resources are selectively distributed or invested among the diversity of activities and experiences that have become personally meaningful to an individual as a consequence of his or her past experiences, cultural background, and current circumstances. Because personal investment is seen in this theory as being dependent on an individual's sense of personal competence and beliefs about investment options, Maehr's approach is consistent with the many theories that highlight the role of personal agency beliefs in motivational patterns.

It also suggests, however, the importance of recognizing the multiplicity and variety of goals that an individual may come to value as a consequence of his or her personal and social-cultural history and his or her current task, social, and organizational contexts. In this respect it is consistent with idiographic theories of goal content [30]. As is generally the case, emotions receive little attention in this theory; nevertheless, the theory of personal investment provides an unusually strong foundation from which to address questions focused on individual, developmental, and cultural differences in motivational patterns.

27. Self-Efficacy Theory/Social Cognitive Theory. Not long after Rotter [12] and Seligman [21] helped elevate the study of context beliefs to the center stage of psychological research, Bandura generated a similar level of excitement and outpouring of empirical work with regard to capability beliefs by introducing the concept of self-efficacy and explaining its key role in facilitating behavior change. Although self- esteem theorists had previously focused attention on this motivational component, Bandura successfully and justifiably criticized their efforts by arguing that only a very limited amount of motivationally relevant information could be gained from global assessments of self-evaluative thoughts. Instead, he argued for, and has repeatedly demonstrated the utility of, an approach that focuses on how people think about their capabilities for effective action in specific behavior episodes—that is, at a level where such thoughts are much more likely to have a direct and substantial impact on behavior.

Although self-efficacy is only one of a number of motivational constructs in Bandura's larger social cognitive theory, it is regarded as the motivationally most decisive process in terms of regulating what a person actually does. The contributions of context beliefs (i.e., behavior-outcome expectancies) are recognized (e.g., Bandura, 1982), but clearly not to the extent of giving them equal status with self-efficacy expectancies. Similarly, emotional states are usually included in descriptions of motivational patterns, but they are generally not regarded as "equal partners" with the cognitive-evaluative processes in "motivational headquarters," as illustrated by Bandura's (1986) comment that "thought can guide action without having to depend upon being stirred up emotionally" (p. 264). On the other hand, like personal investment theory, self-efficacy theory addresses the directive component of motivational patterns more explicitly than most theories organized around personal agency belief concepts. Perhaps most notably, Bandura and Schunk have successfully integrated the important and broadly applicable concepts of goal-setting theory [28] into their conceptual framework.

28. Goal-Setting Theory/High Performance Cycle Theory. As a consequence of Locke and Latham's prolific and persuasive research program, as well as their willingness to adopt useful ideas from a number of other conceptual frameworks, goal-setting theory has emerged as the leading position in the field of work motivation. In addition to its core focus on more versus less productive ways of thinking about task goals, goal-setting theory has recently been expanded to include concepts from self-efficacy theory and expectancy theories of work motivation (among others), thus transforming it from a relatively narrow set of motivational principles to a broad (albeit primarily cognitive) theory of motivation. Locke and Latham have also developed the integrative concept of a "high performance cycle" to describe behavior episodes in which capable people working in a responsive environment commit themselves to challenging goals that they believe they can attain. Interestingly, this concept bears more than a superficial resemblance to Csikszentmihalyi's description of a "flow" experience [24].

29. Goal Orientation Theories. During the 1970s personal agency belief concepts effectively filled the void in motivational theory and research that had been created by the demise of drive theory and the emergence of operant learning and information-processing models as mainstream positions in psychology. In the decade of the 1980s these concepts gained widespread acceptance and became institutionalized in academic journals and textbooks, and goal concepts replaced PABs on the cutting edge of motivational theorizing. This trend is illustrated not only by theories focused on goal-setting and goal-evaluation processes [15, 16, 24, 27, 28], but also by an eclectic group of theories grouped here under the label of goal-orientation theories. In each of these theories two or three qualitatively distinct styles of goal pursuit involving different patterns of goal setting and/or goal content are described in terms of their component processes and behavioral consequences. In most cases a preferred or more adaptive goal orientation is contrasted with an orientation that is regarded as less optimal or even maladaptive in terms of the pursuit and attainment of individual and/or group goals (see Table 6.1 and Chapter 4 for specific examples). This has proven to be a heuristically useful tactic in dealing with a range of motivational problems at both the situation-specific (behavior episode) and personality (BES) levels of analysis.

30. Idiographic Theories of Goal Content. Another development that has further raised the profile of goal concepts in contemporary motivational theorizing is the recent proliferation of conceptual frameworks and assessment procedures designed to promote a better understanding of the content and organization of personal goal hierarchies. Unlike early theories of instincts and needs [2, 3], or even more recent theories organized around one or two powerful motivational principles, idiographic theories of goal content have been constructed using an approach that assumes that one is likely to find substantial within-person variability and across-person idiosyncracy in individual goal hierarchies (see Table 6.1 and Chapter 4 for examples of this approach). This is quite congruent with the emphasis in MST on the organized complexity of motivational patterns within and across individuals. As the development of the Ford and Nichols Taxonomy of Human Goals implies, however, it is also recognized in MST that for some applications a nomothetic approach may be needed. (See Chapter 4 for a detailed discussion of this issue.)

31. Control System Theories of Human Motivation. Just as D. Ford (1987) found it useful to anchor his Living Systems Framework in part around concepts from control system models, a diversity of motivation theorists have found such models useful in describing the processes involved in the direction and regulation of complex behavior patterns. As noted in Chapter 2, such models are particularly adept at accounting for the organization of variable patterns of activity directed by multiple goals and regulated by multiple sources of feedback and feedforward information. They also are useful in facilitating efforts to integrate the concepts and principles of seemingly discrepant theoretical approaches. Indeed, both social cognitive theory and goal-setting theory have increasingly come to resemble control system approaches to human motivation. As with most other contemporary theories of motivation, however, control system models do not adequately highlight, much less precisely describe, the crucial role played by emotional processes in energizing and regulating behavior. They also are prone to the use of jargon terms (e.g., reference criteria, error sensitivity, amplifying processes) that detract from their accessibility to "uninitiated" scholars and professionals.

32. Motivational Systems Theory. As has been repeatedly emphasized in earlier chapters of this book, MST in an integrative theory in which human motivation is conceptualized in terms of the organized patterning of personal goals, emotional arousal processes, and personal agency beliefs. It is not designed to replace other productive and useful frameworks; rather, it is designed to provide a theoretical umbrella for the field and suggest ways in which different streams of theoretical and empirical work might be enriched—for example, by expanding the range of motivational phenomena considered; by incorporating more precise conceptualizations of goals, emotions, and personal agency beliefs into such work; and by placing motivational phenomena in the context of the whole person-in-context system. In addition, MST uses numerous conceptual heuristics and relatively straightforward concepts and concept labels in an effort to promote the application of motivation theory and research to practical, real-world problems.

The major concepts and principles comprising Motivational Systems Theory are summarized in Table 6.1 and in Chapter 8 of this book.

Conclusions

As outlined in Table 6.1, the history of motivational theorizing can be summarized in terms of an evolving conception of the basic nature of human functioning and development. Early theories of motivation portrayed humans as reactive organisms compelled to act by internal and/or external forces (e.g., instincts, needs, drives, incentives, reinforcers, etc.) that were essentially beyond their control. It was assumed that if one could "push" or "pull" the right buttons, motivation would result—a highly mechanistic view that is still the way many people think about human motivation in parenting, education, business, and other daily life settings. Because the human capacity for self-direction and self-regulation was generally not appreciated, directive properties of the person were assumed to be relatively fixed, and self-referent beliefs were irrelevant. Consequently, the emphasis was on homeostatic, stability-maintaining mechanisms (e.g., arousal reduction, self-preservation, need satisfaction).

In the next phase of theorizing attention began to be focused on motivational qualities associated with incremental and transformational change processes (e.g., motivator factors, actualizing tendency, behavior shaping through contingency management, hope for success, desires for understanding and mastery). In addition, a serious interest in and appreciation for the role of self-evaluative thoughts in motivational patterns emerged, at least in rudimentary form. Unfortunately, the increased attention given to cognitive concepts such as expectancy, causal attribution, and locus on control seemed to be at the expense of emotion-related concepts. The concept of motivation became more closely associated with "cool" decision making and judgment rather than "hot" emotions and desires. Indeed, the entire field of motivation seemed to be in danger of being subsumed under the rubric of cognitive or social-cognitive theory.

In the last 15 years, however, the field of motivation has made an impressive comeback. Led by powerful and increasingly sophisticated theories organized around personal agency belief concepts (e.g., learned helplessness theory, self-efficacy theory, cognitive evaluation theory) and goal-related processes (e.g., goal-setting theory, goal orientation theories, idiographic theories of goal content), motivation has reemerged as a potentially powerful and useful construct. Although still largely cognitive in orientation, these theories have carved out territory that is clearly motivational in content. Combined with the continuing elaboration of various differential emotion theories, the elements for theoretical integration are clearly in place, as evidenced not only by the present effort, but also by a number of other recent attempts to promote conceptual mergers and expansions (e.g., Hyland, 1988; Klein, 1989; Locke & Latham, 1990b; Maehr & Pintrich, 1991; Pervin, 1989). Among these efforts, MST provides the most comprehensive integrative conceptual framework for understanding and influencing human motivation that is presently available.

Suggestions for Further Reading

See Table 6.1 (and the reference section at the end of this book) for suggested readings corresponding to each of the 32 theories and categories of theories summarized in that table.

TABLE 6.1 Summary of Motivation Theories in Terms of MST Component Processes

Theory of Motivation	Concepts Related to Personal Goals	Concepts Related to Personal Agency Beliefs	Concepts Related to Emotions or Arousal	Other Major Concepts
1. **Psychoanalytic Theory** (e.g., Freud, 1901/1951, 1915/1934, 1915/1957, 1920/1948, 1923/1947, 1933/1964; also relevant are systems of psychotherapy that have elaborated, transformed, or reconceptualized motivationally relevant psychoanalytic concepts—e.g., Adler, 1924; Erickson, 1963; Hartmann, 1958; Horney, 1945; Rapaport, 1960; see also D. Ford & Urban, 1963)	**Instinctual (Id) drives/wishes** (particularly those related to sex and aggression; i.e., the life and death instincts) **Self-preservation (Ego) drives** (e.g., competence and mastery) **Cathexis** (energy bound to some object) **Ego Ideal** (a component of the Superego that represents valued states, actions, and outcomes)		**Nirvana Principle** (reduce level of arousal to the lowest possible level) **Pleasure Principle** (maximize pleasure, reduce displeasure, especially anxiety) **Anxiety** (response of the ego to stimulation it is unable to control) **Guilt/Shame/Dread** (from violations of Conscience, a component of the Superego that represents forbidden thoughts, feelings, and actions)	**Ego** (self-preservative functions, including displacement, sublimation, and defense mechanisms such as repression, projection, reaction formation, etc. these are governed by the Reality Principle [withhold wish fulfillment/discharge of cathexis until appropriate time, setting, or substitute object is available]) **Ego Strength** (a primary indicator of mental health) **Primary Process** (direct discharge of Id wishes) **Secondary Process** (continuous reality testing by the ego, i.e., integration of Pleasure

174

		Principle with Reality Principle)
		Superego (internalized values, ethics, morals, ideals, taboos, etc.)
2. Instinct Theory/Hormic Psychology (e.g., McDougall, 1908, 1933)	**Instinct/Propensity** (inherited disposition to respond in a purposeful way to various kinds of objects, events, or ideas)	Emotions associated with particular instincts / propensities and sentiments
	Sentiment (learned clustering of instincts and associated emotions around the idea of an object or class of objects)	
3. Need Theories (e.g., Aldefer, 1969, 1972; Maslow, 1943, 1966, 1970; Murray, 1938)	**Multiple needs and hierarchy of needs** (motivational forces or concerns that organize thoughts, feelings, and actions)	**Deficiency, Being,** and **Unified motivational orientations** (Maslow) Contextual influences on needs (e.g., environmental presses)

continued

TABLE 6.1 Continued

Theory of Motivation	Concepts Related to Personal Goals	Concepts Related to Personal Agency Beliefs	Concepts Related to Emotions or Arousal	Other Major Concepts
4. Two-Factor Theory (e.g., Herzberg, 1966; Herzberg, Mausner, & Snyderman, 1959)	**Hygiene Factors** (facilitating or constraining elements of the job context associated with survival and stability maintenance goals) **Motivator Factors** (job elements that afford the attainment of goals associated with personal growth and development)		**Job Satisfaction/ Dissatisfaction** (hypothesized to result primarily from motivator and hygiene factors, respectively)	
5. Drive Theory (e.g., Amsel, 1958; Brown & Farber, 1951; Dollard, Miller, Doob, Mowrer, & Sears, 1939; Miller, 1944, 1951, 1959; Hull, 1931, 1943, 1951, 1952; Mowrer, 1939, 1960; Spence, 1956, 1958; Taylor, 1956)	**Drive Stimuli** (stimuli associated with a particular habit pattern that help provide direction to behavior) **Incentive** (an environmental component that is valued or desired because of its drive-reducing properties)	**Fractional Anticipatory Goal Responses** (learned associations that maintain or inhibit progress toward a goal; functions like an expectancy, although cognitive constructs are explicitly rejected in this theory—note, however, that Tolman (1926, 1932, 1938, 1951, 1952, 1955) used the concept of	**Drive** (a general energizing force caused by deficits in biologically based needs (primary drives), or conditions associated with a primary drive state (secondary drives) **Frustration** (a drive-incrementing emotion aroused by thwarting of progress	**Excitatory Potential** (tendency to act) **Habit** (learned behavior pattern associated with a particular drive state) **Reactive Inhibition** (temporary reduction of excitatory potential for a particular response after its use)

176

Theory				
	Goal Conflicts (especially conflicts between approach and avoidance tendencies)	expectancy (and other cognitive constructs such as belief-value matrices and cognitive maps) in his alternative to traditional drive theory, which ultimately resembled Lewin's field theory and early expectancy-value theories more than drive theory)	toward an important goal) Other learned emotional responses (e.g., anxiety, fear, hope, disappointment)	Conditioned Inhibition (enduring reduction of excitatory potential for a particular response as a consequence of repeated experiences of reactive inhibition)
6. Field Theory (e.g., Lewin, 1935, 1936, 1951; Lewin, Dembo, Festinger, & Sears, 1944)	Need (a potential or current concern) Quasi-need (a specific intention) Valence/Goal (a property of the environment that affords satisfaction of a need or quasi-need) Goal Conflicts (between multiple approach and/or avoidance forces) Level of Aspiration (difficulty of standards for goal attainment)	Potency (expectancies for success and/or failure)	Tension (a state of arousal associated with an unmet need) Frustration (emotion associated with blockage of goal attainment or a goal conflict)	Force (overall magnitude and direction of a motivational pattern) Psychological Distance (cognitive salience of a goal based on, e.g., temporal or situational proximity) Life Space (a concept emphasizing the need to understand the totality of factors operating in the current situation)

continued

TABLE 6.1 Continued

Theory of Motivation	Concepts Related to Personal Goals	Concepts Related to Personal Agency Beliefs	Concepts Related to Emotions or Arousal	Other Major Concepts
7. Actualization Theory (e.g., Rogers, 1946, 1951, 1961; others contributing to this stream of influence include, e.g., Allport, 1955; Lecky, 1945; Maslow, 1943, 1971)	**Actualizing Tendency** (striving toward psychological growth and fulfillment, especially in terms of self-actualization) **Need for Positive Regard** and **Need for Positive Self-Regard** **Organismic Valuing Process** (process by which satisfaction or value is derived from experience)		Emotions associated with successful or unsuccessful need fulfillment or striving toward actualization	**Conditional** and **Unconditional Positive Regard** (constraining and facilitating influences, respectively, on need fulfillment and actualizing tendency) **The Fully Functioning Individual**

8. Cognitive Dissonance Theory (e.g., Brehm & Cohen, 1962; Festinger, 1957, 1964; Wicklund & Brehm, 1976)	Need to Maintain Consistency/Avoid Incongruity among personally relevant beliefs, attitudes, opinions, actions, and so on (based on underlying needs for understanding, positive self-evaluation, and social validation)	Tension (resulting from cognitive dissonance)
9. Optimal Level Theories (e.g., Apter, 1982; Berlyne, 1960, 1971; Dember & Earl, 1957; Hebb, 1949, 1955; Hunt, 1965; Malmo, 1959; Scott, 1966)		Optimal Level of Arousal, Stimulation, or Incongruity (generally with an ultimate focus on a preferred level of emotional arousal)
10. Equity Theory (e.g., Adams, 1963, 1965; Huseman, Hatfield, & Miles, 1987; Walster, Berscheid, & Walster, 1973; Walster, Walster, & Berscheid, 1978)	Need to Maintain Equity/Avoid Inequity in social exchange relationships (especially with regard to employee compensation) Equity Sensitivity (degree to which equity is a salient personal goal)	Guilt (if favored) Anger (if others favored)

continued

179

TABLE 6.1 Continued

Theory of Motivation	Concepts Related to Personal Goals	Concepts Related to Personal Agency Beliefs	Concepts Related to Emotions or Arousal	Other Major Concepts
11. **Operant Learning Theory** (e.g., Skinner, 1953, 1957, 1959, 1974, 1984)	**Environmental Contingencies** ("selection by consequences" of behavior patterns through reinforcement, punishment, and extinction—although *thoughts* about desired consequences (goals) are explicitly rejected as meaningful variables in this theory)	**Schedules of Reinforcement** (procedures that alter context beliefs through specific changes in the responsiveness of the environment—although cognitive concepts such as beliefs are explicitly rejected in this theory)		**Respondent Behaviors** **Operant Behaviors** **Discrimination and Generalization** **Behavior Shaping**
12. **Social Learning Theory** (e.g., Lefcourt, 1976; Phares, 1976; Rotter, 1954, 1966; Rotter, Chance, & Phares, 1972; not to be confused with other theories using the same label, e.g., Bandura, 1977a; Mischel, 1973)	**Need Value and Need Potential** (importance and probability of activating a need associated with a particular reinforcement history)	**Expectancy** (of reinforcement for a particular behavior in a particular situation) **Locus of Control** (generalized expectancy regarding internal versus external control of reinforcement)		**Behavior Potential** (probability that a learned behavior pattern associated with a set of reinforcers will occur)

13. Expectancy-Value Theories of Achievement Motivation (e.g., Atkinson, 1957, 1964; Feather, 1966; Feather, 1982; McClelland, 1961, 1985; McClelland, Atkinson, Clark, & Lowell, 1953; Raynor & McFarlin, 1986; see also the Dynamics of Action elaboration of this basic framework, e.g., Atkinson & Birch, 1970, 1974; Blankenship, 1985; Kuhl & Blankenship, 1979; Revelle & Michaels, 1976)	Need for Achievement (Motive for Success and Motive to Avoid Failure)	Expectancy for (subjective probability of) success or failure	Hope for Success (anticipated pleasure or pride in accomplishment);	Motivational Tendency/Instigating and Inhibiting Forces (overall direction and magnitude of a success- or failure-oriented motivational pattern)
	Other unconscious motive systems (e.g., needs for affiliation, power, intimacy, etc.)		Fear of Failure (anticipated shame or feelings of distress as a consequence of failure)	Cognitions, Skills, Habits
	Incentive (a property of the environment that affords satisfaction of a need)		Other fears (e.g., of success, power, rejection, etc.)	Opportunity to satisfy motive
	Incentive Value (psychological value of achieving success or avoiding failure; closely associated with anticipated emotional states, which are in turn closely linked to underlying motive systems)			

continued

TABLE 6.1 Continued

Theory of Motivation	Concepts Related to Personal Goals	Concepts Related to Personal Agency Beliefs	Concepts Related to Emotions or Arousal	Other Major Concepts
14. Expectancy Theories of Work Motivation (e.g., Graen, 1969; J. Klein, 1990; Kopelman, 1977; Kopelman & Thompson, 1976; Lawler, 1971; Porter & Lawler, 1968; Vroom, 1964; Zedeck, 1977)	**Valence/Value** (emotionally laden desire or preference for a particular state or outcome)	**Expectancy** (belief regarding whether a desired or preferred state is attainable); **Instrumentality** (belief regarding whether job activities are effective means to desired or preferred states or outcomes—implies a responsive environment)		**Force** (overall magnitude and direction of a motivational pattern) Skills and Abilities Role Perceptions
15. Theory of Action Control (e.g., Halisch & Kuhl, 1986; Heckhausen & Kuhl, 1985; Kuhl, 1984, 1985, 1986; Kuhl & Beckmann, 1985, in press)	**Value/Valence** (of an anticipated goal/outcome) **Goal Relevance: Wishes, Wants, and Intentions** (goals that vary along a continuum of potential for producing action, as determined through goal evaluations on multiple criteria associated with value or expectancy: opportunity, time, **Expectancy** (belief	regarding whether a desired or preferred state is attainable) **Instrumentality** (belief regarding whether job activities are effective means to desired or preferred states or outcomes—implies a responsive environment)		**Action (Volitional) Control** (self-regulatory and self-control strategies that "shield" intentions against competing motivational tendencies, thus facilitating the maintenance of activated intentions)

182

importance, urgency, and means (OTIUM)) **Action versus State Orientation** (attentional focus on the actions required to change current states into preferred states versus a noninstrumental focus on the states themselves— may reflect variations in goal content (e.g., task versus affective goals), a stability maintaining versus change goal orientation, or differences in action control capabilities)	**Behavioral Attitudes** (evaluative thoughts/feelings derived from beliefs about interacting with a task or person) **Behavioral Intentions** (currently activated goals formed as a result of attitudes and normative beliefs regarding performance of an action)	**Behavioral Beliefs** (about the outcomes of interacting with a particular task or person) **Behavioral Expectations** (degree of confidence that one has volitional control over intended actions—hypothesized to be the most direct predictor of a person's actions)	**Normative Beliefs** (about the social desirability of performing a particular action) **Volitional Control** (over the enactment of an intention as a result of having or not having prerequisite skills, opportunities, etc.)
16. **Theory of Reasoned Action** (Ajzen & Fishbein, 1977, 1980; Fishbein & Ajzen, 1975; note that this theory is a special case of the more general Theory of Planned Behavior (e.g., Ajzen, 1985), with the former theory applying only to cases in which volitional control can be assumed.			

continued

183

TABLE 6.1 Continued

Theory of Motivation	Concepts Related to Personal Goals	Concepts Related to Personal Agency Beliefs	Concepts Related to Emotions or Arousal	Other Major Concepts
17. **Differential Emotion Theories** (e.g., Ekman, 1972; Ekman & Friesen, 1978; Izard, 1977, 1979, 1991; Plutchik, 1962, 1980; Tomkins, 1962, 1963; also relevant here are theories about particular emotion patterns and their functional and developmental consequences —e.g., Averill, 1968, 1978; Bowlby, 1969, 1973, 1980; Hoffman, 1982; Smith, 1981; Spielberger, 1972; Sroufe & Waters, 1976; etc.)	Emotion-laden perceptions and cognitions that function to direct and organize behavior patterns		**Qualitatively distinct emotion patterns** (ranging in number from approximately 8-10), each functioning to regulate and energize behavior in different kinds of situations involving pervasive, prototypical adaptive problems and opportunities (i.e., each emotion produces a readiness to respond in a particular way to events of personal significance, with interest functioning as a particularly ubiquitous source of energy and evaluative experience)	

Theory			
18. Causal Attribution Theory of Motivation and Emotion (e.g., B. Weiner, 1974, 1979, 1980, 1985, 1986)	General desire for understanding and mastery	Causal Attributions for success and failure (especially attributions involving ability, effort, luck, and task difficulty) Beliefs about the locus, stability, globality, and controllability of causes for success and failure Expectancies for success and failure (as influenced by causal attributional patterns)	Attribution-specific emotional consequences (e.g., pride, anger, gratitude, guilt, pity, hopelessness, etc.)
19. Reactance Theory (e.g., Brehm, 1966, 1972; Brehm & Brehm, 1981)	General desire to maintain a sense of personal freedom Important outcome at stake in current situation	Psychological experience of loss (or threat of loss) of personal freedom (especially the loss of an attractive and available behavioral option)	Psychological Reactance (i.e., annoyance- anger-rage emotion pattern and associated actions, e.g., defiance, aggression, sabotage, rebellion, refusal to act, minimal compliance, constructive problem solving, cognitive distortion) Helplessness (if loss or denial of freedom is prolonged)

continued

TABLE 6.1 Continued

Theory of Motivation	Concepts Related to Personal Goals	Concepts Related to Personal Agency Beliefs	Concepts Related to Emotions or Arousal	Other Major Concepts
20. Personal Causation Theory (e.g., deCharms, 1968, 1976, 1984)	**General desire for agency** (i.e., being effective or being the cause of desired changes) **Intrinsic versus Extrinsic Motivation** (defined by whether goals are self-set versus contextually imposed)	**Personal Causation/Agency** (i.e., locus of causality, or feeling like an "Origin" versus feeling like a "Pawn"—implies freedom, ownership, and choice within strong contextual boundaries that facilitate the exercise of personal agency)		
21. Learned Helplessness/Hopelessness/Optimism Theory (e.g., Abramson, Metalsky, & Alloy, 1989; Abramson, Seligman, & Teasdale, 1978; Miller & Norman, 1979; Peterson & Seligman, 1984; Seligman, 1975, 1991)	**Important personal goals activated by negative life events**	**Explanatory Style** (especially internal, stable, and global versus external, unstable, and specific causal interpretations for negative life events; also applicable to causal interpretations of positive life events) **Learned Helplessness** (belief in response-outcome noncontingency)	**Anxiety** and/or **Depression** (resulting from learned helplessness and especially from generalized hopelessness) **Hope** (resulting from optimistic thinking)	**Cognitive Rumination** (obsessive analysis of negative life events)

Generalized Hopelessness (Helplessness plus expectancy that outcomes will be negative in many areas of life)

Circumscribed Pessimism (helplessness plus negative outcome expectancy that is limited to a particular domain)

Learned Optimism (belief in response- outcome contingency and possibility of favorable outcomes)

Flexible Optimism (optimism anchored in but not overly constrained by realistic thinking)

22. **Self-Worth Theories** (e.g., Covington, 1984a, 1984b, 1992; Covington & Beery, 1976; Harter, 1990; Tesser, 1986; Tesser & Campbell, 1985; some general self-esteem theories are also relevant to this category, e.g.,	Ubiquitous need to protect one's sense of personal value, personal competence, or worth as a person	**Overall sense of value/competence/ ability/success/worth as a person** (in contrast to domain-specific or task-specific evaluations of one's competence or ability)	**Affective consequences of positive and negative evaluations of self-worth** (especially happy versus depressed mood and pride-satisfaction in accomplishment versus shame/guilt/humiliation in failure)	**Social feedback and social relationships as highly significant sources of self-evaluative information** (e.g., through social comparison, social reflection, and social support processes)

continued

TABLE 6.1 Continued

Theory of Motivation	Concepts Related to Personal Goals	Concepts Related to Personal Agency Beliefs	Concepts Related to Emotions or Arousal	Other Major Concepts
Coopersmith, 1967; Rosenberg, 1979)		Tendency to take personal responsibility for successes but not failures (i.e., to attribute failures to an unresponsive environment rather than to a lack of personal capabilities), with helplessness or hopelessness often resulting from failures to protect one's basic sense of self-worth		**Strategies for protecting one's sense of self-worth** (e.g., not trying, procrastination, making excuses, avoiding competitive situations, choosing very low or very high standards for success, selectively attending to self-enhancing feedback) **Role of competitive environments in fostering vulnerability to negative self-worth;** need to construct environments in which failure is less motivationally debilitating (e.g., mastery-oriented environments or environments with cooperative goals)

23. Effectance Motivation Theories (e.g., Harter, 1978, 1981b; White, 1959)	General desire to explore and master one's environment (i.e., to be competent, with manifestations of this general motive varying in strength across domains as a function of emotions, personal agency beliefs, and contextual support for exploration and mastery) Optimal Challenge (task or activity affording attainment of a goal that is particularly meaningful in terms of personal efficacy and feelings of pleasure)	Sense of personal efficacy/competence/mastery versus personal inefficacy	Feelings of pleasure or anxiety in situations involving exploration and mastery
24. Optimal Experience Theory (e.g., Csikszentmihalyi, 1975, 1978, 1990; Csikszentmihalyi & Csikszentmihalyi, 1988)	Intrinsic Motivation (clear and definite personal goals in the context of an optimally challenging task/activity)	Sense of personal control and effectiveness	Enjoyment/Pleasure (versus boredom, anxiety, or frustration) Flow (overall subjective experience of focused attention, sense of control, personal meaning, and pleasure)

continued

189

TABLE 6.1 Continued

Theory of Motivation	Concepts Related to Personal Goals	Concepts Related to Personal Agency Beliefs	Concepts Related to Emotions or Arousal	Other Major Concepts
25. **Self-Determination Theory** (e.g., Deci, 1975, 1980; Deci & Ryan, 1985, 1987, 1991; Deci, Vallerand, Pelletier, & Ryan, 1991; Ryan, 1982; Ryan, Connell, & Deci, 1985; note that this is an integration of three subtheories: Cognitive Evaluation Theory, Organismic Integration Theory, and Causality Orientations Theory)	**Innate need to maintain a sense of self-determination** (i.e., a sense of being able to act out of choice rather than obligation or coercion—including the choice of letting others have control over one's actions or outcomes) **Innate need to maintain a sense of personal competence** **Innate need to "seek and conquer" optimal challenges,** thereby facilitating a sense of self-determination and perceived competence (i.e., intrinsic motivation)	**Internal Versus External Locus of Causality (Self-Determination)** **Perceived Competence** (versus **Incompetence**) **Autonomous Orientation** (tendency to approach a situation with a sense of competence and self-determination) **Control Orientation** (tendency to approach a situation with a sense of being pressured by external or internal controls) **Impersonal Orientation** (tendency to approach a situation with a sense of incompetence and helplessness)	Emotions associated with a sense of competence and self-determination; external or internal pressures and controls; or a sense of incompetence and helplessness	**Informational aspects of an (external or intrapersonal) event** (those providing effectance-relevant feedback in the context of choice or autonomy; facilitates intrinsic motivation and self-determined functioning) **Controlling aspects of an event** (those experienced as involving pressure to think, feel, or act in a certain way, e.g., powerful or seductive rewards, threats of punishment, deadlines, surveillance, excessive ego involvement; undermines intrinsic motivation and facilitates compliance or defiance)

A motivational aspects of an event (those signifying a lack of competence; undermines both intrinsic and extrinsic motivation)

Internalization (degree to which externally defined demands and values are integrated into self-regulatory systems characterized, at least in part, by qualities associated with intrinsic motivation)

Importance of combining opportunities for self-determination with informational limit setting (thus avoiding the amotivational consequences of permissiveness)

continued

191

TABLE 6.1 Continued

Theory of Motivation	Concepts Related to Personal Goals	Concepts Related to Personal Agency Beliefs	Concepts Related to Emotions or Arousal	Other Major Concepts
26. Theory of Personal Investment (e.g., Maehr, 1984; Maehr & Braskamp, 1986)	**Personal Incentives** (differential valuing of events and activities associated with success due to current circumstances, past experiences, and cultural background, especially with regard to action possibilities/ opportunities, one's sense of personal competence, and salient personal goals) **Personal Investment** (of motivational resources in particular kinds of goal-directed activity, primarily as a function of the personal meaning of those activities, as manifested in choice, persistence, continuing motivation, intensity, and performance)	**Sense of Personal Competence** **Perceived Options** for investment of personal resources (whether clear action possibilities/ opportunities are believed to exist)		**Emphasis on *distribution* rather than *availability* of motivational resources** (with a corresponding emphasis on the utility of such an approach for cross-cultural research, human resource management, career and life decision making, etc.) Influence of social expectations, task design, and the organizational/social-cultural context on personal incentives, sense of competence, and perceived options

27. Self-Efficacy Theory/Social Cognitive Theory (e.g., Bandura, 1977b, 1978, 1981, 1982, 1986, 1989; Schunk, 1984, 1991a, 1991b; Wood & Bandura, 1989)	**Goals/Incentives** (desired and expected outcomes that serve as current guides and motivators of behavior) **Intention** (psychological determination to perform an activity or to change a current state into a preferred state) **Proximal Subgoals** (clear, specific goals that, in contrast to vague, distal goals, facilitate immediate action (by strengthening intentions), yield informative feedback, and help maintain or enhance self-efficacy **Internal Standards** (evaluative criteria representing acceptable levels of goal attainment; behavior is regulated primarily through self-evaluative [and associated emotional] reactions based on these criteria)	**Self-Efficacy expectancies** (beliefs about personal capabilities that may vary in level (difficulty of performance accomplishment), generality [range of contexts represented], and strength (vulnerability to disconfirming information]) **Behavior-Outcome expectancies** (beliefs about the contingencies and outcomes associated with particular actions) **Collective Efficacy** (shared beliefs about the capabilities of a group, organization, or nation for effective action) **Optimal Challenge** (a task or activity that matches one's perceived capabilities, provides informative feedback, and offers a rising standard of success)	**Affective states** that may (or may not) be associated with evaluative self-reactions to meeting or not meeting internal standards of achievement, morality, and so on (i.e., evaluative thoughts are seen as the primary regulators of activity)	**Five fundamental cognitive capabilities: generative symbolization, forethought, symbolic communication, evaluative self-regulation, and reflective self-consciousness;** cognitive biases and misjudgments also important in understanding mechanisms underlying behavior patterns (e.g., misjudgments of personal efficacy, unrealistic standards, self-exonerative reactions to reprehensible conduct) **Four sources of self-efficacy information: mastery experiences, modeling, social persuasion, and affective body state information;** attributional and social comparison processes may also influence self-efficacy judgments

continued

TABLE 6.1 Continued

Theory of Motivation	Concepts Related to Personal Goals	Concepts Related to Personal Agency Beliefs	Concepts Related to Emotions or Arousal	Other Major Concepts
27. Self-Efficacy Theory/Social Cognitive Theory (continued)				**Crucial role of social environment in shaping thought and behavior patterns (e.g., through observational learning and other forms of symbolic communication, which serve as uniquely efficient means of conveying information about concepts, rules, and predictive relationships among events)**

28. Goal-Setting Theory/High Performance Cycle Theory (e.g., Latham & Lee, 1986; Latham & Yukl, 1975; Locke, 1968; Locke, Bryan, & Kendall, 1968; Locke, Latham, & Erez, 1988; Locke, Shaw, Saari, & Latham, 1981; Locke & Latham, 1984, 1990a, 1990b; Lee, Locke, & Latham, 1989)	Goal (a valued future end state that one wants to accomplish) Goal Setting (consciously conceiving of desired future states in terms that are more or less specific and/or challenging) Goal Commitment (degree to which individuals or groups are truly trying to attain a goal; i.e., the goal is an intended outcome that is actively being pursued)	Expectancies for success and failure/Self-Efficacy (as defined by expectancy theories of work motivation and Bandura's Social Cognitive Theory)	Job Satisfaction (emotional consequence of (a) effectively completing tasks that are personally engaging and significant, and/or (b) being rewarded for effective performance, assuming such rewards are regarded by the employee as meaningful and equitable)	**High Performance Cycle** (highly productive pattern of activity characterized by challenging goals, strong goal commitment, high expectancy of success, availability of informative feedback, adequate ability, and a responsive environment) **Four mechanisms by which specific, challenging goals, positive expectancies, and informative feedback facilitate high performance: direction of attention and action, increased effort, increased persistence, and the development of task strategies and plans**

continued

195

TABLE 6.1 Continued

Theory of Motivation	Concepts Related to Personal Goals	Concepts Related to Personal Agency Beliefs	Concepts Related to Emotions or Arousal	Other Major Concepts
29. **Goal Orientation Theories** (e.g., C. Ames & R. Ames, 1984a, 1984b; Dweck, 1986; Dweck & Leggett, 1988; Elliott & Dweck, 1988; Kuhl, 1981, 1984, 1985; Kuhl & Beckmann, in press; Nicholls, 1984a, 1984b, 1990; Wicklund, 1986; Winell, 1987)	**Goal Orientations** (styles of goal pursuit involving qualitatively different patterns of goal setting and/or goal content, usually represented in terms of an adaptive versus maladaptive dichotomy [e.g., active versus reactive, approach versus avoidance, change versus maintenance, thriving versus coping, action versus state, mastery versus helpless, task-involved versus ego-involved, etc.])	Adaptive goal orientations generally associated with positive PABs; maladaptive goal orientations often linked to vulnerable or negative PABs		
30. **Idiographic Theories of Goal Content** (e.g., Cantor & Fleeson, 1991; Cantor & Langston, 1989; Emmons, 1986, 1989; Little, 1983, 1989; Markus & Nurius, 1986; Markus & Ruvolo, 1989; Nichols, 1990, 1991)	Various concepts representing goals or goal-directed patterns of activity that are (a) personally meaningful, often at a deep or fundamental level; (b) currently or potentially high in priority; and (c)		Personal goals that are meaningful and high in priority are often linked to strong emotions such as deep satisfaction/dissatisfaction, pride/guilt, excitement/anxiety, etc.	

continued

			Amplifying Processes	
31. Control System Theories of Human Motivation (e.g., Campion & Lord, 1982; Carver & Scheier, 1981, 1982, 1985, 1990; Hollenbeck, 1989; Hyland, 1989; H. Klein, 1989; Lord & Hanges, 1987; Lord & Kernan, 1989; Powers, 1973, 1989; also relevant are historically prominent control system theories (e.g., Ashby, 1956, 1962; Koestler, 1967, 1978; Miller, Galanter, & Pribram, 1960; von Bertalanffy, 1968, 1975; N. Weiner, 1948)	**Reference Criteria/Internal Standards/System Goals** (desired internal states or outcomes of system activity) **Goal Hierarchies** (organization of system goals in multilevel means-ends hierarchies) **Error Sensitivity** (salience or importance of discrepancies between desired and perceived or anticipated states and outcomes)	**Feedforward/Expectancies** (evaluative thoughts representing anticipated states or outcomes of system activity)		**Perceptual Input** (especially input representing internal states or outcomes of system activity) **Comparator** (process by which desired states or outcomes are compared to perceived and/or anticipated states and outcomes) **Behavioral Output** (actions designed to respond to perceived or anticipated disturbances or discrepancies) **Negative Feedback loops** (discrepancy-reducing patterns of system activity) **Positive Feedback loops** (deviation-amplifying patterns of system activity)

powerful in terms of organizing behavior and personality (e.g., core goals, personal strivings, possible selves, life tasks, personal projects, etc.)

TABLE 6.1 Continued

Theory of Motivation	Concepts Related to Personal Goals	Concepts Related to Personal Agency Beliefs	Concepts Related to Emotions or Arousal	Other Major Concepts
31. Control System Theories of Human Motivation (continued)				Control System model often regarded as a basis for integrating other motivation theories (e.g., expectancy theory, attribution theory, goal-setting theory, social cognitive theory, cognitive evaluation theory)
32. Motivational Systems Theory (MST) (e.g., M. Ford, 1992)	**Personal Goals** (Thoughts about desired or undesired consequences that one would like to achieve) **Goal Content** (the consequence represented in a particular goal; may be described in idiographic terms or classified into broad goal categories, e.g., the Ford and Nichols Taxonomy of Human Goals)	**Personal Agency Beliefs** (cognitive evaluations pertaining to the attainability of a goal) **Capability Beliefs** (evaluations of whether one has the personal skills needed to function effectively; these beliefs may pertain to a diversity of instrumental capabilities) **Context Beliefs** (evaluations of whether	**Emotional Arousal Processes** (organized functional patterns consisting of an affective (neuropsychological) component, a physiological component, and a transactional component; these processes serve both a regulatory and energizing function) Emotions evolved to help people maintain or facilitate effective functioning in	MST is anchored in Donald Ford's **Living Systems Framework**, a comprehensive theory of human functioning and development **Behavior Episode** (a context-specific, goal-directed pattern of behavior) **Behavior Episode Schema** (an internal representation of a set of related behavior episode experiences)

			Concepts and Propositions (abstracted BES components and component relationships)
Goal Hierarchies (coordinated patterning of multiple goals within and across behavior episodes; may result in goal conflict or goal alignment within episodes, and goal balance or imbalance across episodes)	one has the responsive environment needed to support effective functioning; these evaluations may pertain to the goals afforded by a particular context, the "goodness of fit" with one's capabilities, the material and informational resources available in that context, or the social-emotional climate provided by that context)	circumstances requiring the rapid and efficient mobilization and deployment of energy resources and transactional capabilities; they are therefore particularly influential in motivating immediate or short-term action	**Personality** (the person's repertoire of stable, recurring BES)
Goal-Setting Processes (methods or strategies used to represent goals within a behavior episode [e.g., focusing on specific short-term goals versus global long-term goals])	**PAB Patterns** (10 qualitatively distinct combinations of capability and context beliefs: **Robust, Tenacious, Modest, Antagonistic, Accepting, Fragile, Vulnerable, Discouraged, Self-Doubting and Hopeless**)	**14 different kinds of emotional patterns** evolved to help people deal with different kinds of pervasive, prototypical problems (8 instrumental emotions and 6 social emotions)	**Achievement** (the attainment of a personally or socially valued goal in a particular context)
Goal Orientations (general styles of goal pursuit across behavior episodes)		**Nonemotional Affective States** (e.g., pain and fatigue) can also serve a motivational function	**Competence** (the attainment of relevant goals in specified environments, using appropriate means and resulting in positive developmental outcomes)
Wishes, Current Concerns, and Intentions (goals varying from a low level to a high level of commitment based on various goal evaluation criteria)			**MST Formula for Effective Functioning** (Achievement/ Competence = Motivation × Skill × Biology Responsive Environment)

continued

TABLE 6.1 Continued

Theory of Motivation	Concepts Related to Personal Goals	Concepts Related to Personal Agency Beliefs	Concepts Related to Emotions or Arousal	Other Major Concepts
32. Motivational Systems Theory (MST) (continued)	**Goal Evaluation Criteria** goal relevance, goal importance, goal attainability, and emotional salience) **Standards for Goal Attainment**			**Motivation (a** psychological, [future-oriented anticipatory], and evaluative phenomenon; defined as the organized patterning of an individual's personal goals, emotional arousal processes, and personal agency beliefs) **17 Principles for Motivating Humans**

CHAPTER SEVEN

How to "Motivate" People: Principles and Applications

I was born motivated, like you all were . . . [but beware]—people try to demotivate you.

Dr. Mae Jemison

Purpose of This Chapter

As noted in chapter 1, a basic assumption of (and rationale for) Motivational Systems Theory is that **motivation is at the heart of many of society's most pervasive and enduring problems, both as a developmental outcome of demotivating social environments and as a developmental influence on behavior and personality.** If that is indeed the case, it is vital that researchers, practitioners, and policymakers recognize the fundamental importance of this aspect of human functioning and acquire sound knowledge about the role of motivational processes in effective functioning. Recognition and understanding are not enough, however. One must also be capable of designing and implementing courses of action that can effectively alter problematic motivational patterns and promote the development and use of more adaptive patterns. The purpose of this chapter is help the reader acquire that capability. This is accomplished by first explaining, in terms of general principles, how to approach the problem of trying to "motivate" someone. Then specific applications of these principles are made to the four major problems selected for analysis in Chapter 1: social responsibility and caring behavior in youth, facilitating motivation for learning and school achievement, understanding and facilitating job satisfaction and work productivity, and leading an emotionally healthy life.

Motivating Humans: General Principles

Framing the Problem

First and foremost, the problem of motivating humans must be understood not in simple, mechanistic terms, but, rather, in terms of a more complex and somewhat idiosyncratic process of trying to *facilitate* desired motivational patterns. In other words, there are no magic motivational buttons that can be pushed to "make" people want to learn, work hard, and act in a responsible manner. Similarly, no one can be directly "forced" to care about something, to feel a particular emotion, or to be optimistic about his or her chances for success. One must try, rather, to arrange experiences, circumstances, opportunities, and contingencies in such a way that they increase the *probability* that a person's behavior will be guided by a motivationally powerful BES. Thus an attempt to "motivate" someone should *not* be viewed as a power struggle or an opportunity to assert one's authority. **Facilitation, not control, should be the guiding idea in attempts to motivate humans.** Even when one is in a position of power or authority, efforts to motivate people will generally be more successful if they are viewed as *collaborations* between people who may or may not share the same feelings, expectations, and agenda of personal goals. **Motivational interventions that do not respect the goals, emotions, and personal agency beliefs that a person brings to a situation may produce short-term effects, but in the long run they are likely to fail or backfire.**

Given this orientation, the problem of motivating humans can be understood at two different levels. At the level of a particular behavior episode, the objective is to produce some *temporary change* in a person's functioning. This is accomplished by influencing the person's goals, emotions, and/or personal agency beliefs in a way that facilitates *achievement* of a particular outcome in a particular context (e.g., completing a homework assignment, performing to a high standard on a task, resolving a disagreement, terminating a child's inappropriate conduct). Highly controlling motivational strategies such as real or implied threats, strong punishments, compelling rewards, and forced competition are sometimes effective means of producing these short-term results; that is why they are so commonly used. Because such strategies tend to activate goals, emotions, and personal agency beliefs that are incompatible with longer-term competence develop-ment, however, they are likely to produce negative developmental consequences if they are repeated across many different behavior episodes. **Thus the strategy of trying to motivate people through direct control of their actions—as opposed to indirect facilitation of their goals, emotions, and personal agency beliefs—should be reserved for situations in which swift attainment of a goal is urgent and no other means are available** (e.g., preventing destructive or highly inappropriate behavior, meeting an urgent deadline). When the problem of motivating humans is viewed from a longer-term or *developmental* perspective (i.e., at the "personality" or BES level of analysis), the objective is to try to produce *enduring, elaborative change* in the person's steady state functioning with respect to a particular set of goals and contexts. Such change is accomplished by trying to facilitate the construction, strengthening, or more frequent activa-tion of BES with powerful motivational components, thereby en-hancing the person's *competence* to deal with similar kinds of circum-stances in the future. Of course, short-term and longer-term motivational objectives often go hand-in-hand; for example, helping a person adopt an optimistic approach to a particular problem may help facilitate a more generally positive outlook with regard to similar problems in the future. As noted in the preceding paragraph, however, there are some circumstances in which short-term motiva-tional gains may come at the expense of longer-term motivational developments. Thus, one should always carefully consider whether efforts to promote a particular achievement will also facilitate the development of an individual's competence to deal with similar situations in the future.

For example, there is a compelling literature on the motivational consequences of controlling experiences that indicates that people often lose interest in activities when they feel coerced or manipulated to engage in those activities, even when the motivational strategies used were intended to be positive and rewarding (Baumrind, 1978; Deci, 1975; Deci & Ryan, 1985; Kunda & Schwartz, 1983; Lepper, 1981; Lepper & Greene, 1978; Ryan, 1982; Ryan & Stiller, 1991). This is a particularly disheartening phenomenon to observe when the activities were at one point highly motivating, as when a child's initial interest and enthusiasm for schoolwork or a "fun" activity is replaced by resentment and avoidance as a consequence of parental pressure to achieve. Another illustration of how short-term efforts to enhance motivation can backfire is provided by the literature on the motivational effects of praise and helping behavior. For instance, Brophy's thoughtful and revealing review of the literature on teacher praise (Brophy, 1981) suggests that praise may be just as likely to undermine motivation as to facilitate it because praise is often discounted, interpreted as a strategy for controlling behavior, or viewed as a signal that one's current capabilities are in need of significant improvement. Graham and Barker (1990) also observed this latter phenomenon in their research on helping behavior as a low-ability cue.

Examples from other areas of life further illustrate the need to attend to the longer-term consequences of attempts to motivate humans. Appropriate but insensitively communicated demands for increased productivity may produce irreparable harm to an employee's morale and commitment to an organization. Attempts to inhibit sexual activity in young people (e.g., by encouraging them to feel guilty about their sexual desires and feelings) may produce intensely conflicted motivational patterns that last a lifetime. Sympathetic efforts designed to help a student preparing for an exam feel less anxious and self-doubting may be misguided if the student needs to study more and has time to do so (Bandura, 1986; Tobias, 1985). In short, **even well-intentioned efforts to facilitate motivation can undermine competence development if insufficient attention is given to the enduring consequences of such efforts.**

Principles for Motivating Humans

Whether one focuses on short-term achievements or longer-term competence development, there are several general principles one can use to guide specific attempts to facilitate a person's motivation.

1. The Principle of Unitary Functioning. In driver education classes, students are urged to expand their field of vision and "get the big picture." Analogously, motivational interventionists must understand that they are *always* dealing with a whole person who is bringing a personality and developmental history to a context in which mutually influential psychological, biological, and environmental processes are interrelated in complexly organized functional patterns. Several important implications flow from this understanding: (a) the individuality of humans and the uniqueness of their motivational patterns *must* be respected, (b) changes in motivational parameters are likely to influence other motivational processes and other parts of the person-in-context system (and vice versa), and (c) motivational interventions may sometimes produce unanticipated consequences. Rather than seeing these as constraints, however, one should try to capitalize on both the predictable and unexpected opportunities that may arise as a result of the unitary functioning of the whole person-in-context.

2. *The Motivational Triumvirate Principle.* As explained in Chapter 3, motivation is a concept representing the *patterning* of three interacting psychological components: goals, emotions, and personal agency beliefs. Consequently, **all three motivational components must ultimately be influenced to "motivate" someone successfully.** For example, if goals are activated in the absence of positive emotions and personal agency beliefs, they will be much like leaders who have lost the enthusiasm and confidence of their followers—they will lead no one nowhere. Similarly, much like a person who is "all dressed up with no place to go," energizing emotions that lack direction will generate activity but not much productivity. Of course, the processes in motivational headquarters will occasionally have their conflicts and disagreements and will sometimes "do their own thing." Nevertheless, to produce strong motivational patterns they must be dealt with as an interdependent team. "Negotiating" with just one member of the motivational triumvirate is therefore a risky strategy.

For example, many educators are concerned about gender inequities in math, technology, and science participation that begin to emerge in early adolescence. Because the demotivating influences on girls' involvement and achievement in these areas are so pervasive, however, this problem defies simple solutions, as illustrated by Miura's (1987) research on computer interest and use in middle-school students. In this series of LSF-guided studies, very sizable gender differences favoring males were observed across several samples in a broad range of variables reflecting personal goals (e.g., willingness to consider a computer-related career), emotional arousal processes (e.g., affective responses to the computer), capability beliefs (e.g., self-efficacy for computer use), and context beliefs (e.g., peer reactions to computer involvement). One can conclude from these findings that interventions designed to address just one aspect of this problem would probably yield disappointing results.

3. The Responsive Environment Principle. Whenever someone tries to motivate a person, he or she becomes a part of that person's environment, and therefore a part of that individual's "equation" for effective functioning (i.e., Achievement/Competence = Motivation x Skill x *Responsive Environment*). Consequently, motivational interventionists must be concerned not only with the specific techniques they intend to use, but also with the more general features of their relationship with that person. Following the list outlined in Chapter 5, there are four major dimensions along which this relationship should be monitored: (a) the interventionist's objectives must be congruent with the person's "agenda" of personal goals (i.e., the two sets of goals must be aligned); (b) the interventionist's objectives must be congruent with the person's biological, transactional, and cognitive capabilities; (c) the interventionist's objectives must be realistic and appropriate given the material and informational resources available to facilitate goal attainment; and (d) the interventionist must provide an emotional climate that supports and facilitates effective functioning.

This latter dimension is particularly crucial in terms of the long-term success of the motivational relationship. For example, if the person does not trust the interventionist to act in his or her best interests, efforts to facilitate motivation will be significantly weakened as such efforts are processed through the perceptual filter created by this negative context belief.

4. The Principle of Goal Activation. If no relevant goal is activated with respect to a desired behavior pattern, there will be no relevant behavior. Moreover, one cannot capitalize on positive personal agency beliefs and emotional strengths unless there is some goal in place against which to anchor these thoughts and feelings (see Chapter 5). Thus, although goal activation is just one step in the process of facilitating effective functioning, it is an essential prerequisite for the entire process. A job, activity, task, or experience *must* afford the attainment of personally relevant goals that are of sufficient strength to generate some degree of commitment if there is to be any hope of effective functioning (Maehr, 1984; Maehr & Braskamp, 1986).

What particular goals should one try to activate? That depends on the circumstances and the nature of the desired behavior pattern. One should first try to imagine what kinds of goals would be most likely to promote effective functioning with regard to the problem being addressed (perhaps using the Taxonomy of Human Goals as a tool for ensuring that the full range of possibilities has been considered). Is performing to a standard of excellence (mastery) or seeking order and organization (management) a key goal? Is safety or social responsibility a central concern? To what extent would a belonging-ness or self-determination goal facilitate effective functioning? Next, try to facilitate the activation of these directly relevant goals rather than alternative goals that are less closely linked—or perhaps even an obstacle to—effective functioning. For example, if a task or a job requires teamwork and high standards for performance, as is often the case in education and in business, it would make more sense to emphasize social responsibility and mastery goals than to highlight potentially competing goals such as superiority and material gain.

How can one facilitate the activation of directly relevant goals in the context at hand when a person does not already have BES anchored by those goals? In some cases this may indeed be a very difficult task (e.g., trying to activate social responsibility goals in a sociopath; trying to activate management goals in a habitually sloppy person). In such cases one may have little choice but to reorganize the context in such a way that it also affords the attainment of other, less directly relevant goals that are a prominent part of the person's BES reper-toire—a process often called "extrinsic" motivation. This is not nec-essarily a "cop-out," however. If done carefully and wisely, this process may lead to the design of jobs, tasks, and activities that afford the attainment of multiple, mutually reinforcing goals, as illustrated by the use of engaging simulations, cooperative goal struc-tures, and self-managed work teams in education and business. "Ex-trinsic" motivational techniques (e.g., monetary incentives, social pres-sures to achieve, earning of privileges or "perks") may also be justified if they are used in a way that tends to facilitate the development of goals more directly linked to competence development. For example, such techniques may promote engagement in tasks and experiences that a person might not otherwise try, thus providing the intervention-ist with opportunities to: (a) demonstrate or clarify the goals that are afforded by a particular context, (b) link positive emotions to the outcomes one would like the person to value, and/or (c) enhance personal agency beliefs with respect to those same outcomes. Indeed, in some cases it may be surprisingly easy to facilitate some degree of liking for a previously uninteresting or unattractive activity by simply getting a person to try it, by recasting the emotional tone of the experi-ence, or by ensuring that the person has some consistent, incremental successes with that activity (e.g., Bandura & Schunk, 1981).

5. The Principle of Goal Salience. Successful application of the Prin-ciple of Goal Activation will facilitate effective functioning only to the extent that the goals that have been activated are conceived of by the actor in terms that are sufficiently clear and compelling for that person to be able to direct his or her behavior in concrete ways in the here and now (Ajzen, 1985; Csikszentmihalyi, 1990; Heckhausen & Kuhl, 1985; Locke & Latham, 1984, 1990a, 1990b; Schunk, 1990b, 1991b; Tubbs & Ekeberg, 1991). In other words, one must try to help people think about their goals in ways that elevate *current concerns* to the status of specific *intentions* that can guide current behavior, and that facilitate the development of a person's *commitment* to pursue those goals in future behavior episodes. Such efforts might take the form of: (a) stating or suggesting clear, optimally challenging "targets" for behavior (Harackiewicz & Sansone, 1991; Locke & Latham, 1984, 1990a, 1990b); (b) linking the attainment of a desired future outcome to specific subgoals that indicate progress toward that outcome (Bandura & Schunk, 1981; Morgan, 1985); (c) focusing attention on the specific actions that are needed in the here and now (Barden & Ford, 1990; Kuhl, 1985; Kuhl & Beckmann, in press); (d) explaining why an activity is meaningful in terms of personally relevant goals (Barden & Ford, 1991; Nichols, 1991); (e) using a goal assessment to help bring difficult-to-access information into consciousness, where it can be expressed in a concrete, perceptible form (Ford & Nichols, 1991); or (f) organizing the context so that it clearly affords certain goals and not others.

6. The Multiple Goals Principle. As noted earlier in Chapter 4, the strongest motivational patterns are those anchored by multiple goals. For example, high GPA students are much more likely than are low GPA students to report trying to accomplish a variety of different cognitive, social, and task goals in the classroom, often simultaneously (D. Bergin, 1987; Wentzel, 1989, 1991a, 1991b). Similarly, well-designed cooperative learning arrangements that emphasize a combination of group rewards and individual accountability appear to activate powerful, unified motivational patterns that synergistically link peer approval and responsibility goals with understanding and mastery goals (Slavin, 1981, 1984, 1987, 1989). Thus, in attempts to motivate people to do something that they might not otherwise do, one should try to organize, design, or modify tasks, activities, and experiences so that they afford the attainment of as many different kinds of goals as possible (Brophy, 1987).

Even in cases where this strategy fails to activate a strong motivational pattern directed by multiple goals, it may provide some motivational insurance against the possibility that *no* relevant goal will be activated. For example, attempts to motivate children to perform distasteful chores may be more productive if they suggest a variety of reasons for getting the job done (e.g., to avoid punishment, gain approval, retain a privilege, master a challenge, demonstrate maturity, feel good about one's self, take pleasure in helping out a family member, feel good about being part of the family "team," escape future nagging, etc.). Similarly, efforts to help people quit smoking may be more likely to succeed if they combine health information that may or may not activate safety or physical well-being goals with compelling evidence (from their own or others' experience) emphasizing the monetary loss, social disapproval, and social isolation that accompanies heavy smoking, as well as the sense of self-respect and self-determination that can result from successful efforts to stop smoking.

7. The Principle of Goal Alignment. In trying to facilitate the activation of multiple goals, or simply in dealing with an existing motivational pattern, one must be wary of goal conflicts that may constrain the power or clarity of a person's motivation. For example, unless they are highly unethical, professionals who are being paid by the hour to provide efficient services (e.g., lawyers and auto mechanics) are likely to have many behavior episodes in which they must resolve conflicts between integrative goals (e.g., social responsibility and equity) and material gain goals. One should avoid assuming, however, that such conflicts are inevitable. One should try, rather, to think of creative ways to facilitate the alignment of multiple goals. For instance, one might offer a bonus for swift completion of a quality job, or one might negotiate a deal in which payment for services rendered is capped and contingent upon meeting certain agreed upon standards of performance, quality, or efficiency. When multiple goals are aligned within and between people in this manner, motivation is strong and productivity is high. Indeed, goal alignment is arguably the primary factor in facilitating harmonious interaction between people and "optimal experience" within an individual (Csikszentmihalyi, 1990).

The Principle of Goal Alignment also applies to the problem of aligning proximal and distal goals in such a way that current activities facilitate progress toward desired futures (see Chapters 4 and 5). When short-term and long-term goals are misaligned, the results can be sad indeed. For example, people may waste a great deal of time on situationally compelling but essentially meaningless activities such as hanging out or watching TV, perhaps even failing to "get around" to the most important things in life before it is too late to do so (e.g., spending time with a family member, acquiring training for a desirable profession, publishing enough to earn tenure). People may also begin to experience a loss of coherence and balance in their goal-seeking efforts and feel that their life lacks purpose. Thus a primary strategy in trying to facilitate motivation and effective functioning is to help people focus on immediate subgoals that signify progress toward the outcomes that will ultimately have the most significance and meaning for them (Bandura, 1986; Barden & Ford, 1991). One should also try to facilitate a general orientation toward goal pursuit that is congruent with committed action and long-term competence development—that is, a *thriving* approach to goal setting and goal seeking in which the commanders in "motivational headquarters" are actively pushing the "instrumental troops" to keep moving toward desired futures, rather than a *coping* approach emphasizing defensive maintenance of current steady state positions that may be increasingly ineffective in the face of changing circumstances (Winell, 1987).

8. The Feedback Principle. People cannot continue to make progress toward their personal goals in the absence of relevant feedback information. Without feedback, motivational headquarters is effectively shut off from the action—it can only guess, using *feedforward* information, how the instrumental troops are doing in their efforts to carry out system directives. Thus feedback is a critical element in efforts to motivate humans. Feedback can facilitate realistic goal setting, trigger adaptive emotional responses, and provide a solid basis for constructing and modifying personal agency beliefs. It can also suggest opportunities to pursue goals other than those that initiated the behavior episode. In contrast, when feedback is absent, it is easy for goals—even important goals—to lose salience and priority, and eventually end up "on the shelf." That is a key reason why focusing one's attention on "controllable short-term goals" is such a productive motivational strategy (Barden & Ford, 1990, 1991).

9. The Flexible Standards Principle. When people receive feedback indicating that they are not performing up to the standards that they have set for themselves or that the context has defined for them, they may become anxious, discouraged, self-doubting, or otherwise demotivated. This is especially likely to occur when these standards appear unattainable in the foreseeable future (e.g., "I'll never be able to break that record/make the Dean's list/wear a size 7/make as much money as my brother"). Motivation can be protected to some extent, however, by trying to facilitate a flexible approach to goal setting in which standards may vary, in an adaptive, realistic fashion, according to the circumstances. For example, a golfer who plays poorly at the beginning of a round, thus foreclosing any chance of earning a low overall score, might be encouraged to define a new standard for the goal of "scoring well" (e.g., scoring well on the remaining holes, or the back nine holes, or on at least some of the holes on the course) as a way of helping the person avoid continued frustration and self-loathing. Similarly, a student who blows a test and can no longer earn an "A" grade in a course might motivationally regroup around a different standard for defining good performance (e.g., raising a currently low grade to a significantly higher level) (Barden & Ford, 1991).

The Flexible Standards Principle also applies more generally to efforts to facilitate an active, improvement-oriented goal orientation. As noted in Chapter 4, people often derive their greatest pleasure from activities and experiences for which there are no concrete or "fixed" standards for goal attainment. In such episodes people can either escape the evaluative pressure of meeting a specific standard for goal attainment or define flexible, evolving standards that become more difficult as expertise increases (i.e., accelerating standards). This goal orientation facilitates learning and skill development without the pressure and worry that often accompanies high-stakes, "do-or-die" standards of evaluation, especially if the increments are small and manageable and are viewed as such. Indeed, over time, such an approach can lead to remarkable achievements and the creation of a truly sound motivational foundation.

It is important to emphasize that making a standard flexible does not mean making it vague or "wishy-washy"; rather, it means being willing and able to replace one clear, challenging standard (e.g., a weight loss goal, a sales or profit goal) with another clear, challenging standard (either harder or easier than the first) when the first one has been accomplished or evaluated as unrealistic. Thus the Flexible Standards Principle is a tool—a powerful tool—for ensuring that the flow of behavior episodes continues in such a way as to maximize productivity, satisfaction, and competence development, during good times and bad.

10. The Optimal Challenge Principle. A pervasive theme in contemporary theories of motivation that is closely related to the Flexible Standards Principle is the idea that motivation is maximized under conditions of "optimal challenge"—that is, conditions in which standards for goal attainment are difficult given the person's current level of expertise, but still attainable with vigorous or persistent effort (Bandura, 1986; Csikszentmihalyi, 1975, 1990; Deci & Ryan, 1985; Harter, 1978; White, 1959). Under such circumstances, successes are unusually satisfying and exciting in terms of emotional arousal and highly empowering in terms of personal agency beliefs. Indeed, PABs have their greatest impact in precisely these kinds of situations. Failures are also more likely to be seen as an intrinsic part of the process of pursuing a goal than in circumstances where trivially easy or unrealistically difficult standards apply. Of course, it may not always be easy to estimate or practical to arrange what would constitute an optimal challenge for a particular person in a particular context at a particular point in time. Nevertheless, the motivational power of optimally challenging circumstances is a well-documented phenomenon that makes the goal of creating such circumstances a worthy ideal to include in one's repertoire of guiding motivational principles.

11. The Principle of Direct Evidence. As noted in Chapter 5, effective functioning can easily be compromised by personal agency belief patterns in which at least one component is weak or negative. As a result, many formal and informal motivational interventions are designed to "boost confidence," "build trust," "reduce negative self-talk," and the like—that is, to facilitate positive capability or context beliefs (or both). In implementing such interventions, however, one must keep in mind, that experiences that focus directly on the vulnerable aspects of an individual's PABs will generally have much more impact than will experiences that are only vaguely or tangentially relevant to the problem at hand (Bandura, 1986). For example, efforts to promote employee morale may have little impact on negative context beliefs if such efforts do not address the concerns that originally led workers to view their environment as unresponsive (e.g., low pay, unrealistic demands, lack of resources, arbitrary rules and regulations, dangerous working conditions, lack of congruence with core personal goals). Similarly, because attempts to facilitate a person's general self-esteem are likely to have little effect on self-doubts about particular capabilities (e.g., ability to use a computer; ability to manage one's time, ability to maintain a relationship), they are only likely to be useful when the primary vulnerability to be addressed is itself a very general problem (e.g., pervasive feelings of unhappiness or worthlessness).

The Principle of Direct Evidence also has implications for the kinds of behavior episode experiences one might try to design to facilitate positive PAB patterns. For example, if all that is needed is to *activate* existing BES with Robust, Modest, or Tenacious PABs already in place, then thinking episodes (e.g., reminding, encouraging, mental rehearsal) may be sufficient—further evidence of one's capabilities or the environment's responsiveness may not be needed. If, however, one is trying to facilitate the *creation* of new BES or the modification of existing BES that have become permeated with self-doubt and discouragement, it may be necessary to begin with observational episodes (e.g., episodes in which similar others are observed to succeed) that demonstrate that there is reason to hope for success (Schunk, 1984, 1991a; Snyder et al., 1991). Such episodes may then lead to thinking episodes in which one imagines the possibility of being able to act like the efficacious model. Once sufficient hope has been generated or restored through observational and/or thinking episodes, one can proceed to have the person engage in instrumental episodes that provide evidence of progress and accomplishment caused, at least in part, through that person's own efforts. Because such evidence is unusually direct and compelling, this is generally the most powerful technique for facilitating positive personal agency beliefs (Bandura, 1986; Schunk, 1984, 1991a). Only the most stubbornly persistent BES can resist direct and repeated evidence demonstrating the power of one's capabilities and the congeniality of one's environment.

12. The Reality Principle. The preceding principle leads directly to a warning about the limitations of motivational interventions and a powerful way of thinking about the interactions among the four major ingredients for effective functioning (i.e., motivation, skill, biological readiness, and a responsive environment). To some extent personal agency beliefs can help compensate for weaknesses in the nonmotivational parts of the system by facilitating efforts to increase skills, improve one's health, or create or seek out responsive aspects of one's environment. In the long run, however, strong capability beliefs are difficult to maintain in the absence of *actual skills* and concrete evidence of those skills. This is particularly true for individuals with a BES repertoire infused with thoughts and feelings of hopelessness, self-doubt, or fraudulence (Kolligian, 1990). Similarly, to maintain positive context beliefs people ultimately need a *truly responsive environment*, especially when they are prone to thoughts and feelings of hostility, discouragement, or resignation. In other words, sometimes the best motivational intervention may be simply to make a straightforward attempt to promote learning, skill development, or optimal health (e.g. through better instruction or training, more study or practice, or life-style changes) or to enhance the quality of the conditions in which people live and work (e.g., through social, organizational, or economic reform).

Interestingly, the Reality Principle appears to be somewhat more flexible for young children than for adolescents and adults. Up until about third grade, and perhaps to some extent continuing into pre-adolescence, children appear to have difficulty integrating feed-back—especially comparative feedback—about personal limitations and environmental unresponsiveness into their personal agency be-liefs (Phillips & Zimmerman, 1990; Ruble, 1983; Stipek, 1984; Stipek & MacIver, 1989). Consequently, children are more likely than adults to display optimistic and resilient motivational patterns and are less likely to manifest the affective consequences of persistently negative personal agency beliefs (e.g., chronic anxiety, helplessness, and de-pression). This phenomenon may be attributable in part to a strong tendency among young children to engage in "wishful thinking" (e.g., believing that desired outcomes will magically become actual outcomes) (Stipek & Hoffman, 1980) and to associate effort with ability (Nicholls, 1978), but it may also simply reflect more general cognitive-developmental limitations (Case, 1985). Some have even speculated that this optimistic bias may have an evolutionary basis— that is, it is clearly adaptive for young members of a species to be somewhat insensitive to information that might demotivate them (Bjorklund & Green, 1992). This is not to say, of course, that children are invulnerable to failure and mistreatment; even in infancy one can discern striking individual differences in patterns of personal agency beliefs (Ford & Thompson, 1985; Sroufe, 1983). The point is simply this: luckily, it generally takes more direct and more persistent evidence of deficits in ability and environmental responsiveness to demotivate young children than to demotivate their wiser but sadder elders.

Consistent with this last point, there is clear evidence that motiva-tion and mental health are better served by "flexible optimism" (i.e., optimism that is grounded in but not overly constrained by current reality) than by "realistic pessimism" (i.e., pessimism that is an-chored in and inhibited by reality—not to be confused with strategic pessimism that is simply designed to protect one's self from the possibility of disappointment) (Seligman, 1991). This suggests that many adults might be able to enjoy a happier and more productive life if they were able to think more like children—that is, if they could learn to: (a) disattend to failure feedback unless it is persistent and pervasive, (b) disregard comparisons with others as much as possi-ble when evaluating one's competence, (c) place more value on effort than on ability as a criterion for self-worth, and (d) let negative events fade away quickly rather than amplifying their meaning and significance through cognitive rehearsal and rumination. There are some circumstances in which it is clearly unreasonable to expect either adults or children to maintain a robust motivational pattern, but adolescents and adults are particularly likely to contribute to the demotivating effects of these circumstances—or even demotivate themselves—by the way they attend to and think about the problems and opportunities in their lives.

13. The Principle of Emotional Activation. Strong motivational patterns almost always have strong emotions embedded within them. Thus one way to approach the problem of trying to motivate someone is to try to activate those emotional patterns—both positive and negative—that are most directly linked to effective functioning for the purpose at hand. This requires sound knowledge of the different kinds of emotional patterns humans are capable of experiencing and the specific functions each of those emotions serve (see Chapter 5). For example, if a person is passively accepting injurious or unfair treatment, it may be productive to try to instigate a safe and appropriate degree of resentment, anger, or contempt in the victim. Conversely, it may be useful to try to facilitate a healthy degree of embarrassment, shame, or guilt in someone who tends to view victimizing behavior as normal or justifiable. Thus, rather than viewing emotions as obstacles or distractions, they should be seen as powerful motivational "tools"—tools designed by our evolutionary history and shaped by our cultural and developmental history—that can help facilitate learning, task engagement, prosocial behavior, corrective action, self-protective behavior, and other highly valued outcomes. The trick is to facilitate use of precisely the right "tool" (or combination of tools) for the task at hand at a magnitude that is neither too weak nor too strong for the job to be accomplished.

Of course, this is not always an easy "trick" to pull off. The difficulty of activating a particular emotion pattern, and doing so to the proper degree, may vary considerably depending on a person's general temperament and specific history of emotional learning (Lerner, 1982, 1984; Thompson, 1991). For example, it may be much easier to elicit fear of victimization in people who characteristically are inhibited by dangerous or unfamiliar circumstances and in people who have witnessed or experienced a relevant victimizing event. One should therefore avoid "emotional overkill" by starting with a relatively gentle or subtle method of activating an emotion, and then "turning up the heat" only to the extent that it seems necessary to produce meaningful activation of the desired emotion pattern.

In applying the Principle of Emotional Activation it is also important to understand that it may not be easy to "deactivate" an emotion once it has been activated, at least for a while, even if the circumstances that activated the emotion change. In other words, emotions are difficult to "turn on" or "turn off" at will. For example, people will generally remain frightened for some time after averting a dangerous situation. Similarly, they may remain angry about some obstacle to goal attainment even after the obstacle has been removed, especially if they give the "emotional flywheel" another push by engaging in thinking episodes that recreate the emotionally arousing event (D. Ford, 1987). On the other hand, it is also important to understand that, in the absence of such reenactments, emotions will tend to wane in magnitude over time even when the circumstances that activated them do *not* change. That is one reason why patience is such a virtue in emotionally volatile situations—well-intentioned actions may be just as likely to add "fuel" to the emotional "fire" as to improve the situation. Conversely, this phenomenon also helps explain why it is so useful to have celebrations, retrospectives, award ceremonies, story telling, and other formal and informal events that are designed to repeat, recount, or remind group members of their past accomplishments, thus generating renewed satisfaction, pride, and enthusiasm for future episodes in that context.

14. The "Do It" Principle. Many motivational problems involve unrealistically negative or conflictual messages from one or more of the evaluators in motivational headquarters, thus resulting in the inhibition of potentially productive behavior. A person might be avoiding romantic relationships due to a recent bad experience. A perfectionistic writer might be having difficulty putting anything down on paper. A self-doubting actor might be unnecessarily ruling out more challenging roles. When such problems arise, and it is clear that the person would like to and is capable of functioning effectively in the problematic context, an approach that can sometimes work wonders is to do whatever it takes to get the person to do *something*— make a date, write down whatever comes to mind, go to an audition for a big role—anything that is likely to facilitate activation of their competent BES. This provides a concrete way of displacing the problematic motivational pattern and an opportunity to initiate a feedback process that is likely to yield information contradicting the inhibiting messages in the original motivational pattern (i.e., accomplishment and satisfaction are likely to follow before too long). Repeated application of this principle can also help build unusually strong BES (i.e., "habits") that are likely to emerge automatically even under conditions of stress, anxiety, and emotional distraction. For example, with such BES students, athletes, musicians, and actors in performance situations can proceed to just "do it," confidently knowing that if they simply execute the routines they have rehearsed and learned so well, they will perform effectively.

The "Do It" Principle may also apply to some cases in which the person is not fully capable of effective functioning; however, such cases are risky in that the person is more likely to receive feedback that confirms the negative thoughts and feelings that were inhibiting his or her behavior. Thus when applying this principle to circumstances with unpredictable outcomes, one should take steps to try to ensure that the person is as fully prepared as possible to deal with those circumstances (i.e., facilitate the *skill* component of effective functioning). In addition, one should try to maximize the likelihood that the person will be entering a safe and supportive environment that is likely to yield motivating rather than demotivating feedback (i.e., facilitate the *responsive environment* component of effective functioning). Under such circumstances the person is likely to maintain motivation and engagement while he or she develops a more effective BES that can be readily transferred to future relevant episodes.

15. The Principle of Incremental Versus Transformational Change. The "Do It" Principle is primarily relevant to situations in which one is trying to facilitate stability maintenance (thus reestablishing an effective steady state pattern) or a modest degree of incremental change. In some circumstances, however, the problem to be addressed requires somewhat more drastic action. For example, a person might be operating on the basis of a long, demotivating history of poverty, abuse, or unresponsive caregiving, or be suffering from the entrenched effects of a traumatizing event in which he or she was victimized, rejected, or unable to accomplish a cherished goal. Major changes in motivational patterns may also be needed in cases where people have developed strong motivational habits associated with socially disapproved, personally dangerous, or highly unproductive behavior patterns.

To achieve the kinds of qualitative changes just described, one can either construct a series of incremental change experiences designed to produce significant additive effects, or initiate a disorganization-reorganization process designed to produce transformational change.

For example, one might try to facilitate teenagers' motivation to avoid unsafe sexual encounters by offering a steady diet of warnings and informative facts, or by trying to shock them with stories, pictures, or real people that portray the horrible physical and social consequences of contracting a sexually transmitted disease. Similarly, one might try to resolve family pathology by slowly but surely teaching family members conflict-resolution skills, or by intentionally *escalating* conflict until it reaches the point where some transformation in relationship patterns is likely (e.g., Brendler, Silver, Haber, & Sargent, 1992).

Because evolutionary change is generally safer and more reliable than revolutionary change, a good rule of thumb in such cases is: increment if you can, transform if you must (D. Ford, 1987). In other words, dramatic, disorganizing motivational maneuvers should be reserved for truly extreme cases, and even then only as a last resort. Moreover, such maneuvers should only be attempted in conjunction with transition protection processes (e.g., strong social support mechanisms; expert professional guidance; time to "work through" the change process), and with a clear understanding of the urgency of maintaining a high stability-instability ratio.

16. The Equifinality Principle. In human affairs, it is rarely the case that there will be only one possible or "correct" pathway to a goal. People and contexts are simply too variable and multifaceted for things to be that simple. Therefore, instead of looking for the one "best" or "right" way of motivating a particular person in a particular context, one should think in terms of the Equifinality Principle: there may be a variety of pathways that will ultimately lead to the desired outcome. This implies that, rather than simply relying on one or two motivational procedures that may or may not "work" in a particular case, one should adopt a much more creative and determined problem-solving approach guided by the belief that, if at first you don't succeed, keep trying! Otherwise, the personal agency beliefs of the motivational interventionist may also be vulnerable to thoughts and feelings of discouragement, self-doubt, and hopelessness.

17. The Principle of Human Respect. Of all the MST principles for motivating humans, perhaps the most important is this: *always* treat people with respect. People are not simply bodies in a classroom or boxes in an organizational chart or information-processing machines—they are thinking, feeling, self-directed human beings with a very personal repertoire of goals, emotions, and self-referent beliefs that *must* be treated with respect and care if efforts to facilitate desired motivational patterns and the development of human competence are to succeed. This is true not only in parenting and in counseling, where more intimate exchanges are likely to occur, but also in education and business—perhaps *especially* in education and business because that is where people are most likely to be treated as interchangeable parts in an organizational machine. For example, consider the contrast between: (a) an impersonal goal-setting intervention in which it is assumed that students or workers will automatically commit themselves to the target goals of concern to the teacher or manager assigning the goals, and (b) a goal-setting intervention in which a flexible framework of goal options is suggested that has been designed collaboratively with students' or workers', or with their current concerns and core goals in mind. This latter way of proceeding is not only much more likely to facilitate goal alignment and enduring goal commitment, it is also less likely to produce unanticipated negative consequences such as alienation or resentment. Thus two motivational procedures that appear very similar on the surface may produce very different effects—in this case, half-hearted, temporary effects versus an enduring sense of ownership, trust, and loyalty—depending on whether they incorporate the Principle of Human Respect.

The 17 MST principles for motivating humans are summarized in Table 7.1.

Application of MST to the Problem of Promoting Social Responsibility and Caring Behavior in Youth

Parents often say that the thing they want most for their children is for them to be happy and successful. The concern that seems to dominate parents' actions on an everyday basis, however, is whether or not their children are behaving in a responsible and caring manner—that is, are their children following the rules, doing what they "ought" to be doing, and being "nice" to other people. This impression is supported by a recent study (Krumboltz, Ford, Nichols, & Wentzel, 1987) in which parents of high-school students were asked to evaluate a diversity of goals in terms of "How important is it that people achieve this outcome by age 18?" Goal statements were constructed to represent five academic domains (verbal, math, science, social studies, and fine arts) and five nonacademic domains (health, interpersonal competence, moral development, career development, and attitudes

TABLE 7.1   The 17 Motivational Systems Theory Principles for Motivating
Humans

The MST Principles	Core Idea
The Principle of Unitary Functioning	One *always* deals with a whole person-in-context
The Motivational Triumvirate Principle	Goals, emotions, and PABs must all be influenced to facilitate motivation
The Responsive Environment Principle	*Relationships* are as important as techniques
The Principle of Goal Activation	Little else matters if there is no relevant goal in place
The Principle of Goal Salience	Goals must be clear and compelling to transform concerns into intentions
The Multiple Goals Principle	Multiple goals can strengthen motivation substantially
The Principle of Goal Alignment	Multiple goals must be aligned rather than in conflict to enhance motivation
The Feedback Principle	Goals lose their potency in the absence of clear and informative feedback
The Flexible Standards Principle	Flexible, standards protect against demotivation and facilitate self-improvement
The Optimal Challenge Principle	Challenging but attainable standards enhance motivation
The Principle of Direct Evidence	Clear, specific evidence is needed to influence capability and context beliefs
The Reality Principle	PABs ultimately require real skills and a truly responsive environment
The Principle of Emotional Activation	Strong emotions indicate and facilitate strong motivational patterns
The "Do It" Principle	If a person is capable, just try to get them started
The Principle of Incremental Versus Transformational Change	Incremental change is easier and safer; transform and only with care and as a last resort
The Equifinality Principle	There are many ways to motivate humans— if progress is slow, keep trying!
The Principle of Human Respect	People *must* be treated with respect to produce enduring motivational effects

toward self and learning). The results indicated that the top four
goals (from a pool of 120 goal statements) were all concerned with
aspects of socially responsible and mature behavior:

1. Know right from wrong and act accordingly.
2. Be honest in dealing with other people.
3. Understand and avoid the harmful effects of prescription and illegal
   drugs.

4. Avoid stealing or damaging other people's property.

A variety of other goals were also rated highly (including goals focused on various aspects of happiness and success), but none higher than those listed above.

Motivational Patterns and Principles Associated With Social Responsibility and Caring Behavior in Youth

In a recent series of studies, M. Ford and several colleagues and collaborators (Estrada, 1987; M. Ford, 1987b; Ford, Wentzel, Siesfeld, Wood, & Feldman, 1986; Ford, Wentzel, Wood, Stevens, & Siesfeld, 1989; Ford, Chase, Love, Pollina, & Ito, 1992; Wood, 1990) have demonstrated the power and utility of a Motivational Systems Theory approach to understanding practical human problems. Using a variety of questionnaire, journal, and interview techniques, these researchers have confirmed and clarified several recurring findings in the literature on prosocial motivation and contributed new information regarding the patterns of goals, emotions, and personal agency beliefs that appear to be most closely associated with social responsibility and caring behavior in youth. Their findings and the practical implications of these findings in terms of MST principles can be summarized as follows:

1. Compared to their less prosocial peers, highly prosocial adolescents are more likely to be interested in and concerned about a diversity of personal goals. This supports the MST hypothesis that strong motivational patterns will generally be anchored by multiple goals and suggests that the Multiple Goals Principle should be a key part of any effort to facilitate social responsibility and caring behavior. Indeed, Ford et al. (1992) found that one of the most distinctive features of highly uncaring adolescents was the large number of goals they regarded as unimportant. Although endorsement of a broad range of goals was no guarantee of prosocial competence, highly caring students virtually never manifested the narrowness that tended to characterize the goal hierarchies of many of those scoring low in caring competence.

2. Socially responsible adolescents and highly caring youth place particularly high priority on the three integrative goals of resource provision, social responsibility, and equity. In other words, they care deeply about the welfare of others and "doing right" by other people. In contrast, socially irresponsible adolescents and highly uncaring youth manifest a remarkably self-serving motivational

pattern in which self-enhancing goals such as material gain, self-determination, and resource acquisition are not balanced by integrative concerns or other goals that may facilitate social responsibility and caring behavior (see next three paragraphs). This suggests that interventions designed to enhance prosocial behavior that do not attend carefully to the Principles of Goal Activation and Goal Alignment are unlikely to be effective.

3. Responsible, caring teenagers consistently affirm the importance of goals related to learning, task completion, and task mastery. This appears to be part of a general pattern involving high standards for personal conduct and a strong desire to meet those self-evaluative standards. Conversely, people with weak internal standards are particularly prone to expedient, self-serving behavior (Bandura, 1991b). The Principle of Goal Salience may be an appropriate antidote to this pattern (i.e., standards and expectations for social conduct should be crystal clear and consistently enforced).

4. Young people who behave in a consistently prosocial manner appear to be unusually interested in a diversity of goals associated with inherently meaningful aspects of human experience. For example, Ford et al. (1992) found that, compared to their less caring peers, highly caring adolescents were more interested in: (a) creative experiences; (b) experiences reflecting feelings of unity or spiritual connectedness with people, nature, or a greater power; and (c) experiences that contribute to a sense of feeling unique, special, or different from others. Thus caring for others may be, in many cases, a part of a larger pattern of seeking to engage life in ways that are particularly or even profoundly rich in meaning. Efforts to link such goals to prosocial actions might therefore be a productive strategy (the Principle of Goal Activation).

5. Social responsibility and caring behavior are also associated with a variety of goals reflecting self-acceptance and mental, emotional, and physical well-being. Thus investment in self-enhancing goals does not seem to be a major factor inhibiting prosocial behavior as long as integrative goals are also in place. Indeed, it appears that one of the primary rewards of behaving in a responsible or helpful manner is increased self-comfort and a more positive self-image (Wood, 1990)—a finding that again implicates the Principles of Goal Activation and Goal Alignment.

6. Socially responsible and caring behavior patterns are associated with several emotion patterns: (a) strong feelings of guilt about breaking rules and commitments, (b) compelling feelings of empathic concern for distressed or victimized people, (c) a sense of pride or pleasure in helping others, and (d) a fear of negative social consequences. These emotions appear to have an additive effect. For example, Ford et al. (1989) found that, whereas the anticipated activation of one of these emotions was generally enough to lead students to say they would "probably" choose a responsible course of action over a competing irresponsible action, the modal response when three or more of these emotions were simultaneously activated was to "definitely" choose to behave in a responsible manner. Thus it would appear that, at least in this domain, interventions based on the Principle of Emotional Activation would be very likely to yield powerful results.

7. Consistent with their hierarchy of personal goals, consistently irresponsible and uncaring youth manifest a combination of strong self-interest emotions (e.g., happiness, resentment, or disappointment under conditions of personal gain or loss) and remarkably weak emotions reflecting concern for others (especially guilt). This finding further underlines the importance of the Principle of Emotional Activation.

8. Though clearly not as dominant as personal goals and emotional arousal processes, capability beliefs also play an important role in prosocial motivational patterns. Interestingly, prosocial adolescents not only feel confident in their ability to behave in a responsible and caring manner, they also doubt their ability to justify irresponsible or uncaring behavior to others or themselves. Indeed, the ability to dismiss, explain away, or make excuses for social transgressions is a hallmark of irresponsible behavior (Bandura, 1991b). This suggests the need for careful monitoring and clear feedback regarding desired and undesired behavior patterns (the Feedback Principle).

9. Although prosocial behavior patterns are not consistently linked with positive context beliefs, there is evidence suggesting that highly negative context beliefs may promote an antagonistic motivational pattern that is antithetical to prosocial behavior (Dodge, 1980; Dodge & Frame, 1982; Dodge & Somberg, 1987). This finding implicates not only the Responsive Environment Principle, but also the Principle of Direct Evidence (i.e., because only direct,

compelling evidence of environmental responsiveness is likely to influence strong feelings of mistrust and hostility).

10. On average, female adolescents are more likely than their male counterparts to behave in a caring and responsible manner, apparently because they are more likely to prioritize goals reflecting concern for others (Ford et al. 1986; Ford et al., 1992) and more likely to experience strong emotions supporting prosocial behavior (especially guilt and empathic concern) (Ford et al., 1989; Ford et al., 1992). The Equifinality Principle and the Principle of Incremental versus Transformational Change may therefore be particularly applicable to prosocial interventions with adolescent males.

Application of MST to the Problem of Increasing Motivation for Learning and School Achievement

A great deal of concern has been expressed recently regarding the large number of students who either drop out of school prematurely (approximately one fourth of all public school students in the United States and nearly half of all low-SES minority students) or who complete their schooling without developing the skills expected of a high school graduate and necessary for success in modern societies (Wlodkowski & Jaynes, 1990). A less dramatic but even more pervasive problem is the tendency of many academically capable students to invest themselves in the learning process in a minimal or superficial way. Indeed, this motivational pattern seems to become increasingly common as students progress through the educational system (Harter, 1981a). Teachers who have to deal with disinterested students on a daily basis often become discouraged and leave the profession or passively accept the low standards that many students adopt for their schoolwork.

Why is it that so many students learn to dislike school and academic learning? Cross (1990) framed the question in a more positive way:

> How can we make school matter to students? How can we connect school learning to their lives? How can we change the image of schooling from a rite of passage to what it really is: an opportunity to develop our most valuable resource, young people's *minds*? (p. 22)

If motivation is indeed the foundation on which learning and skill development must be built, these are truly fundamental questions that education scholars, professionals, and policymakers need to address with much more vigor, persistence, and determination than is evident in most current reform efforts.

Motivational Patterns and Principles Associated With Learning and School Achievement

In Goodlad's (1983) widely read survey, "A Place Called School," high school teachers ranked "lack of student interest" as the most serious obstacle to their educational efforts. From the students' perspective, however, this is simply a reflection of the fact that, for many students, school does not afford the attainment of relevant personal goals (the Principle of Goal Activation). Even worse, some schools tend to become associated with strong avoidance goals (e.g., avoiding negative social and self-evaluations) (Covington, 1984a, 1984b; Kagan, 1990). As a result, many students manifest a "minimum effort" motivation pattern characterized by a "coping" (i.e., reactive, avoidant, stability-maintaining) goal orientation, vulnerable personal agency beliefs, and emotions of boredom and anxiety.

It is important to note that the motivation pattern just described is more likely to characterize average and low-achieving students than their higher-achieving peers. For example, in Wentzel's research on the goals associated with academic competence at school (Wentzel, 1989), high GPA students reported that they consistently tried to accomplish all of the goals most closely associated with learning and academic success, namely, mastery, management, understanding, and social responsibility (the Multiple Goals Principle). With the exception of social responsibility, however, these goals were only occasionally salient for medium GPA students, who were generally more concerned with belongingness and entertainment goals—goals that might be expected to conflict with academic success in the classroom (the Principle of Goal Alignment). Low GPA students also placed high priority on these latter two goals, but because of their remarkably low concern with management and social responsibility goals, lacked the "motivational insurance" needed to maintain a respectable GPA (the Multiple Goals Principle).

This is not to say, of course, that high-achieving students are free from motivational problems. A coping, "play it safe" goal orientation is also common among these students. Moreover, because many such students adopt (or are expected to meet) unrealistically high performance standards (the Principle of Flexible Standards), they too are likely to suffer from anxiety and fragile or vulnerable personal agency beliefs from time to time.

Nevertheless, it appears that the demotivating effects of school environments are especially problematic for students who, for one reason or another, do not "fit" into the academic culture of the school (the Principle of Goal Alignment). What is the nature of that culture? In many (perhaps most) junior and senior high schools, the academic culture is individualistic, highly controlling, intensely evaluative, and often overtly competitive (Paris, Lawton, Turner, & Roth, 1991):

> As children progress through school, public evaluations of ability and normative comparisons become more common. Emphasis on letter grades and tests can encourage a focus on ability perceptions, competition, social comparison, and negative self-evaluations. . . . Use of grades and standardized test scores to provide recognition for students (e.g., honor roll, gifted classes) leads students to focus on the "currency value" of achievement rather than on its more intrinsic value. In addition, such narrow definitions of academic success further separate the "haves" from the "have nots." (p. 17)

Ironically, schools become more likely to manifest these qualities just as students are becoming more skilled at making social comparisons and ability evaluations, more capable of reflecting on and ruminating about their inadequacies and failures, and more interested in opportunities for self-determination and self-regulation. This developmentally alarming trend has helped generate interest in alternative forms of school organization, especially in early adolescence (Eccles & Midgley, 1989):

> Does it make sense to put these developing children in a classroom environment . . . that promotes ability evaluations and social comparison, that decreases opportunities for student self-management and choice, and that is more formal and impersonal? We suggest that there is a developmental mismatch resulting from changes in the classroom environment that are at odds with physiological, psychological, and cognitive changes in the young adolescent. (p. 174)

This all-too-common way of organizing school environments inevitably leads to demotivating experiences for all but the most successful students. For example, such contexts tend to produce negative social comparisons with "smarter" peers, a lack of peer support for achievement, and an emphasis on avoiding failure or avoiding "hassles" rather than on learning new content or mastering new skills. This pattern is particularly likely to characterize "at-risk" students. As Kagan (1990) explains:

> Factors within classrooms and schools transform students at risk into a discrete subculture that is incompatible with academic success. The result is a feeling of estrangement and failure . . . at-risk students have low educational aspirations, low self-esteem, an external locus of control, and negative attitudes toward school along with a history of academic failure, truancy, and misconduct, *with no indication that they lack requisite aptitudes* [italics added]. (pp. 105-106)

Although this alienated motivational pattern may manifest consistency within the academic context, and therefore appear to school observers to be a stable "trait" associated with "defective" (i.e., lazy, irresponsible, immature) students, it is more accurately described as a context-specific motivational pattern that is activated and maintained by the belief that school is a persistently unresponsive, uncaring environment that is incongruent with, or even hostile toward, one's interests, concerns, and capabilities (Kagan, 1990; Wehlage & Rutter, 1986). This is evidenced by the fact that when students move to a more responsive environment, motivational patterns tend to change, sometimes dramatically (Edmonds, 1986; Kagan, 1990; Sexton, 1985).

Perhaps the most disturbing aspect of academic environments that emphasize individualistic and competitive goal structures is that they are generally not like other important life contexts, even those that are performance-oriented. In other words, contrary to common wisdom, such environments do *not* provide relevant training for other domains of life—they only serve to separate the "winners" from the "losers" in an academic "game" that many students would prefer not to play. Bishop (1989) eloquently summarizes this disparity between academic and "real" life:

> Young people are not lazy. In their jobs after school and on the football field, they work very hard. In these environments they are part of a team where individual efforts are visible and appreciated by teammates. Competition and rivalry are not absent, but they are offset by shared goals, shared successes and external measures of achievement. . . . On the sports field, there is no greater sin than giving up, even when the score is hopelessly one-sided. On the job, tasks not done by one worker will generally have to be completed by another. In too many high schools, when it comes to academics, a student's success is purely personal. (p. 9)

Perhaps, then, the problem is not as intractable as one might think. By reorganizing tasks and classrooms so that they routinely feature group goals, teamwork, and individual accountability to the group (Slavin, 1981, 1989) rather than competition and individualism, it may be possible, even with at-risk students, to: (a) minimize the demotivating effects of academic life on students' personal agency beliefs, (b) activate academic goals and align these goals with powerful peer responsibility and approval goals, and (c) facilitate the development of motivational patterns that are infused with energy and enthusiasm (Principles of Goal Activation, Goal Alignment, and Emotional Activation). The motivational power derived from an emphasis on shared goals, cooperative involvement, and personal responsibility can be even further amplified by generalizing this collaborative strategy to interactions between parents and teachers (e.g., through family participation initiatives) and interactions between teachers and administrators (e.g., through an understanding that principals should facilitate the work of empowered teachers rather than constrain their autonomy and creativity) (cf. Levin, 1987, 1991). This prescription is consistent with an emerging consensus in the scholarly and professional literature on the characteristics of effective schools, as summarized in a recent PBS documentary anchored by Roger Mudd (Devaney, 1990):

> What makes these schools work? . . . "Simple, pervasive commitment that *all* children can learn." Collegiality among teachers. A new "empowering" role for the principal, treating teachers as professionals and sharing decisions with them. Children learning in cooperative rather than competitive ways in schools with a strong community spirit. Parents viewed as partners with the school in their children's learning. (p. 1)

Such reorganization may be easier to describe than to implement, however. The tendency of educators to rely on competition and other forms of social comparison to motivate students has become so habitual that even the most well-intentioned efforts tend to incorporate these core features of the traditional academic culture. For example, each year a major corporation sponsors an essay-writing contest designed to motivate junior and senior high school students by having them describe inspirational people in their lives. Because of the individualistic way in which the contest is organized, however, only a very few of the most academically able students (i.e., those who least need motivational facilitation) can earn recognition. It would be easy to reorganize the contest so that *classrooms* or *schools* rather than individuals were competing against each other; such a system would result in many students being honored, including less able students whose efforts were just as crucial to group success as those of the best essay writers. This more effective motivational strategy never occurred to the contest organizers, who persist in running the contest in a traditional individualistic/competitive format.

The entrenched nature of the academic culture makes it all the more critical that educational leaders and policymakers come to appreciate the motivationally debilitating effects of competition and performance-oriented social evaluation. As C. Ames (1987) emphasizes in her analysis of the practical implications of motivational research in education:

> The most basic recommendation must be that the classroom should not focus students on comparing themselves with others. This social comparison involves blatant methods such as grading on a curve or posting students' achievements to less obvious practices such as not informing students of evaluation criteria in advance. . . . In other words, instructional practices which actually impose social comparison standards as well as those which encourage or make social comparison salient should not be used. (p. 143)

The alternative to social comparison is clear and strongly advocated by motivational researchers in education: students should be compared with *themselves* over time (C. Ames, 1987; Covington, 1991; Paris et al., 1991). Thus, rather than emphasizing grades and test scores, teachers should concentrate on helping students make progress toward specific, optimally challenging academic goals that will naturally increase in difficulty as learning proceeds (Principle of Goal Salience, Optimal Challenge Principle, Flexible Standards Principle).

In contrast to the more collaborative and less evaluative orientation outlined in the preceding paragraphs, educational policymakers attempting to cope with the problem of enhancing student motivation often suggest solutions that are likely to exacerbate rather than remove the demotivating features of the traditional academic culture (e.g., curriculum mandates, high-stakes testing of students, rigid performance evaluations of teachers, stronger controls on student and teacher behavior) (Paris et al., 1991; Ryan et al., 1985; Ryan & Stiller, 1991). Even many education scholars endorse these kinds of tactics, apparently not appreciating the deep and pervasive damage that controlling, bureaucratic, hierarchical organizational arrangements can inflict on the emotions and personal agency beliefs of students and teachers (Deci et al., 1991; Ryan et al., 1985). The warning at the beginning of this chapter about the potential trade-off between short-term achievement and long-term competence development is particularly relevant to such solutions.

> While strong controls may bring immediate behavioral results, every indication is that they will impair learning and be deleterious to autonomy, enduring motivation, and self-esteem. These unfortunate consequences have been shown to result even from the more positive events like rewards, affirming feedback, and ego involvement. Imagine the psychological costs of such control systems for the children who fare more poorly—those at the end of the normal curves, who get the bad grades and continuous negative feedback. (Ryan et al., 1985, p. 27)

Transforming competitive, controlling, "coping" school environments into collaborative, caring, "thriving" school environments that strive for "motivational equity" (Covington, 1991) is a necessary step in addressing the problem of "lack of student interest." Additional strategies must be applied at the level of specific tasks and activities, however, if motivational enhancements are to be realized and maintained in the classroom. Specifically, everyday tasks and activities must be selected and organized in such a way as to make them as engaging and interesting as possible (Principles of Goal and Emotional Activation). There are many different ways to accomplish this objective (Equifinality Principle). For example, one can: (a) clearly state learning objectives (Principle of Goal Salience) and their relevance to students' lives, (b) emphasize learning rather than performance goals, (c) try to make abstract content more concrete or familiar, (d) link tasks and activities to students' personal interests and experiences, (e) offer students choices and opportunities for autonomy and creativity, (f) introduce novelty and variety into classroom daily routines, (g) mix frequent instrumental and observational episodes in with the usual menu of thinking (e.g., reading and listening) episodes, and (h) provide students with frequent opportunities to interact with their classmates (Brophy, 1987; Malone & Lepper, 1987).

More generally, whether through teacher training programs or less formal means, teachers must become much more aware of the basic motivational requirements underlying effective teaching (e.g., as outlined in the 17 principles described in this chapter) and much more practiced at applying these principles on a daily basis (Brophy, 1987). Motivation for learning must be regarded as a vital and ubiquitous goal in teaching, both as a prerequisite for the achievement of specific curricular objectives and as a desired long-term outcome of schooling (Krumboltz et al., 1987).

Application of MST to the Problem of Understanding and Facilitating the Links Between Job Satisfaction and Work Productivity

The two most common outcome variables in the literature on work motivation are job satisfaction and job productivity (Campbell & Pritchard, 1976; Iaffaldano & Muchinsky, 1985; Porter & Lawler, 1968; Schwab & Cummings, 1970; Steers & Porter, 1979; Vroom, 1964). In fact these two variables are often studied together. In such studies it is generally assumed that a satisfied worker should be a productive worker; however, in most research examining the association between job satisfaction and job performance, the relationship is weak or nonexistent. As Iaffaldano and Muchinsky (1985) concluded in their recent review of this literature:

> The ideals of high job satisfaction and high productivity are valued in our society, and attempts to design work so as to jointly achieve these goals are continuous. Indeed, both management and union representatives generally endorse the notion that greater productivity would result if workers were more satisfied . . . thus, the finding that these variables are not highly correlated questions the assumptions implicit in organizational programs and policies, our research endeavors, and even in the expectations of those who review the satisfaction-performance literature. . . . It appears that the satisfaction-performance relation qualifies as a long-standing fad among organizational researchers, and researchers feel compelled to reinvestigate the topic despite a profusion of empirical non-support. (pp. 268-269)

The characterization of this line of research as a "fad" is unfortunate. From the perspective of MST, job satisfaction reflects the successful attainment of the worker's personal goals, whereas job productivity reflects the successful attainment of the organization's goals. Thus, rather than simply dismissing this literature as a misguided effort to connect "naturally" independent outcomes, it should be interpreted as a warning that there may be something seriously wrong with the way that many work environments are organized. Specifically, these findings suggest a pervasive lack of alignment between the personal goals of employees and their employers (the Principle of Goal Alignment). If this interpretation is accurate, facilitating the degree of synergy between the goals of workers and organizations may be the key to a more motivated and more productive work force (Baird, 1976; Bhagat, 1982; Lawler & Porter, 1967).

It is important to understand that goal alignment does not necessarily imply similarity in goal content. Although workers must have a clear understanding of what the organization is trying to accomplish, and a clear understanding of what they are expected to accomplish in their own jobs (the Principle of Goal Salience), all that is truly required is that the job thus defined affords the attainment of the worker's core personal goals (Maehr & Braskamp, 1986; Nichols, 1990). To the extent that being productive on the job leads to the attainment of *multiple* core goals, the job should be highly satisfying indeed (the Multiple Goals Principle). Although it may be unreasonable to expect most jobs to provide this level of goal alignment on a continuous basis (i.e., very high correlations between job satisfaction and performance are probably not attainable), significant progress toward this ideal can be achieved through careful and consistent application of the Principle of Goal Alignment.

Motivational Patterns and Principles Associated With the Simultaneous Achievement of Job Satisfaction and Work Productivity

There are at least three different ways to facilitate goal alignment between workers and their employers:

1. effective communication of organizational goals to individual workers;
2. application of the Multiple Goals Principle to jobs and work environments, especially those that are incongruent with the core goals of a diverse work force; and
3. selection of personnel with motivational characteristics that are compatible with the opportunities and requirements of a particular job context.

Communication of Organizational Goals. It has become commonplace for scholars and professionals in business to cite the development of an organizational "vision" or "mission" as one of the prerequisites for organizational success (e.g., Labich, 1988; Maehr, 1987; Schein, 1985). Less well understood are the steps that organizational leaders need to take to facilitate goal awareness, understanding, and commitment among members of the organization (the Principle of Goal Salience). Failure to take these steps is surprisingly common and a tremendous obstacle to progress in aligning worker and organizational goals. For example, Farnham (1989) cites the results of a study indicating that less than a third of the employees surveyed believed that management was providing them with clear goals and direction. He also notes other data suggesting that many business leaders are unaware of the mediocre job they are doing in this regard. Given that workers are generally quite willing to commit themselves to the legitimate goals of an employer (Locke & Latham, 1990a, 1990b), this is a rather appalling discrepancy with enormous motivational consequences.

Perhaps the clearest statement outlining the specific steps that organizational leaders can take to facilitate goal activation with regard to the organization's goals is provided by Collins (1988) in an article titled "How to Pass Your Passion On." What is particularly striking about his analysis is the salience of energizing emotions in the process of motivating workers (as implied by the use of the word "passion" in the title of the article). It appears that when organizational goals are communicated to workers with excitement, enthusiasm, and sincerity, they are hard to resist (the Principle of Emotional Activation).

> A sense of purpose, shared by all and to which all are committed, is perhaps the single most important factor in the success of any organized effort. Coming up with such a mission is a vital function of leadership. But coming up with such a mission isn't enough. A leader must instill the mission as a shared sense of purpose throughout the organization or team. How do you go about that? There are four basic components: (1) Make an unwavering personal commitment to the mission. People have to see that you have conviction about what you are trying to get the team to do—that it is something you care a great deal about . . . (2) Focus. Great leaders . . . remain obsessively intent on the primary aim at all times and seldom allow complexities, problems or irrelevant opportunities to distract them from the central theme of their work . . . (3) Reinforce the mission by defining and measuring progress. Develop benchmarks for keeping track of how well the team is doing . . . (4) Communicate! Take advantage of every opportunity to convey the mission and emphasize its central and dominant role. (pp. 1-2PC)

Design of Jobs and Work Environments. When a job is organized in a way that tends to facilitate the attainment of a particular worker's core personal goals, motivation will flourish (Nichols, 1990). When the same job is organized in a way that tends to violate these goals, demotivation will occur. Thus, to the extent that jobs and work environments can be altered to avoid such violations and facilitate core goal attainment (the Principle of Goal Alignment), motivation can be enhanced without changing workers (Hackman & Oldham, 1976). Maehr (1987) provides an unusually clear explanation of this contextual perspective on work motivation:

Motivational "problems" are not, in the main, attributable to a *lack* in motivational potential. Rather, "motivational problems" are largely a matter of how people choose to invest their time and energy. . . . Thus, the inevitable question of concern is—why in this but not that case? What is there about a particular job or job context that does not serve to elicit work investment? There is not really anything "wrong" with the person—she is not lacking in drive, she is not lazy; she simply is not attracted to the task in this case. In such instances the manager may be well-advised to ask: What is there about the job or the job context that does not serve to elicit her investment? (p. 290)

The first step in conducting such an analysis is to consider whether workers believe that their work environment is *fair* (Adams, 1963, 1965) and *trustworthy* (Zand, 1972)—that is, whether they think that *any* core goal opportunities afforded by the context are real (the Responsive Environment Principle). For example, it may be difficult for workers to accept the sincerity of efforts to promote teamwork or improve efficiency if top managers and executives are being paid exorbitant salaries (the Reality Principle) (Farnham, 1989). Similarly, efforts to empower workers may have little impact if no one believes that management is truly committed to the principle of shared decision making (Conger, 1989). In contrast, when workers believe that management can be trusted to behave in a responsible and competent manner, motivation is generally high (Farnham, 1989). Fairness and trust thus provide the fundamental foundation for constructing a work environment that facilitates goal alignment between workers and employers (Zand, 1972).

The next step in considering how jobs and work environments might be reorganized to promote job satisfaction and performance is to try to identify the core goals of workers in particular job circumstances. As the diversity of the work force grows, this becomes an increasingly challenging task. Nevertheless, there are recurring themes in the literature that suggest that many cases could be accommodated by designing jobs and work environments so that they better afford the attainment of several key goals. For example, in Nichols' (1990) study testing the predictive utility of his *Assessment of Core Goals* (Nichols, 1991), the following goal statements (generated by 10 different subjects) were found to be the most predictive of specific episodes of job dissatisfaction (i.e., violations of these goals were highly demotivating):

I want to feel a sense of belonging; a bond or camaraderie.

I want to be genuinely cared about.

I want to feel that I'm great, or that my work is great.

I want to feel a sense of peacefulness that comes from losing touch with my self-critical thoughts and doubts.

I want to be seen by others as very capable.

I want to be admired and respected for my high level of skill and ability.

I don't want to feel helpless, stuck, or held down.

I don't want to feel controlled, pressured, or dumped on.

I want a feeling of shared love and caring.

I want to feel a sense of acceptance, caring, and camaraderie. (p. 115)

The emphasis in this list on goals such as belongingness, resource acquisition, mastery, self-determination, and positive self-evaluations is consistent not only with the findings of management consultants (e.g., Farnham, 1989; Smith, 1991), but also with a number of motivation theories that emphasize the central importance of these categories of goal content (e.g., self-determination theory, effectance motivation theories, self-worth theories, optimal experience theory—see Table 6.1 for relevant references).

The process of altering a particular job or work environment to better afford the attainment of these kinds of goals (or other core goals of particular relevance to a specific set of workers) is a very context-specific matter that is largely dependent on "local knowledge." Creativity and persistence are also great virtues in this regard (the Equifinality Principle). Based on the Responsive Environment Principle and the Principles of Goal Activation and Goal Alignment, however, some general ideas can be offered that are likely to have broad utility in addressing such problems. For example, one might concentrate on developing: (a) a pervasive atmosphere of acceptance, caring, and cooperation; (b) employee involvement programs (and policies that facilitate involvement, such as open-door policies, face-to-face communication between workers and top management, and regular surveys of employee attitudes); (c) employee empowerment programs (e.g., reducing organizational layers, rewarding initiative and personal responsibility, forming self-managed teams, offering choices and flexibility in scheduling, benefits, etc.); (d) employee recognition programs (especially those that emphasize the contributions of work groups rather than a few specific individuals); and (e) removal of arbitrary or inefficient rules and procedures that highlight the unresponsiveness of the work environment (Conger, 1989; Deci & Ryan, 1985; Dumaine, 1990; Farnham, 1989; Maehr, 1987; Hackman & Oldham, 1976).

In the previous section on applying Motivational Systems Theory to education, cooperative goal structures were discussed as a useful tool for facilitating goal alignment between students and teachers. This is also a powerful strategy for enhancing goal alignment between workers and organizations. Covey (1990) describes a vivid example of the powerful results one can anticipate in terms of job satisfaction and work productivity when the "win/win" philosophy of a cooperative goal structure is effectively applied:

> This kind of thinking can . . . affect every area of organizational life if people have the courage . . . to concentrate on Win/Win. I am always amazed at the results that happen, both to individuals and to organizations, when responsible, proactive, self-directing individuals are turned loose on a task. . . . I worked for several years with a very large real estate organization in the Middle West. My first experience with this organization was at a large sales rally where over 800 sales associates gathered for the annual reward session. . . . Out of the 800 people there, around forty received awards for top performance. . . . There was no doubt that those forty people had *won*; but there was also the underlying awareness that 760 people had *lost*. We immediately began educational and organizational development work to align the systems and structures of the organization toward the Win/Win paradigm. . . . At the next rally one year later, there were over 1,000 sales associates present, and about 800 of them received awards. . . . The remarkable thing was that almost all of the 800 who received the awards that year had produced as much per person in terms of volume and profit as the previous year's forty. . . . The spirit of Win/Win had [released] enormous energy and talent. The resulting synergy was astounding to almost everyone involved. (pp. 226, 229-230)

Whatever strategies are used, it is important to keep in mind that the ultimate objective is not simply to enhance motivation, but also to *jointly* facilitate motivation and work productivity. Organizational commitment to policies and procedures that respect and facilitate the attainment of workers' core goals is likely to be sustained only if such policies and procedures contribute to the attainment of the organization's goals (the Principle of Goal Alignment). Thus the "trick" for business leaders and consultants is to ensure that productive work behavior is an instrumental part of the process of pursuing core personal goals.

Selection of Personnel With Motivational Characteristics That Are Compatible With the Job and Work Environment. The first two strategies for promoting goal alignment between workers and organizations represent ways to facilitate motivation by creating more responsive work environments. An additional (or alternative) strategy focusing more on the person side of the equation for effective functioning is to select or reassign personnel in a way that capitalizes on the motivational strengths that workers bring to the job (i.e., as a result of their existing repertoire of work-related BES). In other words, given a clear understanding of the motivational requirements of a job and appropriate assessment tools (e.g., Ford & Chase, 1991; Ford & Nichols, 1992; Nichols, 1991), it should be possible to identify prospective employees who already have goals, emotions, and personal agency beliefs that "fit" that job well.

Based on interviews with exceptionally effective people in business and industry, Maehr and Braskamp (1986) constructed a general motivational profile that probably fits a wide variety of jobs, but appears to be especially important for leadership positions. This profile is characterized by: (a) an active, challenge-seeking goal orientation; (b) an emphasis on personal rather than competitive standards for goal attainment); (c) robust personal agency beliefs; and (d) "boundless" emotional energy. This is consistent with Covey's (1990) description of highly effective people, although he places additional emphasis on the ability of such people to facilitate goal alignment, both in their own goal seeking ("put first things first") and in their relationships with other people (think "win/win" and "synergize"). This latter ability is particularly crucial for leaders who are responsible for managing diverse work groups, as it tends to mesh rather than conflict with the goal of facilitating motivation and productivity in such groups: "the essence of synergy is to value differences—to respect them, to build on strengths, to compensate for weaknesses" (Covey, 1990, p. 263).

A different kind of selection problem that is in some ways even more challenging is that of identifying workers who can maintain a high level of motivation under conditions that are, at least in some respects, highly unresponsive. For example, as Gerlach-Downie (1990) relates, child care workers who report being satisfied with their jobs tend to have a distinctive goal profile that enables them to tolerate the low pay and high-energy demands of the job:

> Child care workers often speak of their jobs in terms of it being a "mission" and they seem willing to sacrifice some of the comforts of other jobs if they feel that others recognize their suffering and/or are also suffering for the same goals. . . . This does not mean that child care workers do not yearn for more extrinsic rewards and reduced energy

demands for the job. They do. But their attitudes regarding job satisfaction seem to adapt well to an environment where few extrinsic rewards and a wide range of energy demands are expected. (pp. 206-207)

A somewhat more dramatic example of this same kind of selection problem is illustrated by the results of an LSF/MST-guided study conducted by Karimi, 1988; Behravesh, Karimi, & Ford, 1989 of the factors associated with effective performance among inspection personnel in nuclear power plants. Specifically, this investigation focused on the common problem of poor performance among inspectors responsible for identifying the possible presence of invisible cracking in the main coolant pipes of boiling water reactors. The consequences of failing to detect and correct such flaws are potentially quite severe, not only in terms of environmental safety, but also in terms of costs to the plant.

Previous research on this topic had focused, rather unproductively, on technical (i.e., skill-related) aspects of inspectors' performance. By collecting detailed descriptions of highly competent workers and behavior episodes characterized by superior, typical, and unusually poor performance, however, Karimi was able to demonstrate that performance problems were primarily attributable to an unresponsive physical and social environment that placed extreme motivational demands on workers (a violation of the Optimal Challenge Principle). Although some of these contextual obstacles to effective functioning were, in principle, alterable—for example, inadequate levels of performance feedback (the Feedback Principle); conflicting directives and inconsistent performance standards (the Principles of Goal Salience and Goal Alignment); and a lack of faith in management's concern about inspector safety and accuracy (the Responsive Environment Principle)— others were not (e.g., high levels of heat, noise, humidity, and radiation; long working hours; time pressures and delays). Thus, even under the best of circumstances, workers needed to be able to draw upon their own motivational resources to sustain effective functioning. Specifically, highly competent inspection personnel tended to manifest the following qualities: (a) a high degree of initiative and self-direction; (b) strong task goals and high standards for performance (i.e., they cared about doing a good job, and took pride in being able to meet standards of professional conduct); (c) powerful feelings of enjoyment and excitement in overcoming the challenges posed by a demanding job in a hostile environment, and an ability to avoid the negative emotional consequences often associated with such jobs; and (d) virtually invulnerable capability beliefs, even in the face of strong social-evaluative pressures. Workers without these qualities were generally less likely to be able to maintain effective functioning in this potentially demotivating context.

Application of MST to the Problem of Helping People Lead an Emotionally Healthy Life

Increasing recognition of the impact of psychological (especially motivational) processes on behavioral and physiological functioning has made the use of concepts such as "stress" and "coping" widespread not only in everyday language, but also in scientific and professional journals. For example, many researchers and practitioners (e.g., Benight, 1992; Chesney & Rosenman, 1985; Low, 1991; Pattillo, 1990; Taylor & Arnow, 1988; Thoresen & Pattillo, 1988; Williams, Barefoot, & Shekelle, 1985) have become concerned about the long-term health consequences of certain patterns of emotional functioning (e.g., angry and depressive patterns). Others have focused on the emotional and physical health consequences of negative personal agency beliefs (e.g., Bandura, 1986; Beck, 1976; Benight, 1992; Ellis, 1982; Peterson, Seligman, & Vaillant, 1988; Pierce, Gardner, Cummings, & Dunham, 1989; Seligman, 1991). Still others have emphasized the importance of how people think about and pursue their goals as a determinant of emotional well-being (e.g., Csikszentmihalyi, 1990; Emmons, 1989; Ford & Nichols, 1991; Klinger, 1975, 1977; Markus, Cross, & Wurf, 1990; Nichols, 1991; Pervin, 1983; Schutz, 1991; Winell, 1987). Indeed, virtually all systems of psychotherapy emphasize motivational processes in some form (Ford & Urban, 1967).

Such efforts are consistent with the MST premise that a strong motivational foundation is the key to overcoming the anxieties, obstacles, and stressful experiences of everyday living and developing the kind of BES that will enable one to lead an emotionally healthy life. Evidence for this premise is provided by two literatures focusing on the extreme outcomes of attempted suicide and enduring happiness.

Motivational Patterns and Principles Associated With Attempted Suicide and Enduring Happiness

Attempted Suicide. Baumeister (1990) has provided a careful theoretical analysis of the psychological events leading to the most common category of suicide attempts, namely, those motivated by an attempt to escape the psychological consequences of negative life events. In the first of six steps in Baumeister's (1990) escape theory, current outcomes or circumstances fall far below self-set standards and/or other people's expectations. This discrepancy may reflect very bad events that are well below very reasonable standards (the Principle of Direct Evidence), or not-so-bad events that are well below unrealistic and highly inflexible standards (the Principle of Flexible Standards). The person then blames himself or herself for the real or imagined failure, thus activating a Self-Doubting or Hopeless PAB pattern characterized by a deep sense of inadequacy, worthlessness, and self-condemnation. This leads to powerful negative emotions such as depression, loneliness, anxiety, or guilt, and an aversive state in which "the person is . . . acutely aware of self as inadequate, incompetent, unattractive, or guilty" (p. 91). This self-awareness motivates the person to try to escape this unhappy state, which is accomplished primarily through a process Baumeister calls "cognitive deconstruction." This process refers to the filling of consciousness with concrete, meaningless content, and to an intentional (and to some extent adaptive) failure to attend to the broader goals and values that normally provide meaning to a person's thoughts, feelings, and actions. The resulting sense of meaninglessness, when combined with thoughts and feelings of hopelessness, is potentially lethal: "Suicide thus emerges as an escalation of the person's wish to escape from meaningful awareness of current life problems and their implications about the self" (p. 91).

This analysis reveals that changes in goals, emotions, and personal agency beliefs are heavily implicated in, and necessary prerequisites for, most suicide attempts. This means that a suicide attempt is not likely to occur until major damage has occurred to all three motivational components (the Motivational Triumvirate Principle). A practical implication of this conclusion is that suicide attempts may be preventable if just one of these components can be facilitated during or prior to the onset of an episode in which suicide is being contemplated. That is why the cognitive deconstruction step is so crucial in escape theory—in this phase the person focuses his or her attention on controllable short-term goals (normally an effective motivational strategy), but does so in ways that are arbitrary and unconnected to anything of significance, and, as a result, becomes disengaged from their last remaining motivational lifeline (i.e., meaningful personal goals). This suggests that, in addition to the Principles of Emotional Activation (for positive emotions) and Direct Evidence (for positive PABs), the Principle of Goal Activation may be an important tool in suicide prevention efforts (i.e., encouraging the person to consciously think about meaningful past events and future possibilities).

Enduring Happiness. The hallmark of emotional health is a steady state pattern in which happiness, in its various forms (e.g., satisfaction, pride, pleasure, joy), is the dominant emotion. This, according to Csikszentmihalyi (1990), is apparently not an easy pattern to achieve:

> Genuinely happy people are few and far between. How many people do you know who enjoy what they are doing, who are reasonably satisfied with their lot, who do not regret the past and look to the future with genuine confidence? (p. 11)

If it is indeed the case that enduring happiness is a relatively rare achievement, why might that be so? Frijda (1988) offers a particularly interesting, albeit somewhat speculative answer to this question:

> There exists, it would seem, misery that one does not get used to; there is deprivation to which one does not adapt. This fact has, it appears, no counterpart for positive emotions. Joy, bliss, and fascination invariably tend to fade toward neutrality or some pale contentment. One must, I think, posit a *law of hedonic asymmetry*. . . . : *Pleasure is always contingent upon change and disappears with continuous satisfaction. Pain may persist under persisting adverse conditions.* . . . That the net quality of life, by consequence, tends to be negative is an unfortunate result. . . . On the other hand, the law's outcomes are not unavoidable. . . . Enduring happiness seems possible, and it can be understood theoretically. However, note that it does not come naturally, by itself. It takes effort. (pp. 353-354)

The idea that enduring happiness is something that people must actively strive for is a powerful idea, one that is congruent with the MST emphasis on self-direction and effective functioning. This same emphasis is found in several other theories as well, but perhaps most notably in White's (1959) effectance motivation theory, Deci and Ryan's (1985) self-determination theory, and Csikszentmihalyi's (1990) optimal experience theory. In each of these theories there is a strong view that enduring happiness will not result simply from coping successfully with negative life events and problems. One must, rather, adopt a thriving goal orientation in which one actively seeks out and chooses goals that are personally compelling, optimally challenging, and flexible with regard to standards for goal attainment. To make this a truly meaningful process that yields deep and continuous satisfaction, these goals must be interconnected in a hierarchy of short-term and longer-term goals characterized by a high level of balance and commitment (Winell, 1987).

Both Csikszentmihalyi (1990) and Deci and Ryan (1985) emphasize how emotional well-being can be undermined by social demands, pressures, and expectations that promote negative context beliefs (the Responsive Environment Principle), and that may also activate potentially distracting goals and emotions (the Principle of Goal Alignment). Csikszentmihalyi (1990), however, offers a way around this problem that he clearly sees as the key to optimal experience— namely, the mental conversion of problems and constraints into opportunities and challenges:

> A person can make himself happy, or miserable, regardless of what is happening "outside," just by changing the contents of consciousness. We all know individuals who can transform hopeless situations into challenges to be overcome. . . . This ability to persevere despite obstacles and setbacks is the quality people most admire in others, and justly so; it is probably the most important trait not only for succeeding in life, but for enjoying it as well. To develop this trait, one must find ways to order consciousness so as to be in control of feelings and thoughts. (p. 24)

Thus the "secret to happiness" is not doing away with negative events, or waiting for some major positive event to occur. In fact, happiness and misery are surprisingly unrelated to the objective quality of events, as evidenced, for example, by the fact that suicides are more common in societies with higher standards of living and in areas with better weather (Baumeister, 1990). Enduring happiness is more the result of an everyday "motivational life-style"—a (a) proactive, change-oriented life-style guided by a dynamically evolving BES repertoire in which a (b) rich and balanced mixture of clear, attainable short-term goals and (c) multiple, powerful long-term goals is supported by (d) a philosophy of "flexible optimism" (Seligman, 1991), (e) clear but flexible standards for goal attainment, (f) an "ability to transform adversity into an enjoyable challenge" (Csikszentmihalyi, 1990, p. 200), and (g) a consistent habit of enjoying and reliving the real and anticipated joys and successes in life.

Another productive way to address the problem of facilitating enduring happiness is to focus on the *content* of the goals and motivational patterns characterizing people who see themselves, and are seen by others, as experiencing a great deal of happiness in their lives. This is the approach taken by Chase and Ford (1992) in their MST-guided study of happy and unhappy adolescents. Using both the *Assessment of Personal Goals* and *Assessment of Personal Agency Beliefs* (see Chapters 4 and 5), Chase and Ford (1992) discovered that happy teenagers were significantly more likely than their unhappy peers to be concerned about, and optimistic about the possibility of attaining, four sets of goals:

1. experiencing positive affective states (e.g., happiness and relaxation);
2. maintaining positive self-evaluative thoughts and a positive outlook on life;
3. experiencing a sense of connectedness with others, both in terms of caring for and feeling accepted by partners in ongoing social relationships; and
4. staying physically active and productive.

These data, which are quite congruent with Baumeister's (1991) analysis of the "meanings of life," suggest that a particularly effective strategy for promoting an enduring sense of happiness in others (or in one's self) might be to focus one's attention directly and explicitly on these four broad categories of goals and the means and obstacles associated with their attainment.

Suggestions for Further Reading

Ames, C., & Ames. R. (Eds.) (1985). *Research on motivation in education, Vol. 2: The classroom milieu*. Orlando, FL: Academic Press.

Baumeister, R. F. (1991). *Meanings of life*. New York: Guilford.

Covey, S. R. (1990). *The 7 habits of highly effective people*. New York: Simon & Schuster.

Maehr, M. L., & Ames, C. (Eds.) (1989). *Advances in motivation and achievement, Vol. 6: Motivation enhancing environments*. Greenwich, CT: JAI Press.

Maehr, M. L., & Kleiber, D. A. (Eds.) (1987). *Advances in motivation and achievement, Vol. 5: Enhancing motivation*. Greenwich, CT: JAI Press.

Slavin, R. E. (1984). Students motivating students to excel: Cooperative incentives, cooperative tasks, and student achievement. *The Elementary School Journal, 85*, 53-63.

CHAPTER EIGHT

Summary of Motivational Systems Theory

Go confidently in the direction of your dreams. Live the life you have imagined.

Henry David Thoreau

Rationale for Motivational Systems Theory

THE PRIMARY THEORETICAL RATIONALE for Motivational Systems Theory (MST) is the urgent need for a conceptual framework that addresses the lack of consensus, cohesion, and integration in the field of motivation (see Chapter 1). MST attempts to bring coherence to the field by providing a clear, precise, and comprehensive conceptualization of the basic substance and organization of motivational patterns (Chapters 3, 4, and 5) and by showing how other theories can be understood within this integrative framework (Chapter 6).

The primary applied rationale for MST is the premise that motivation is at the heart of many of society's most pervasive and enduring problems, both as a developmental outcome of demotivating social environments and as a developmental influence on behavior and personality. Linked to this premise is the fundamental proposition that motivation provides the psychological foundation for the development of human competence in everyday life (Chapter 7).

General Nature of Motivational Systems Theory

Motivational Systems Theory is derived from D. Ford's Living Systems Framework (D. Ford, 1987; M. Ford & D. Ford, 1987), a comprehensive theory of human functioning and development that is designed to represent all of the component processes of the person and how they are organized in complex patterns of unitary functioning in variable environments (Chapter 2). The anchoring of MST in this broader framework makes it possible to describe how motivational processes interact with biological, environmental, and nonmotivational psychological and behavioral processes to produce effective or ineffective functioning in the person as a whole (Chapters 3, 4, and 5). The LSF thus provides the foundation for constructing a conceptualization of motivation that has broad theoretical, empirical, and practical utility.

MST is designed to represent all three sets of phenomena that have traditionally been of concern in the field of human motivation: the selective *direction* of behavior patterns (i.e., where people are heading and what they are trying to do), the selective *energization* of behavior patterns (i.e., how people get "turned on" or "turned off"), and the selective *regulation* of behavior patterns (i.e., how people decide to try something, stick with it, or give up).

Concepts and Principles Representing the Overall Person-in-Context System

A person always functions as a unit in coordination with the environments in which he or she is functioning (the Principle of Unitary Functioning) (D. Ford, 1987).

The basic unit of functioning is the *behavior episode*. A behavior episode is a context-specific, goal-directed pattern of behavior that unfolds over time until one of three conditions is met: (a) the goal organizing the episode is accomplished, or accomplished "well enough"; (b) the person's attention is preempted by some internal or external event, and another goal takes precedence (at least temporarily); or (c) the goal is evaluated as unattainable, at least for the time being (D. Ford, 1987). Three different types of behavior episodes can be distinguished. In an *instrumental episode*, the person is actively engaged in some motor or communicative activity ("output") de-signed to influence his or her environment in some way and is actively seeking feedback information ("input") from the environment about the results of that activity. In an *observational episode*, the person is actively seeking relevant informational "input" from the environment about someone else's instrumental activity. There is no "output" to speak of because the person is not trying to influence the environment. In a *thinking episode*, both the output and input processes associated with instrumental activity are inhibited, and no effort is made either to influence or watch others influence the environment. The purpose of a thinking episode is, rather, to experience, enjoy, or try to improve the organization of some information in a person's repertoire or to construct or rehearse a plan for future action from such information.

People guide their behavior in new episodes using *behavior episode schemata (BES)*. A BES is an internal representation of a set of related behavior episode experiences (including episodes that have only been imagined or observed) (D. Ford, 1987). A BES represents the functioning of the whole person-in-context because that is what is involved in any given behavior episode. A BES provides guidance about what one should pay attention to and how one should think, feel, and act in a specific behavior episode.

Goals and *contexts* are the anchors that organize and provide coherence to the activities taking place within a particular behavior episode. They also organize the functions represented within a specific BES.

The anchoring of BES to goals and contexts, while facilitating the process of constructing clear and specific guides to behavior, can constrain the process of transferring useful BES components to other relevant BES. To overcome this limitation, humans have developed the capability for constructing cognitive representations of BES components and component relationships, typically called *concepts* (or constructs) and *propositions* (or rules or theories), respectively (D. Ford, 1987). It is only when concepts and propositions are embedded back into personalized and conceptually anchored BES that they become infused with personal meaning and utility, however.

Once a BES has been constructed, it can be elaborated or combined with other BES and BES components. Over time this can yield a very powerful BES encompassing a diverse repertoire of optional behavior patterns organized around a related set of goals and contexts. By combining a number of such BES together, a qualitatively superior kind of expertise called *generative flexibility* can emerge.

BES can also be elaborated by linking components together in sequential fashion to produce a "script." A script serves as a template for a stereotyped sequence of events. Well-rehearsed scripts (sometimes also called habits) can greatly facilitate the execution of precise, efficient behavior patterns; however, they tend to be lacking in generative flexibility. In fact, the essential value of "automated" scripts or habits is to eliminate such variability.

Personality is defined as the person's repertoire of stable, recurring BES.

Achievement is the concept used in MST to describe effective functioning at the behavior episode level of analysis. Achievement is defined as the attainment of a personally or socially valued goal in a particular context.

Competence is the concept used in MST to describe effective functioning at the BES (i.e., personality) level of analysis. Competence is defined as the attainment of relevant goals in specified environments using appropriate means and resulting in positive developmental outcomes.

Concepts and Principles Representing the Components of Effective Functioning

In any behavior episode, there are four major prerequisites for effective functioning:

1. The person must have the *motivation* needed to initiate and maintain activity until the goal directing the episode is attained.

2. The person must have the *skill* needed to construct and execute a pattern of activity that will produce the desired consequence (this category includes all of the nonmotivational psychological and behavioral processes of the person).

3. The person's *biological structure and functioning* must be able to support the operation of the motivation and skill components.

4. The person must have the cooperation of a *responsive environment* that will facilitate, or at least not excessively impede, progress toward the goal.

Thus at a broad level it is possible to describe the processes contributing to effective person-in-context functioning using the following heuristic formula—the MST formula for effective functioning:

$$\text{Achievement/Competence} = \frac{\text{Motivation} \times \text{Skill}}{\text{Biology}} \times \text{Responsive Environment}$$

In other words, effective functioning requires a motivated, skillful person whose biological and behavioral capabilities support relevant interactions with an environment that has the informational and material properties and resources needed to facilitate (or at least permit) goal attainment. If *any* of these components is missing or inadequate, achievements will be limited and competence development will be thwarted.

Motivation is a *psychological, future-oriented* (anticipatory), and *evaluative* (rather than instrumental) phenomenon. Based on these defining criteria, motivation is defined in MST as the organized patterning of an individual's personal goals, emotional arousal processes, and personal agency beliefs. Symbolically this can be represented as a formula of three interacting components:

$$\text{Motivation} = \text{Goals} \times \text{Emotions} \times \text{Personal Agency Beliefs}$$

In LSF terms the nonmotivational components of effective functioning include (a) environmental processes, (b) biological processes, (c) information processing and memory functions, (d) attention and consciousness arousal processes, (e) activity arousal processes, (f) control cognitions (planning and problem-solving thoughts and means evaluations), (f) transactional processes (e.g., motor and communicative actions), and (g) regulatory feedback cognitions (performance evaluations). All but (a) and (b) are referred to as instrumental or skill-related processes in MST.

Concepts and Principles Pertaining to Personal Goals

Personal goals are thoughts about desired (or undesired) states or outcomes that one would like to achieve (or avoid). *Goal evaluation processes* are cognitive evaluations of the goals being pursued or contemplated in terms of their continuing or potential relevance or priority.

Personal goals have two basic properties: they represent the consequences to be achieved (or avoided), and they direct the other components of the person to try to produce those consequences (or prevent them from occurring). Goals thus play a leadership role in motivational patterns by defining their content and direction.

The concept of *goal content* is used in MST to describe the desired or undesired consequence represented by a particular goal. The 24-category Ford and Nichols Taxonomy of Human Goals provides a comprehensive description of the different kinds of goals that people may pursue within and across behavior episodes (see Chapter 4).

Behavior is often (perhaps usually) guided by multiple goals simultaneously. Indeed, the most motivating activities and experiences in life are those that involve the simultaneous pursuit and attainment of many different kinds of goals.

The term *goal hierarchy* is used to describe the coordination of multiple goals within and across behavior episodes. At the level of a specific behavior episode, goal hierarchies consist of organized sequences of embedded subgoals that serve as targets or markers of progress toward the overall goal (or goals) of the episode. Effective functioning requires a strategic emphasis on attainable short-term goals combined with a periodic review of the long-term goals that give meaning and organization to one's short-term pursuits.

Goal conflict and *goal alignment* are the terms used in MST to describe motivational patterns in which multiple goals are organized in conflictual or mutually facilitative ways within behavior episodes. Achievement and competence are greatly facilitated by efforts to enhance goal alignment, both in terms of the goals afforded by the context and the goal coordination skills of the individual.

Goal balance and *goal imbalance* are the terms used in MST to describe patterns of goal pursuit that are broad and multifaceted versus narrow or "empty" with regard to important life goals. Finding ways to balance goal pursuits across episodes is an important prerequisite for effective overall functioning. Goal hierarchies at this broader level of analysis also provide a useful way of describing an individual's personality.

At the behavior episode level, the cognitive methods or strategies used to represent a goal are called *goal-setting processes*. When goals are conceived of in sufficiently concrete terms, they can define a precise "target" that an individual or group can try to "hit" or approach with their goal-seeking efforts. Moreover, if the target is set at an optimally challenging level of difficulty—that is, at a level that is "hard" but attainable—progress and continuing motivation are likely to be maximized (assuming an adequate level of feedback).

At the BES/personality level of analysis, one can identify qualitatively distinct styles of goal pursuit called *goal orientations* (e.g., coping versus thriving orientation; see Chapter 4 for a complete list). Goal orientations can have pervasive effects on motivation, achievement, and competence development.

The influence of goals on behavior is a function of the extent to which they are prioritized by cognitive and emotional regulatory processing. *Wishes* are goals that fail to gain priority (beyond their role in thinking episodes) because they are associated with strong inhibiting emotions (e.g., fear or guilt) or are evaluated as highly unrealistic or so discrepant from one's current state that meaningful progress toward the goal is impossible, at least under present circumstances. *Current concerns* are goals that have "passed" a set of general evaluative "tests" (e.g., goal importance and emotional valence tests) and are now influencing the rest of the system through their selective organizing function (i.e., a *general commitment* has been made to pursue these goals). *Intentions* are goals that are highly prioritized and currently producing or ready to produce instrumental action (i.e., the person has made a *specific commitment* to achieving the goal in the current behavior episode).

Four criteria may be used by the psychological evaluators in "motivational headquarters" to determine which goals should be prioritized in the context of a specific behavior episode:

1. *goal relevance* (i.e., what goals are meaningful or appropriate in a particular context);
2. *goal importance* (i.e., to what extent are the relevant goals in a particular context personally significant to the individual);
3. *goal attainability* (i.e., personal agency beliefs);
4. the *emotional salience* of the actions and consequences associated with pursuing and achieving the goal.

The motivational burden tends to shift from goals to personal agency beliefs and emotions once a commitment has been made to pursue a goal.

Concepts and Principles Pertaining to Personal Agency
Beliefs

Personal agency beliefs are evaluative thoughts involving a comparison between a desired consequence (i.e., some goal) and an anticipated consequence (i.e., what the person expects to happen if they pursue that goal). Consequently, personal agency beliefs pertaining to a particular goal have no meaning or functional significance if that goal is dormant or of no value to the individual (i.e., personal agency beliefs only matter if there is a relevant goal in place).

There are two kinds of personal agency beliefs. *Capability beliefs* are evaluations of whether one has the personal SKILL needed to function effectively (e.g., "Am I capable of achieving this goal? Do I have what it takes to accomplish this goal?"). *Context beliefs* are evaluations of whether one has the RESPONSIVE ENVIRONMENT needed to support effective functioning (e.g., "Does my context afford the opportunity to try to achieve my goal? Will my context make it easier or harder for me to attain my goal? Can I trust this context to support me or cooperate with me in what I try to do, or will I be ignored/rejected/attacked?").

Personal agency beliefs are often more fundamental than the actual skills and circumstances they represent in the sense that they can motivate people to create opportunities and acquire capabilities they do not yet possess. Positive capability and context beliefs are not sufficient, however, for desired outcomes to occur. Ultimately people must still have relevant skills and a responsive environment.

Personal agency beliefs play a particularly crucial role in situations involving challenging but attainable goals (i.e., goals that are neither impossible nor trivially easy to accomplish).

The precise meaning of a capability belief will vary depending on the particular kind of capability represented in that belief (e.g., ability to perform an athletic feat versus ability to cope with a stressful situation).

The precise meaning of a context belief will vary depending on the kind of environmental unresponsiveness represented in that belief. Specifically, the environment must be congruent with an individual's "agenda" of personal goals; it must be congruent with the person's biological, transactional, or cognitive capabilities; it must have the material or informational resources needed to facilitate goal attainment; and it must provide an emotional climate that supports and facilitates effective functioning.

MST addresses the need to develop theoretically sound and pragmatically useful ways of representing the *patterning* of capability and context beliefs by offering a taxonomy designed to capture the essential qualities of 10 conceptually distinguishable PAB patterns (see Chapter 5).

Concepts and Principles Pertaining to Emotional Arousal Processes

Emotions are organized functional patterns consisting of three components: an *affective* (neural-psychological) *component* (i.e., the general subjective feeling part of the emotion), a *physiological component* (i.e., a supporting pattern of biological processing), and a *transactional component* (i.e., a pattern of motor and communicative actions designed to facilitate goal attainment). Emotions help people deal with varying circumstances by providing evaluative information about the person's interactions with the environment (affective regulatory function) and by supporting and facilitating action designed to produce desired consequences (energizing function).

Emotions can be triggered in several different ways, including by direct perception in circumstances that convey information matching the conditions for which the emotional pattern evolved as a fixed action pattern. This is the way that most emotional experiences are initiated in very young children. In older children and adults, however, emotions are more commonly activated by cognitive evaluations pertaining to current or potential concerns in real or imagined circumstances. Consequently, emotions that are not anchored to a goal that is currently directing or influencing the individual's activity (i.e., an intention or a current concern) will generally have little meaning or personal significance.

Although emotions do not provide direct information about what a person is trying to accomplish or avoid, they provide clues about the content of a person's goals by influencing selective attention, recall, event interpretation, learning, decision making, and problem solving in predictable ways.

Emotions, once activated, tend to take on a life of their own, so that they may persist in some form (e.g., a mood state) even after a goal is attained or some other goal takes precedence. Emotions may also wane in magnitude even when a goal remains strong and active if the conditions eliciting the emotion are not perceptually or cognitively salient. Indeed, every emotional state will eventually dissipate unless it is reactivated in some way (e.g., through cognitive rumination), just as a flywheel on a machine will slowly stop unless periodically given another push.

Cognitive evaluations and emotional arousal patterns function as a regulatory "team," with each "player" contributing to effective decision making in different and unique ways. Personal agency beliefs, because they are more likely to incorporate considerations about long-term consequences and the potential availability of alternative courses of action, are particularly useful for decisions about "big picture" matters, such as whether one should initiate or continue a complex, difficult, or time-consuming course of action. Emotions, on the other hand, are particularly useful when effective functioning requires immediate or vigorous action in the context of a concrete problem or opportunity, such as escape from imminent harm, removal of an obstacle to goal attainment, or inhibition of a personally or socially damaging action.

Different kinds of emotional patterns evolved to help people deal with different kinds of pervasive, prototypical problems and opportunities of living. D. Ford (1987) has identified 14 basic emotional patterns representing different kinds of motivational influences. Four of these are instrumental emotions that evolved to help regulate the initiation, continuation, repetition, and termination of behavior episodes: satisfaction-pleasure-joy, downheartedness-discouragement-depression, curiosity-interest-excitement, and disinterest-boredom-apathy. Four others are instrumental emotions that evolved to help regulate efforts to cope with potentially disrupting or damaging circumstances: startle-surprise-astonishment, annoyance-anger-rage, wariness-fear-terror, and dislike-disgust-loathing. In addition, three social emotions evolved to help regulate interpersonal bonding: sexual arousal-pleasure-excitement, acceptance-affection-love, and loneliness-sorrow-grief; and another set of three social emotions evolved to help regulate conformity to or cooperation with social expectations and patterns of social organization: embarrassment-shame/guilt-humiliation, scorn-disdain-contempt, and resentment-jealousy-hostility.

Principles for Motivating Humans

All of the MST principles for motivating humans must be understood in terms of the general conception that *facilitation*, not control, should be the guiding idea in attempts to motivate humans. Even when one is in a position of power or authority, the strategy of trying to motivate people through direct control of a person's actions—as opposed to indirect facilitation of their goals, emotions, and personal agency beliefs—should be reserved for situations in which swift attainment of a goal is urgent and no other means are available. In addition, because short-term motivational gains often come at the expense of longer-term motivational patterns, one should always carefully consider whether efforts to promote a particular *achievement* will also facilitate the development of an individual's *competence* to deal with similar situations in the future.

The Principle of Unitary Functioning. Motivational interventionists must understand that they are *always* dealing with a whole person who is bringing a personality and developmental history to a context in which mutually influential person and environment processes are organized in complexly organized functional patterns (i.e., "get the big picture").

The Motivational Triumvirate Principle. All three motivational components—goals, emotions, and personal agency beliefs—must be influenced to "motivate" someone successfully.

The Responsive Environment Principle. Whenever someone tries to motivate a person, he or she becomes a part of that person's environment, and therefore a part of that individual's "equation" for effective functioning (i.e., Achievement/Competence = Motivation x Skill x *Responsive Environment*). Consequently, motivational interventionists must be concerned not only with the specific techniques they intend to use, but also with the more general features of their relationship with that person, especially those that directly impact the person's context beliefs (e.g., trustworthiness).

The Principle of Goal Activation. If no relevant goal is activated with respect to a desired behavior pattern, there will be no behavior. Moreover, one cannot capitalize on positive personal agency beliefs and emotional strengths unless there is some goal in place against which to anchor these thoughts and feelings.

The Principle of Goal Salience. The goals that have been activated must be conceived of in terms that are sufficiently clear and compelling to be able to direct a person's behavior in concrete ways in the here and now (i.e., they must facilitate the formation and maintenance of specific *intentions* and a continuing *commitment* to pursue those goals).

The Multiple Goals Principle. The strongest motivational patterns are those anchored by multiple goals. Thus one should try to organize, design, or modify tasks, activities, and experiences so that they afford the attainment of as many different kinds of goals as possible. Even in cases where this strategy fails to activate a strong motivational pattern directed by multiple goals, it may provide some *motivational insurance* against the possibility that *no* relevant goal will be activated.

The Principle of Goal Alignment. When multiple goals are aligned within and between people, motivation is strong and productivity is high. Motivation is also facilitated by aligning proximal and distal goals in such a way that attention is focused on immediate subgoals that signify progress toward meaningful long-term goals.

The Feedback Principle. Even when clear, compelling goals are activated, people cannot continue to make progress toward those goals for very long in the absence of relevant feedback information. Feedback facilitates realistic goal-setting, triggers adaptive emotional responses, and provides a solid basis for constructing and modifying personal agency beliefs. It can also suggest opportunities to pursue goals other than those that initiated the behavior episode.

The Flexible Standards Principle. When people receive potentially demotivating feedback, motivation can be protected to some extent by trying to facilitate a flexible approach to goal setting in which standards may vary, in an adaptive, realistic fashion, according to the circumstances. This same principle also applies to situations in which continuing motivation may be jeopardized by goal attainment. In both cases one must be willing and able to replace one clear, challenging standard with another clear, challenging standard (either harder or easier than the first) when the first one has been accomplished or evaluated as unattainable.

The Optimal Challenge Principle. Motivation is maximized under conditions of "optimal challenge"—that is, conditions in which standards for goal attainment are difficult given the person's current level of expertise, but still attainable with vigorous or persistent effort. Under such circumstances, successes are unusually satisfying and exciting in terms of emotional arousal and highly empowering in terms of personal agency beliefs.

The Principle of Direct Evidence. Experiences that focus directly on the vulnerable aspects of an individual's personal agency beliefs will generally have much more impact than will experiences that are only vaguely or tangentially relevant to the problem at hand.

The Reality Principle. Personal agency beliefs can help compensate for weaknesses in the nonmotivational parts of the system by facilitating efforts to increase skills, improve one's health, or create or seek out responsive aspects of one's environment. In the long run, however, positive capability and context beliefs are difficult to maintain in the absence of *actual skills* and a *truly responsive environment*. Thus one should try to facilitate motivational patterns characterized by "flexible optimism" (i.e., optimism that is grounded in but not overly constrained by current reality) (Seligman, 1991).

The Principle of Emotional Activation. Motivation can be facilitated by activating the emotional patterns—both positive and negative— that are most directly linked to effective functioning for the purpose at hand.

The "Do It" Principle. When a person is demotivated but clearly capable of functioning effectively, a useful strategy is to do whatever it takes to get the person to activate their competent BES. This provides a concrete way of displacing the problematic motivational pattern and an opportunity to initiate a feedback process that is likely to yield information contradicting the inhibiting messages in the original motivational pattern.

The Principle of Incremental Versus Transformational Change. To achieve qualitative changes in motivational patterns, one can either construct a series of incremental change experiences designed to produce significant additive effects or initiate a disorganization-reorganization process designed to produce transformational change. A good rule of thumb in such cases is: increment if you can, transform if you must. Transformational change should only be attempted, however, in conjunction with transition protection processes, and with a clear understanding of the urgency of maintaining a high stability-instability ratio.

The Equifinality Principle. Because there are usually a variety of pathways to a goal in complexly organized systems, motivational interventionists should adopt a creative and determined problem-solving approach guided by the belief that, if at first you don't succeed, keep trying!

The Principle of Human Respect. People are not simply bodies in a classroom or boxes in an organizational chart or information-processing machines—they are thinking, feeling, self-directed human beings with a very personal repertoire of goals, emotions, and self-referent beliefs that *must* be treated with respect and care if efforts to facilitate desired motivational patterns and the development of human competence are to succeed.

References

Abelson, R. P. (1981). Psychological status of the script concept. *American Psychologist, 36,* 715-727.

Abramson, L. Y., Metalsky, G. I., & Alloy, L. B. (1989). Hopelessness depression: A theory-based subtype of depression. *Psychological Review, 96,* 358-372.

Abramson, L. Y., Seligman, M. E. P., & Teasdale, J. D. (1978). Learned helplessness in humans: Critique and reformulation. *Journal of Abnormal Psychology, 87,* 49-74.

Ackoff, R. L., & Emery, F. E. (1971). *On purposeful systems.* Chicago: Aldine.

Adams, J. (1990). *The Honig campaign for State Superintendent 1982.* Paper presented in doctoral seminar on the development of human competence, Stanford University School of Education, Stanford, CA.

Adams, J. S. (1963). Toward an understanding of inequity. *Journal of Abnormal and Social Psychology, 67,* 422-436.

Adams, J. S. (1965). Inequity in social exchange. In L. Berkowitz (Ed.), *Advances in experimental social psychology* (Vol. 2, pp. 267-300). New York: Academic Press.

Adler, A. (1924). *The practice and theory of individual psychology.* New York: Harcourt Brace.

Ajzen, I. (1985). From intentions to actions: A theory of planned behavior. In J. Kuhl & J. Beckmann (Eds.), *Action control: From cognition to behavior* (pp. 11-39). Berlin: Springer Verlag.

Ajzen, I., & Fishbein, M. (1977). Attitude-behavior relations: A theoretical analysis and review of empirical research. *Psychological Bulletin, 84,* 888-918.

Ajzen, I., & Fishbein, M. (1980). *Understanding attitudes and predicting social behavior.* Englewood Cliffs, NJ: Prentice-Hall.

Aldefer, C. P. (1969). An empirical test of a new theory of human needs. *Organizational Behavior and Human Performance, 4,* 142-175.

Aldefer, C. P. (1972). *Existence, relatedness, and growth.* New York: Free Press.

Allport, G. W. (1955). *Becoming: Basic considerations for a psychology of personality.* New Haven, CT: Yale University Press.

Amabile, T. M., DeJong, W., & Lepper, M. R. (1976). Effects of externally imposed deadlines on subsequent intrinsic motivation. *Journal of Personality and Social Psychology, 34*, 92-98.

Ames, C. (1987). The enhancement of student motivation. In M. L. Maehr & D. A. Kleiber (Eds.), *Advances in motivation and achievement, Vol. 5: Enhancing motivation* (pp. 123-148). Greenwich, CT: JAI.

Ames, C., & Ames, R. (1984a). Systems of student and teacher motivation: Toward a qualitative definition. *Journal of Educational Psychology, 76*, 535-556.

Ames, C., & Ames, R. (1984b). Goal structures and motivation. *The Elementary School Journal, 85*, 39-52.

Ames, C., & Ames, R. (Eds.) (1985). *Research on motivation in education, Vol. 2: The classroom milieu.* Orlando, FL: Academic Press.

Ames, C., & Ames, R. (Eds.) (1989). *Research on motivation in education, Vol. 3: Goals and cognitions.* San Diego, CA: Academic Press.

Ames, R. E., & Ames, C. (Eds.) (1984). *Research on motivation in education, Vol. 1: Student motivation.* Orlando, FL: Academic Press.

Amsel, A. (1958). The role of frustrative nonreward in noncontinuous reward situations. *Psychological Bulletin, 55*, 102-119.

Appley, M. H. (1990). Time for reintegration? *Science Agenda, 3*(1), 12-13.

Apter, M. J. (1982). *The experience of motivation: Theory of psychological reversals.* New York: Academic Press.

Arbib, M. A. (1989). *The metaphorical brain 2: Neural networks and beyond.* New York: John Wiley.

Arbib, M. A., & Hesse, M. B. (1986). *The construction of reality.* Cambridge, UK: Cambridge University Press.

Ashby, W. R. (1956). *An introduction to cybernetics.* New York: John Wiley.

Ashby, W. R. (1962). Principles of the self-organizing system. In H. Von Foerster & G. W. Zopf (Eds.), *Principles of self-organization* (pp. 108-118). New York: Pergamon.

Atkinson, J. W. (1957). Motivational determinants of risk-taking behavior. *Psychological Review, 64*, 359-372.

Atkinson, J. W. (1964). *An introduction to motivation.* Princeton, NJ: Van Nostrand.

Atkinson, J. W., & Birch, D. (1970). *The dynamics of action.* New York: John Wiley.

Atkinson, J. W., & Birch, D. (1974). The dynamics of achievement-oriented activity. In J. W. Atkinson & J. O. Raynor (Eds.), *Motivation and achievement* (pp. 271-325). Washington, DC: Winston.

Atkinson, J. W., & Feather, N. T. (Eds.) (1966). *A theory of achievement motivation.* New York: John Wiley.

Averill, J. R. (1968). Grief: Its nature and significance. *Psychological Bulletin, 70*, 721-748.

Averill, J. R. (1978). Anger. In H. H. Howe, Jr., & R. A. Dienstbier (Eds.), *Nebraska Symposium on Motivation* (Vol. 26, pp. 1-80). Lincoln: University of Nebraska Press.

Azuma, H. (1984). Secondary control as a heterogeneous category. *American Psychologist, 39*, 970-971.

Baird, L. S. (1976). Relationship of performance to satisfaction in stimulating and nonstimulating jobs. *Journal of Applied Psychology, 61*, 721-727.

Bakan, D. (1966). *The duality of human existence.* Boston: Beacon Press.

Bandura, A. (1977a). *Social learning theory.* Englewood Cliffs, NJ: Prentice-Hall.

Bandura, A. (1977b). Self-efficacy: Toward a unifying theory of behavior change. *Psychological Review, 84*, 191-215.

Bandura, A. (1978). The self-system in reciprocal determinism. *American Psychologist, 33*, 344-358.

Bandura, A. (1981). Self-referent thought: The developmental analysis of self-efficacy. In J. H. Flavell & L. D. Ross (Eds.), *Development of social cognition* (pp. 200-239). New York: Cambridge University Press.

Bandura, A. (1982). Self-efficacy mechanism in human agency. *American Psychologist, 37,* 122-147.

Bandura, A. (1986). *Social foundations of thought and action: A social cognitive theory.* Englewood Cliffs, NJ: Prentice-Hall.

Bandura, A. (1989). Self-regulation of motivation and action through internal standards and goal systems. In L. A. Pervin (Ed.), *Goal concepts in personality and social psychology* (pp. 19-85). Hillsdale, NJ: Lawrence Erlbaum.

Bandura, A. (1990). Conclusion: Reflections on nonability determinants of competence. In R. J. Sternberg & J. Kolligian, Jr. (Eds.), *Competence considered* (pp. 315-362). New Haven, CT: Yale University Press.

Bandura, A. (1991a). Human agency: The rhetoric and the reality. *American Psychologist, 46,* 157-162.

Bandura, A. (1991b). Social cognitive theory of moral thought and action. In W. M. Kurtines & J. L. Gewirtz (Eds.), *Handbook of moral behavior and development, Vol. 1: Theory* (pp. 45-103). Hillsdale, NJ: Lawrence Erlbaum.

Bandura, A., & Cervone, D. (1983). Self-evaluative and self-efficacy mechanisms governing the motivational effects of goal systems. *Journal of Personality and Social Psychology, 45,* 1017-1028.

Bandura, A., & Cervone, D. (1986). Differential engagement of self-reactive influences in cognitive motivation. *Organizational Behavior and Human Decision Processes, 38,* 92-113.

Bandura, A., & Schunk, D. H. (1981). Cultivating competence, self-efficacy, and intrinsic interest through proximal self-motivation. *Journal of Personality and Social Psychology, 41,* 586-598.

Barden, R. C., & Ford, M. E. (1990). *Optimal performance in golf.* Minneapolis, MN: Optimal Performance Systems.

Barden, R. C., & Ford, M. E. (1991). *Optimal performance in education.* Minneapolis, MN: Optimal Performance Systems.

Baumeister, R. F. (1984). Choking under pressure: Self-consciousness and paradoxical effects of incentives on skillful performance. *Journal of Personality and Social Psychology, 46,* 610-620.

Baumeister, R. F. (1990). Suicide as escape from self. *Psychological Review, 97,* 90-113.

Baumeister, R. F. (1991). *Meanings of life.* New York: Guilford.

Baumrind, D. (1978). Parental disciplinary patterns and social competence in children. *Youth and Society, 9,* 239-276.

Beck, A. T. (1976). *Cognitive therapy and emotional disorders.* New York: International University Press.

Beck, A. T., & Freeman, A. (1990). *Cognitive therapy of personality disorders.* New York: Guilford.

Beck, R. C. (1978). *Motivation: Theories and principles.* Englewood Cliffs, NJ: Prentice-Hall.

Becker, L. J. (1978). Joint effect of feedback and goal setting on performance: A field study of residential energy conservation. *Journal of Applied Psychology, 63,* 428-433.

Behravesh, M. M., Karimi, S. S., & Ford, M. E. (1989). Human factors affecting the performance of inspection personnel in nuclear power plants. *Nuclear Plant Journal, 7,* 16-63.

Benight, C. (1992). *An initial test of the competent-incompetent desperation shift (CIDS) theory of sudden cardiac death.* Unpublished doctoral dissertation, School of Education, Stanford University, Stanford CA.

Bergin, C. A. C. (1987). Prosocial development in toddlers: The patterning of mother-infant interactions. In M. E. Ford & D. H. Ford (Eds.), *Humans as self-constructing living systems: Putting the framework to work* (pp. 121-143). Hillsdale, NJ: Lawrence Erlbaum.

Bergin, D. (1989). Student goals for out-of-school learning activities. *Journal of Adolescent Research, 4,* 92-109.

Bergin, D. A. (1987). *Intrinsic motivation for learning, out-of-school activities, and achievement.* Unpublished doctoral dissertation, School of Education, Stanford University, Stanford, CA.

Berlyne, D. E. (1960). *Conflict, arousal, and curiosity.* New York: McGraw-Hill.

Berlyne, D. E. (1971). Arousal and reinforcement. *Nebraska Symposium on Motivation* (Vol. 15, pp. 1-110). Lincoln: University of Nebraska Press.

Bevan, W. (1991). Contemporary psychology: A tour inside the onion. *American Psychologist, 46,* 475-483.

Bhagat, R. S. (1982). Conditions under which stronger job performance-job satisfaction relationships may be observed: A closer look at two situational contingencies. *Academy of Management Journal, 25,* 772-789.

Bishop, J. H. (1989). Why the apathy in American high schools? *Educational Researcher, 18,* 6-10, 42.

Bjorklund, D. F., & Green, B. L. (1992). The adaptive nature of cognitive immaturity. *American Psychologist, 47,* 46-54.

Blankenship, V. (1985). The dynamics of intention. In M. Frese & J. Sabini (Eds.), *Goal directed behavior: The concept of action in psychology* (pp. 161-170). Hillsdale, NJ: Lawrence Erlbaum.

Bolles, R. C. (1975). *Theory of motivation* (2nd ed.). New York: Harper & Row.

Borke, H. (1971). Interpersonal perception of young children: Egocentrism or empathy? *Developmental Psychology, 5,* 263-269.

Bowlby, J. (1969). *Attachment and loss, Vol 1: Attachment.* New York: Basic Books.

Bowlby, J. (1973). *Attachment and loss, Vol 2: Separation, anxiety, and anger.* New York: Basic Books.

Bowlby, J. (1980). *Attachment and loss, Vol 3: Sadness and depression.* New York: Basic Books.

Brehm, J. W. (Ed.) (1966). *A theory of psychological reactance.* New York: Academic Press.

Brehm, J. W. (1972). *Responses to loss of freedom: A theory of psychological reactance.* Morristown, NJ: General Learning Press.

Brehm, J. W., & Cohen, A. R. (1962). *Explorations in cognitive dissonance.* New York: John Wiley.

Brehm, S., & Brehm, J. W. (1981). *Psychological reactance: A theory of freedom and control.* New York: Academic Press.

Brendler, J., Silver, M., Haber, M., & Sargent, J. (1992). *Madness, chaos, and violence: Therapy with families at the brink.* New York: Basic Books.

Brophy, J. (1981). Teacher praise: A functional analysis. *Review of Educational Research, 51,* 5-32.

Brophy, J. (1987). Socializing students' motivation to learn. In M. L. Maehr & D. A. Kleiber (Eds.), *Advances in motivation and achievement, Vol. 5: Enhancing motivation* (pp. 181-210). Greenwich, CT: JAI.

Brown, J. S. (1961). *The motivation of behavior.* New York: McGraw-Hill.

Brown, J. S., & Farber, I. E. (1951). Emotions conceptualized as intervening variables: With suggestions toward a theory of frustration. *Psychological Bulletin, 48,* 465-495.

Buckley, W. (1967). *Sociology and modern systems theory.* Englewood Cliffs, NJ: Prentice-Hall.

Burger, J. M. (1989). Negative reactions to increases in perceived personal control. *Journal of Personality and Social Psychology, 56,* 246-256.

Camp, B., & Bash, M. A. (1980). Developing self-control through training in problem solving: The "Think Aloud" program. In D. P. Rathjen & J. P Foreyt (Eds.), *Social competence: Interventions for children and adults* (pp. 24-53). New York: Pergamon.

Campbell, J. P., & Pritchard, R. D. (1976). Motivation theory in industrial and organizational psychology. In M. D. Dunnette (Ed.), *Handbook of industrial and organizational psychology* (pp. 63-130). Chicago: Rand McNally.

Campion, M. A., & Lord, R. G. (1982). A control system conceptualization of the goal-setting and changing process. *Organizational and Human Performance, 30,* 265-287.

Campos, J. J., & Barrett, K. C. (1984). Toward a new understanding of emotions and their development. In C. E. Izard, J. Kagan & R. B. Zajonc (Eds.), *Emotion, cognition, and behaviors* (pp. 230-252). Cambridge, UK: Cambridge University Press.

Cannon, W. B (1939). *The wisdom of the body* (2nd ed.). New York: Norton.

Cantor, N., & Fleeson, W. (1991). Life tasks and self-regulatory processes. In M. L. Maehr & P. R. Pintrich (Eds.), *Advances in motivation and achievement* (Vol. 7, pp. 327-369). Greenwich, CT: JAI.

Cantor, N., & Langston, C. A. (1989). Ups and downs of life tasks in a life transition. In L. A. Pervin (Ed.), *Goal concepts in personality and social psychology* (pp. 127-167). Hillsdale, NJ: Lawrence Erlbaum.

Cantor, N., & Kihlstrom, J. F. (1987). *Personality and social intelligence.* Englewood Cliffs, NJ: Prentice-Hall.

Cantor, N., Markus, H., Niedenthal, P., & Nurius, P. (1986). On motivation and the self-concept. In R. M. Sorrentino & E. T. Higgins (Eds.), *Handbook of motivation and cognition: Foundations of social behavior* (pp. 96-121). New York: Guilford.

Carver, C. S., & Scheier, M. F. (1981). *Attention and self-regulation: A control-theory approach to human behavior.* New York: Springer Verlag.

Carver, C. S., & Scheier, M. F. (1982). Control theory: A useful conceptual framework for personality-social, clinical, and health psychology. *Psychological Bulletin, 92,* 111-135.

Carver, C. S., & Scheier, M. F. (1985). A control-systems approach to the self-regulation of action. In J. Kuhl & J. Beckmann (Eds.), *Action control: From cognition to behavior* (pp. 237-265). Berlin: Springer Verlag.

Carver, C. S., & Scheier, M. F. (1990). Origins and functions of positive and negative affect: A control-process view. *Psychological Review, 97,* 19-35.

Casarez-Levison, R. (1991). *An empirical investigation of the coping strategies used by victims of crime and their relation to psychological adjustment.* Unpublished doctoral dissertation, School of Education, Stanford University, Stanford, CA.

Case, R. (1985). *Intellectual development: Birth to adulthood.* San Diego, CA: Academic Press.

Cattell, R. B. (1957). *Personality and motivation: Structure and measurement.* New York: Harcourt Brace & World.

Chapman, M., Skinner, E. A., & Baltes, P. B. (1990). Interpreting correlations between children's perceived control and cognitive performance: Control, agency, or means-ends beliefs? *Developmental Psychology, 26,* 246-253.

Chase, C., & Ford, M. E. (1992). *Happy and unhappy adolescents: Differences in goals and personal agency beliefs.* Paper presented at the annual meeting of the American Educational Research Association, San Francisco, CA.

Chesney, M. A., & Rosenman, R. H. (Eds.). (1985). *Anger and hostility in cardiovascular and behavioral disorders.* Washington, DC: Hemisphere.

Cofer, C. N. (1959). Motivation. *Annual Review of Psychology, 10,* 173-202.

Cofer, C. N., & Appley, M. H. (1964). *Motivation: Theory and research.* New York: John Wiley.

Cohen, S., & Wills, T. A. (1985). Stress, social support, and the buffering hypothesis. *Psychological Bulletin, 98,* 310-357.

Collins, J. (1988, September 18). How to pass your passion on. *San Jose Mercury News,* pp. 1-2PC.

Conger, J. A. (1989). Leadership: The art of empowering others. *The Academy of Management Executive, 3,* 17-24.

Connell, J. P. (1985). A new multidimensional measure of children's perceptions of control. *Child Development, 56,* 1018-1041.

Connell, J. P., & Wellborn, J. G. (1990). Competence, autonomy and relatedness: A motivational analysis of self-system processes. In M. Gunnar & L. A. Sroufe (Eds.), *Minnesota Symposium on Child Psychology* (Vol. 23, pp. 43-77). Hillsdale, NJ: Lawrence Erlbaum.

Coopersmith, S. (1967). *The antecedents of self-esteem.* San Francisco: Freeman.

Corcoran, K. J. (1991). Efficacy, "skills," reinforcement, and choice behavior. *American Psychologist, 46,* 155-157.

Covey, S. R. (1990). *The 7 habits of highly effective people.* New York: Simon & Schuster.

Covington, M. V. (1984a). The self-worth theory of achievement motivation: Findings and implications. *The Elementary School Journal, 85,* 5-20.

Covington, M. V. (1984b). The motive for self-worth. In R. E. Ames & C. Ames (Eds.), *Research on motivation in education, Vol 1: Student motivation* (pp. 77-113). New York: Academic Press.

Covington, M. V. (1991). *Motivation, self-worth, and the myth of intensification.* Paper presented at the annual meeting of the American Psychological Association, San Francisco, CA.

Covington, M. V. (1992). *Emotion, motivation and cognition in school achievement.* New York: Cambridge University Press.

Covington, M. V., & Beery, R. (1976). *Self-worth and school learning.* New York: Holt, Rinehart & Winston.

Covington, M. V., & Omelich, C. L. (1979). Are causal attributions causal? A path analysis of the cognitive model of achievement motivation. *Journal of Personality and Social Psychology, 37,* 1487-1504.

Cross, C. T. (1990). National goals: Four priorities for educational researchers. *Educational Researcher, 19,* 21-24.

Csikszentmihalyi, M. (1975). *Beyond boredom and anxiety.* San Francisco, CA: Jossey-Bass.

Csikszentmihalyi, M. (1978). Intrinsic rewards and emergent motivation. In M. R. Lepper & D. Greene (Eds.), *The hidden costs of reward* (pp. 205-216). Hillsdale, NJ: Lawrence Erlbaum.

Csikszentmihalyi, M. (1990). *Flow: The psychology of optimal experience.* New York: Harper & Row.
Csikszentmihalyi, M., & Csikszentmihalyi, I. (Eds.) (1988). *Optimal experience: Psychological studies of flow in consciousness.* New York: Cambridge University Press.
Danner, F. W., & Lonky, E. (1981). A cognitive-developmental approach to the effects of rewards on intrinsic motivation. *Child Development, 52,* 1043-1052.
deCharms, R. (1968). *Personal causation.* New York: Academic Press.
deCharms, R. (1976). *Enhancing motivation: Change in the classroom.* New York: Irvington.
deCharms, R. (1984). Motivation enhancement in educational settings. In R. E. Ames & C. Ames (Eds.), *Research on motivation in education, Vol 1: Student motivation* (pp. 275-310). Orlando, FL: Academic Press.
deCharms, R. (1987). The burden of motivation. In M. L. Maehr & D. A. Kleiber (Eds.), *Advances in motivation and achievement, Vol. 5: Enhancing motivation* (pp. 1-21). Greenwich, CT: JAI.
Deci, E. L. (1975). *Intrinsic motivation.* New York: Plenum.
Deci, E. L. (1980). *The psychology of self-determination.* Lexington, MA: Lexington.
Deci, E. L., & Ryan, R. M. (1985). *Intrinsic motivation and self-determination in human behavior.* New York: Plenum.
Deci, E. L., & Ryan, R. M. (1987). The support of autonomy and the control of behavior. *Journal of Personality and Social Psychology, 53,* 1024-1037.
Deci, E. L., & Ryan, R. M. (1991). A motivational approach to self: Integration in personality. In R. Dienstbier (Ed.), *Nebraska symposium on motivation, Vol. 38: Perspectives on motivation* (pp. 237-288). Lincoln: University of Nebraska Press.
Deci, E. L., Vallerand, R. J., Pelletier, L. G., & Ryan, R. M. (1991). Motivation and education: The self-determination perspective. *Educational Psychologist, 26,* 325-346.
Dember, W. N., & Earl, R. W. (1957). Analysis of exploratory, manipulatory, and curiosity behaviors. *Psychological Review, 64,* 91-96.
Demetriou, A., & Efklides, A. (1981). The structure of formal operations: The ideal of the whole and the reality of the parts. In J. A. Meacham & N. R. Santilli (Eds.), *Social development in youth: Structure and content* (pp. 20-46). Basel, Switzerland: Karger.
Devaney, K. (Ed.) (1990). Back to school basics. *The Holmes Group forum, 5*(1), 1, 3.
Dewsbury, D. A. (1978). *Comparative animal behavior.* New York: McGraw-Hill.
Dodge, K. A. (1980). Social cognition and children's aggressive behavior. *Child Development, 51,* 162-170.
Dodge, K. A., Asher, S. R., & Parkhurst, J. T. (1989). Social life as a goal-coordination task. In C. Ames & R. Ames (Eds.), *Research on motivation in education, Vol. 3: Goals and cognitions* (pp. 107-135). San Diego, CA: Academic Press.
Dodge, K. A., & Frame, C. L. (1982). Social cognitive biases and deficits in aggressive boys. *Child Development, 53,* 620-635.
Dodge, K. A., & Somberg, D. (1987). Hostile attributional biases among aggressive boys are exacerbated under conditions of threat to the self. *Child Development, 58,* 213-224.
Dollard, J., Miller, N. E., Doob, L. W., Mowrer, O. H., & Sears, R. R. (1939). *Frustration and aggression.* New Haven, CT: Yale University Press.
Dumaine, B. (May 7, 1990). Who needs a boss? *Fortune,* pp. 52-60.
Dweck, C. S. (1986). Motivational processes affecting learning. *American Psychologist, 41,* 1040-1048.
Dweck, C. S., & Leggett, E. L. (1988). A social-cognitive approach to motivation and personality. *Psychological Review, 95,* 256-273.

Earley, P. C., Northcraft, G. B., Lee, C., & Lituchy, T. R. (1990). Impact of process and outcome feedback on the relation of goal setting to task performance. *Academy of Management Journal, 33,* 87-105.

Eccles (Parsons), J. S., Adler, T., & Meece, J. (1984). Sex diffferences in achievement: A test of alternative theories. *Journal of Personality and Social Psychology, 46,* 26-43.

Eccles, J. S., & Midgley, C. (1989). Stage-environment fit: Developmentally appropriate classrooms for young adolescents. In C. Ames & R. Ames (Eds.), *Research on motivation in education, Vol. 3: Goals and cognitions* (pp. 139-186). San Diego, CA: Academic Press.

Edmonds, R. (1986). Characteristics of effective schools. In U. Neisser (Ed.), *The school achievement of minority children* (pp. 93-104). Hillsdale, NJ: Lawrence Erlbaum.

Ekman, P. (1972). Universals and cultural differences in facial expressions of emotion. In J. K. Cole (Ed.), *Nebraska symposium on motivation* (pp. 207-283). Lincoln: University of Nebraska Press.

Ekman, P., & Friesen, W. V. (1978). *Facial action coding system.* Palo Alto, CA: Consulting Psychologist Press.

Ekman, P., Levenson, R. W., & Friesen, W. V. (1983). Autonomic nervous system activity distinguishes among emotions. *Science, 221,* 1208-1210.

Elliott, E. S., & Dweck, C. S. (1988). Goals: An approach to motivation and achievement. *Journal of Personality and Social Psychology, 54,* 5-12.

Ellis, A. W. (Ed.) (1982). *Normality and pathology in cognitive functions.* New York: Academic Press.

Emmons, R. A. (1986). Personal strivings: An approach to personality and subjective well-being. *Journal of Personality and Social Psychology, 51,* 1058-1068.

Emmons, R. A. (1989). The personal striving approach to personality. In L. A. Pervin (Ed.), *Goal concepts in personality and social psychology* (pp. 87-126). Hillsdale, NJ: Lawrence Erlbaum.

Erez, M. (1977). Feedback: A necessary condition for the goal setting-performance relationship. *Journal of Applied Psychology, 62,* 624-627.

Erickson, E. H. (1963). *Childhood and society* (rev. ed.). New York: Norton.

Estrada, P. (1987). *Empathy and prosocial behavior in adolescence.* Unpublished doctoral dissertation, School of Education, Stanford University, Stanford, CA.

Farnham, A. (1989, December 4). The trust gap. *Fortune,* pp. 56-78.

Feather, N. T. (Ed.) (1982). *Expectations and actions: Expectancy-value models in psychology.* Hillsdale, NJ: Lawrence Erlbaum.

Festinger, L. (1957). *A theory of cognitive dissonance.* Evanston, IL: Row, Peterson.

Festinger, L. (Ed.) (1964). *Conflict, decision, and dissonance.* Stanford, CA: Stanford University Press.

Fishbein, M., & Ajzen, I. (1975). *Belief, attitude, intention, and behavior: An introduction to theory and research.* Reading, MA: Addison-Wesley.

Fiske, S. T., & Taylor, S. E. (1984). *Social cognition.* Reading, MA: Addison-Wesley.

Ford, D. H. (1987). *Humans as self-constructing living systems: A developmental perspective on behavior and personality.* Hillsdale, NJ: Lawrence Erlbaum.

Ford, D. H., & Lerner, R. M. (1992). *Developmental systems theory: An integrative approach.* Newbury Park, CA: Sage.

Ford, D. H., & Urban, H.B. (1963). *Systems of psychotherapy.* New York: John Wiley.

Ford, D. H., & Urban, H.B. (1967). Psychotherapy. *Annual Review of Psychology, 18,* 333-372.

Ford, M. E. (1979). The construct validity of egocentrism. *Psychological Bulletin, 86,* 1169-1188.

Ford, M. E. (1981). *Androgyny as self-assertion and integration: Implications for psychological and social competence.* Unpublished manuscript, Stanford University, School of Education, Stanford, CA.

Ford, M. E. (1982). Social cognition and social competence in adolescence. *Developmental Psychology, 18,* 323-340.

Ford, M. E. (1984). Linking social-cognitive processes with effective social behavior: A living systems approach. In P. C. Kendall (Ed.), *Advances in cognitive-behavioral research and therapy, Vol. 3* (pp. 167-211). New York: Academic Press.

Ford, M. E. (1985). The concept of competence: Themes and variations. In H. A. Marlowe & R. B. Weinberg (Eds.), *Competence development* (pp. 3-49). Springfield, IL: Charles C Thomas.

Ford, M. E. (1986). A living systems conceptualization of social intelligence: Outcomes, processes, and developmental change. In R. J. Sternberg (Ed.), *Advances in the psychology of human intelligence* (Vol. 3, pp. 119-171). Hillsdale, NJ: Lawrence Erlbaum.

Ford, M. E. (1987a). Overview of the heuristic utility of the living systems framework for guiding research and professional activities. In M. E. Ford & D. H. Ford (Eds.), *Humans as self-constructing living systems: Putting the framework to work* (pp. 377-393). Hillsdale, NJ: Lawrence Erlbaum.

Ford, M. E. (1987b). Processes contributing to adolescent social competence. In M. E. Ford & D. H. Ford (Eds.), *Humans as self-constructing living systems: Putting the framework to work* (pp. 199-233). Hillsdale, NJ: Lawrence Erlbaum.

Ford, M. E. (in press). A living systems approach to the integration of personality and intelligence. In R. J. Sternberg & P. Ruzgis (Eds.), *Intelligence and personality.* New York: Cambridge University Press.

Ford, M. E., Burt, R. E., & Bergin, C. C. (1984). *The role of goal setting and goal importance in adolescent social competence.* Paper presented at the annual meeting of the American Educational Research Association, New Orleans.

Ford, M. E., & Chase, C. (1991). *Manual: Assessment of Personal Agency Beliefs.* School of Education, Stanford University, Stanford, CA.

Ford, M. E., Chase, C., Love, R., Pollina, S., & Ito, S. (1992). *Qualities associated with caring behavior in adolescence: Goals, emotions, and personal agency beliefs.* Submitted for publication.

Ford, M. E., & Ford, D. H. (Eds.) (1987). *Humans as self-constructing living systems: Putting the framework to work.* Hillsdale, NJ: Lawrence Erlbaum.

Ford, M. E., & Nichols, C. W. (1987). A taxonomy of human goals and some possible applications. In M. E. Ford & D. H. Ford (Eds.), *Humans as self-constructing living systems: Putting the framework to work* (pp. 289-311). Hillsdale, NJ: Lawrence Erlbaum.

Ford, M. E., & Nichols, C. W. (1991). Using goal assessments to identify motivational patterns and facilitate behavioral regulation and achievement. In M. L. Maehr & P. R. Pintrich (Eds.), *Advances in motivation and achievement* (Vol. 7, pp. 51-84). Greenwich, CT: JAI.

Ford, M. E., & Nichols, C. W. (1992). *Manual: Assessment of Personal Goals.* Palo Alto, CA: Consulting Psychologist Press.

Ford, M. E., & Thompson, R. A. (1985). Perceptions of personal agency and infant attachment: Toward a life-span perspective on competence development. *International Journal of Behavioral Development, 8,* 377-406.

Ford, M. E., Wentzel, K. R., Siesfeld, G. A., Wood, D., & Feldman, L. (1986). *Adolescent decision making in real-life situations involving socially responsible and irresponsible choices.* Paper presented at the annual meeting of the American Educational Research Association, San Francisco, CA.

Ford, M. E., Wentzel, K. R., Wood, D., Stevens, E., & Siesfeld, G. A. (1989). Processes associated with integrative social competence: Emotional and contextual influences on adolescent social responsibility. *Journal of Adolescent Research, 4,* 405-425.

Franken, R. E. (1988). *Human motivation* (2nd ed.). Pacific Grove, CA: Brooks/Cole.

Freud, S. (1901/1951). *The psychopathology of everyday life.* New York: New American Library.

Freud, S. (1915/1934). *A general introduction to psychoanalysis.* New York: Washington Square Press.

Freud, S. (1915/1957). Instincts and their vicissitudes. In *The standard edition of the complete psychological works of Sigmund Freud* (Vol. 14, pp. 117-140). London: Hogarth.

Freud, S. (1920/1948). *Beyond the pleasure principle.* London: Hogarth.

Freud, S. (1923/1947). *The ego and the id.* London: Hogarth.

Freud, S. (1933/1964). New introductory lectures on psycho-analysis. In *The standard edition of the complete psychological works of Sigmund Freud* (Vol. 22, pp. 3-182). London: Hogarth.

Frey, K. S., & Ruble, D. N. (1990). Strategies for comparative evaluation: Maintaining a sense of competence across the life span. In R. J. Sternberg & J. Kolligian, Jr. (Eds.), *Competence considered* (pp. 167-189). New Haven, CT: Yale University Press.

Frijda, N. H. (1988). The laws of emotion. *American Psychologist, 43,* 349-358.

Garland, H., & Adkinson, J. H. (1987). Standards, persuasion, and performance. *Group and Organizational Studies, 12,* 208-220.

Geen, R. G., Beatty, W. W., & Arkin, R. M. (Eds.) (1984). *Human motivation: Physiological, behavioral, and social approaches.* Boston: Allyn & Bacon.

Gerlach-Downie, S. (1990). *Worrying about the child care worker: A study of child care workers' job satisfaction and intent to quit.* Unpublished doctoral dissertation, Stanford University, School of Education, Stanford, CA.

Goldstein, A. P., & Kanfer, F. H. (Eds.) (1979). *Maximizing treatment gains: Transfer enhancement in psychotherapy.* New York: Academic Press.

Goodlad, J. (1983). *A place called school.* New York: McGraw-Hill.

Graen, G. (1969). Instrumentality theory of work motivation: Some experimental results and suggested modification. *Journal of Applied Psychology, 53,* 1-25.

Graham, S., & Barker, G. P. (1990). The down side of help: An attributional-developmental analysis of helping behavior as a low-ability cue. *Journal of Educational Psychology, 82,* 7-14.

Gregory, W. L. (1981). Expectancies for controllability, performance attributions, and behavior. In H. M. Lefcourt (Ed.), *Research with the locus of control construct, Vol. 1: Assessment methods* (pp. 27-118). New York: Academic Press.

Gurin, P., & Brim, O. G., Jr. (1984). Change of self in adulthood: The example of sense of control. In P. B. Baltes & O. G. Brim, Jr. (Eds.), *Life-span development and behavior* (Vol. 6, pp. 281-334). New York: Academic Press.

Hackman, J. R., & Oldham, G. R. (1976). Motivation through the design of work: Test of a theory. *Organizational Behavior and Human Performance, 16,* 250-279.

Halisch, F., & Kuhl, J. (Eds.) (1986). *Motivation, intention, and volition.* New York: Springer Verlag.

Harackiewicz, J. M., & Sansone, C. (1991). Goals and intrinsic motivation: You *can* get there from here. In M. L. Maehr & P. R. Pintrich (Eds.), *Advances in motivation achievement* (Vol. 7, pp. 21-49). Greenwich, CT: JAI.

Harter, S. (1978). Effectance motivation reconsidered: Toward a developmental model. *Human Development, 21,* 34-64.

Harter, S. (1981a). A new self-report scale of intrinsic versus extrinsic orientation in the classroom: Motivational and informational components. *Developmental Psychology, 17,* 300-312.

Harter, S. (1981b). A model of intrinsic mastery motivation in children: Individual differences in developmental change. In W. A. Collins (Ed.), *Minnesota symposium on child psychology* (Vol. 14, pp. 215-255). Hillsdale, NJ: Lawrence Erlbaum.

Harter, S. (1982). The perceived competence scale for children. *Child Development, 53,* 87-97.

Harter, S. (1983). Developmental perspectives on the self-system. In E. M. Hetherington (Ed.) & P. H. Mussen (Series Ed.), *Handbook of child psychology, Vol. 4: Socialization, personality, and social development* (4th ed., pp. 275-385). New York: John Wiley.

Harter, S. (1990). Causes, correlates, and the functional role of global self-worth: A life-span perspective. In R. J. Sternberg & J. Kolligian, Jr. (Eds.), *Competence considered* (pp. 67-97). New Haven, CT: Yale University Press.

Hartmann, H. (1958). *Ego psychology and the problem of adaptation.* New York: International Universities Press.

Hebb, D. O. (1949). *The organization of behavior.* New York: John Wiley.

Hebb, D. O. (1955). Drives and the C.N.S. (conceptual nervous system). *Psychological Review, 62,* 243-254.

Heckhausen, H. (1991). *Motivation and action* (2nd ed.). New York: Springer Verlag.

Heckhausen, H., & Kuhl, J. (1985). From wishes to action: The dead ends and short cuts on the long way to action. In M. Frese & J. Sabini (Eds.), *Goal-directed behavior: The concept of action in psychology* (pp. 134-159). Hillsdale, NJ: Lawrence Erlbaum.

Herzberg, F. (1966). *Work and the nature of man.* Cleveland, OH: World.

Herzberg, F., Mausner, B., & Snyderman, B. (1959). *The motivation to work.* New York: John Wiley.

Higgins, E. T., Strauman, T., & Klein, R. (1986). Standards and the process of self-evaluation: Multiple affects from multiple stages. In R. M. Sorrentino & E. T. Higgins (Eds.), *Handbook of motivation and cognition: Foundations of social behavior* (pp. 23-63). New York: Guilford.

Hilgard, E. R., & Atkinson, R. C. (1967). *Introduction to psychology* (4th ed.). New York: Harcourt Brace & World.

Hoffman, L. (1981). *Foundations of family therapy: A conceptual framework for systems change.* New York: Basic Books.

Hoffman, M. L. (1982). Development of prosocial motivation: Empathy and guilt. In N. Eisenberg (Ed.), *The development of prosocial behavior* (pp. 281-313). New York: Academic Press.

Hoffman, M. L. (1986). Affect, cognition, and motivation. In R. M. Sorrentino & E. T. Higgins (Eds.), *Handbook of motivation and cognition: Foundations of social behavior* (pp. 244-280). New York: Guilford.

Hollenbeck, J. R. (1989). Control theory and the perception of work environment: The effects of focus of attention on affective and behavioral reactions to work. *Organizational Behavior and Human Decision Processes, 43,* 406-430.

Hollenbeck, J. R., Williams, C. R., & Klein, H. J. (1989). An empirical examination of the antecedents of commitment to difficult goals. *Journal of Applied Psychology, 74,* 18-23.

Horney, K. (1945). *Our inner conflicts.* New York: Norton.

Holt, E. B. (1931). *Animal drive and the learning process, an essay toward radical empiricism* (Vol. 1). New York: Holt.

Hull, C. L. (1931). Goal attraction and directing ideas conceived as habit phenomena. *Psychological Review, 38,* 487-506.

Hull, C. L. (1943). *Principles of behavior.* New York: Appleton-Century-Crofts.

Hull, C. L. (1951). *Essentials of behavior.* New Haven, CT: Yale University Press.

Hull, C. L. (1952). *A behavior system.* New Haven, CT: Yale University Press.

Hunt, J. McV. (1965). Intrinsic motivation and its role in psychological development. In D. Levine (Ed.), *Nebraska Symposium on Motivation* (Vol. 3, pp. 189-282). Lincoln: University of Nebraska Press.

Huseman, R. C., Hatfield, J. D., & Miles, E. W. (1987). A new perspective on equity theory: The equity sensitivity construct. *Academy of Management Review, 12,* 222-234.

Hyland, M. E. (1988). Motivational control theory: An integrative framework. *Journal of Personality and Social Psychology, 55,* 642-651.

Iaffaldano, M. T., & Muchinsky, P. M. (1985). Job satisfaction and job performance: A meta-analysis. *Psychological Bulletin, 97,* 251-273.

Imai, M. (1986). *Kaizen: The key to Japan's economic success.* New York: Random House.

Izard, C. E. (1977). *Human emotions.* New York: Plenum.

Izard, C. E. (1979). Emotions as motivations: An evolutionary-developmental perspective. In R. A. Dienstbier (Ed.), *Nebraska symposium on motivation* (pp. 163-200). Lincoln: University of Nebraska Press.

Izard, C. E. (1991). *The psychology of emotions.* New York: Plenum.

James, W. (1892). *Psychology: A briefer course.* New York: Holt.

Jantsch, E. (1980). *The self-organizing universe.* Oxford, UK: Pergamon.

Johnson, D. W., & Johnson, R. T. (1975). *Learning together and alone.* Englewood Cliffs, NJ: Prentice-Hall.

Johnson, D. W., Maruyama, G., Johnson, R., Nelson, D., & Skon, L. (1982). Effects of cooperative, competitive, and individualistic goal structures on achievement: A meta-analysis. *Psychological Bulletin, 89,* 47-62.

Kagan, D. M. (1990). How schools alienate students at risk: A model for examining proximal classroom variables. *Educational Psychologist, 25,* 105-125.

Kanfer, R., & Kanfer, F. H. (1991). Goals and self-regulation: Applications of theory to work settings. In M. L. Maehr & P. R. Pintrich (Eds.), *Advances in motivation and achievement* (Vol. 7, pp. 287-326). Greenwich, CT: JAI.

Karimi, S. S. (1988). *Factors that motivate and influence excellence in human performance: A case study of inspection personnel in the complex context of nuclear power plants.* Unpublished doctoral dissertation, School of Education, Stanford University, Stanford, CA.

Katzell, R. A., & Thompson, D. E. (1990). Work motivation: Theory and practice. *American Psychologist, 45,* 144-153.

Kirsch, I. (1982). Efficacy expectations or response predictions: The meaning of efficacy ratings as a function of task characteristics. *Journal of Social and Personality Psychology, 42,* 132-136.

Kirsch, I. (1986). Early research on self-efficacy: What we already knew without knowing we knew. *Journal of Social and Cognitive Psychology, 4,* 339-358.

Klein, H. J. (1989). An integrated control theory model of work motivation. *Academy of Management Review, 14,* 150-172.

Klein, J. I. (1990). Feasibility theory: A resource-munificence model of work motivation and behavior. *Academy of Management Review, 15,* 646-665.

Kleinginna, P. R., Jr., & Kleinginna, A. M. (1981). A categorized list of motivation definitions, with a suggestion for a consensual definition. *Motivation and Emotion, 5,* 263-291.

Klinger, E. (1975). Consequences of commitment to and disengagement from incentives. *Psychological Review, 82,* 1-25.

Klinger, E. (1977). *Meaning and void: Inner experience and the incentives in people's lives.* Minneapolis: University of Minnesota Press.

Klinger, E. (1985). Missing links in action theory. In M. Frese & J. Sabini (Eds.), *Goal directed behavior: The concept of action in psychology* (pp. 311-319). Hillsdale, NJ: Lawrence Erlbaum.

Klinger, E. (1987). The interview questionnaire technique: Reliability and validity of a mixed idiographic-nomothetic measure of motivation. In J. N. Butcher & C. D. Spielberger (Eds.), *Advances in personality assessment* (Vol. 6, pp. 31-48). Hillsdale, NJ: Lawrence Erlbaum.

Kobasa, S. C. (1979). Stressful life events, personality, and health: An inquiry into hardiness. *Journal of Personality and Social Psychology, 37,* 1-11.

Koestler, A. (1967). *The ghost in the machine.* New York: Macmillan.

Koestler, A. (1978). *Janus.* New York: Random House.

Kolligian, J., Jr. (1990). Perceived fraudulence as a dimension of perceived incompetence. In R. J. Sternberg & J. Kolligian, Jr. (Eds.), *Competence considered* (pp. 261-285). New Haven, CT: Yale University Press.

Kolligian, J., Jr., & Sternberg, R. J. (1990). Preface. In R. J. Sternberg & J. Kolligian, Jr. (Eds.), *Competence considered* (pp. ix-xv). New Haven, CT: Yale University Press.

Kopelman, R. E. (1977). Across-individual, within-individual, and return on effort versions of expectancy theory. *Decision Sciences, 8,* 651-662.

Kopelman, R. E., & Thompson, P. H. (1976). Boundary conditions for expectancy theory predictions of work motivation and job performance. *Academy of Management Journal, 19,* 237-258.

Krug, S. E. (1989). Leadership and learning: A measurement-based approach for analyzing school effectiveness and developing effective school leaders. In M. L. Maehr & C. Ames (Eds.), *Advances in motivation and achievement, Vol. 6: Motivation enhancing environments* (pp. 249-277). Greenwich, CT: JAI.

Krumboltz, J. D., Ford, M. E., Nichols, C. W., & Wentzel, K. R. (1987). The goals of education. In R. C. Calfee (Ed.), *The study of Stanford the schools: Views from the inside, Part II.* Stanford, CA: Stanford University.

Kuhl, J. (1981). Motivational and functional helplessness: The moderating effect of state versus action orientation. *Journal of Personality and Social Psychology, 40,* 155-170.

Kuhl, J. (1984). Volitional aspects of achievement motivation and learned helplessness: Toward a comprehensive theory of action control. In B. A. Maher (Ed.), *Progress in experimental personality research* (Vol. 13, pp. 99-170). New York: Academic Press.

Kuhl, J. (1985). Volitional mediators of cognition-behavior consistency: Self-regulatory processes and action versus state orientation. In J. Kuhl & J. Beckmann (Eds.). *Action control: From cognition to behavior* (pp. 101-128). Berlin: Springer Verlag.

Kuhl, J. (1986). Motivation and information processing: A new look at decision making, dynamic change, and action control. In R. M. Sorrentino & E. T. Higgins (Eds.), *Handbook of motivation and cognition: Foundations of social behavior* (pp. 404-434). New York: Guilford.

Kuhl, J., & Beckmann, J. (1985) (Eds.) *Action control: From cognition to behavior.* Berlin: Springer Verlag.

Kuhl, J., & Beckmann, J. (in press). *Volition and personality: Action and state orientation.* Toronto: Hogrefe.

Kuhl, J., & Blankenship, V. (1979). The dynamic theory of achievement motivation: From episodic to dynamic thinking. *Psychological Review, 86,* 141-151.

Kunda, Z., & Schwartz, S. H. (1983). Undermining intrinsic moral motivation: External reward and self-presentation. *Journal of Personality and Social Psychology, 45,* 763-771.

Labich, K. (1988, October 24). The seven keys to business leadership. *Fortune,* pp. 58-66.

Laird, J. D. (1974). Self-attribution of emotion: The effects of expressive behavior on the quality of emotional experience. *Journal of Personality and Social Psychology, 29,* 475-486.

Landy, F. J., & Becker, L. J. (1987). Motivation theory reconsidered. *Research in Organizational Behavior, 9,* 1-38.

Langer, E. J. (1989). *Mindfulness.* Reading, MA: Addison-Wesley.

Langer, E. J., & Park, K. (1990). Incompetence: A conceptual reconsideration. In R. J. Sternberg & J. Kolligian, Jr. (Eds.), *Competence considered* (pp. 149-166). New Haven, CT: Yale University Press.

Laszlo, E. (1972). *The systems view of the world.* New York: George Braziller.

Latham, G. P., & Lee, T. W. (1986). Goal setting. In E. A. Locke (Ed.), *Generalizing from laboratory to field settings* (pp. 101-117). Lexington, MA: Lexington.

Latham, G. P., & Yukl, G. A. (1975). A review of research on the application of goal setting in organizations. *Academy of Management Journal, 18,* 824-845.

Lawler, E. E. (1971). *Pay and organizational effectiveness: A psychological view.* New York: McGraw-Hill.

Lawler, E. E., & Porter, L. W. (1967). The effect of performance on job satisfaction. *Industrial Relations, 7,* 20-28.

Lazarus, R. S. (1982). Thoughts on the relations between emotions and cognitions. *American Psychologist, 37,* 1019-1024.

Lazarus, R. S. (1984). On the primacy of cognition. *American Psychologist, 39,* 124-129.

Lazarus, R. S. (1991a). Progress on a cognitive-motivational-relational theory of emotion. *American Psychologist, 46,* 819-834.

Lazarus, R. S. (1991b). *Emotion and adaptation.* New York: Oxford University Press.

Lazarus, R. S. (1991c). Cognition and motivation in emotion. *American Psychologist, 46,* 352-367.

Lazarus, R. S., & Folkman, S. (1984). *Stress, appraisal and coping.* New York: Springer.

Lecky, P. (1945). *Self-consistency: A theory of personality.* New York: Island.

Lee, S., Ichikawa, V., & Stevenson, H. W. (1987). Beliefs and achievement in mathematics and reading: A cross-national study of Chinese, Japanese, and American children and their mothers. In M. L. Maehr & D. A. Kleiber (Eds.). *Advances in motivation and achievement, Vol. 5: Enhancing motivation* (pp. 149-179). Greenwich, CT: JAI.

Lee, T. W., Locke, E. A., & Latham, G. P. (1989). Goal setting theory and job performance. In L. A. Pervin (Ed.), *Goal concepts in personality and social psychology* (pp. 291-326). Hillsdale, NJ: Lawrence Erlbaum.

Lefcourt, H. M. (1976). *Locus of control.* Hillsdale, NJ: Lawrence Erlbaum.

Lefcourt, H. M. (Ed.) (1981). *Research with the locus of control construct, Vol 1: Assessment methods.* New York: Academic Press.

Lefrancois, G. R. (1980). *Psychology.* Belmont, CA: Wadsworth.

Lepper, M. R. (1981). Intrinsic and extrinsic motivation in children: Detrimental effects of superfluous social controls. In W. A. Collins (Ed.), *Aspects of the development of competence: The Minnesota symposium on child psychology* (Vol. 14, pp. 155-214). Hillsdale, NJ: Lawrence Erlbaum.

Lepper, M. R., & Greene, D. (Eds.) (1978). *The hidden costs of reward*. Hillsdale, NJ: Lawrence Erlbaum.

Lerner, R. M. (1982). Children and adolescents as producers of their own development. *Developmental Review, 2*, 342-370.

Lerner, R. M. (1984). *On the nature of human plasticity*. New York: Cambridge University Press.

Levenson, H. (1981). Differentiating among internality, powerful others, and chance. In H. M. Lefcourt (Ed.), *Research with the locus of control construct, Vol 1: Assessment methods* (pp. 15-63). New York: Academic Press.

Levin, H. M. (1987). Accelerated schools for disadvantaged students. *Educational Leadership, 44*, 19-21.

Levin, H. M. (1991). Accelerated visions. *Accelerated schools, 1*(2), 2-3.

Lewin, K. (1935). *A dynamic theory of personality*. New York: McGraw-Hill.

Lewin, K. (1936). *Principles of topological psychology*. New York: McGraw-Hill.

Lewin, K. (1951). *Field theory in social science*. New York: Harper.

Lewin, K., Dembo, T., Festinger, L., & Sears, P. S. (1944). Level of aspiration. In J. McV. Hunt (Ed.), *Personality and the behavioral disorders* (Vol. 1, pp. 333-378). New York: Ronald.

Little, B. R. (1983). Personal projects: A rationale and method for investigation. *Environment and Behavior, 15*, 273-309.

Little, B. R. (1989). Personal projects analysis: Trivial pursuits, magnificent obsessions and the search for coherence. In D. M. Buss & N. Cantor (Eds.), *Personality psychology: Recent trends and emerging directions* (pp. 15-31). New York: Springer Verlag.

Locke, E. A. (1968). Toward a theory of task motivation and incentives. *Organizational Behavior and Human Performance, 3*, 157-189.

Locke, E. A., Bryan, J. F., & Kendall, L. M. (1968). Goals and intentions as mediators of the effects of monetary incentives on behavior. *Journal of Applied Psychology, 52*, 104-121.

Locke, E. A., Frederick, E., Lee, C., & Bobko, P. (1984). Effects of self-efficacy, goals, and task strategies on task performance. *Journal of Applied Psychology, 69*, 241-251.

Locke, E. A., & Latham, G. P. (1984). *Goal setting: A motivational technique that works*. Englewood Cliffs, NJ: Prentice-Hall.

Locke, E. A., & Latham, G. P. (Eds.) (1990a). *A theory of goal setting and task performance*. Englewood Cliffs, NJ: Prentice-Hall.

Locke, E. A., & Latham, G. P. (1990b). Work motivation and satisfaction: Light at the end of the tunnel. *Psychological Science, 1*, 240-246.

Locke, E. A., Latham, G. P., & Erez, M. (1988). The determinants of goal commitment. *Academy of Management Review, 13*, 23-39.

Locke, E. A., Shaw, K. N., Saari, L. M., & Latham, G. P. (1981). Goal setting and task performance: 1969-1980. *Psychological Bulletin, 89*, 125-152.

Lord, R. G., & Hanges, P. J. (1987). A control system model of organizational motivation: Theoretical development and applied implications. *Behavioral Science, 32*, 161-178.

Lord, R. G., & Kernan, M. C. (1989). Application of control theory to work settings. In W. A. Herschberger (Ed.), *Volitional action* (pp. 493-514). Amsterdam: Elsevier.

Loveland, K. K., & Olley, J. G. (1979). The effects of external reward on interest and quality of task performance in children of high and low intrinsic motivation. *Child Development, 50*, 1207-1210.

Low, K. G. (1991). *Psychosocial variables, Type A behavior pattern, and coronary heart disease in women*. Unpublished doctoral dissertation, School of Education, Stanford University, Stanford, CA.

Maehr, M. L. (1974). Culture and achievement motivation. *American Psychologist, 29*, 887-896.

Maehr, M. L. (1984). Meaning and motivation: Toward a theory of personal investment. In R. Ames & C. Ames (Eds.), *Research on motivation in education, Vol 1: Student motivation* (pp. 115-144). New York: Academic Press.

Maehr, M. L. (1987). Managing organizational culture to enhance motivation. In M. L. Maehr & D. A. Kleiber (Eds.), *Advances in motivation and achievement, Vol. 5: Enhancing motivation* (pp. 287-320). Greenwich, CT: JAI.

Maehr, M. L. (1989). Thoughts about motivation. In C. Ames & R. Ames (Eds.), *Research on motivation in education, Vol. 3: Goals and cognitions* (pp. 299-315). San Diego, CA: Academic Press.

Maehr, M. L., & Ames, C. (Eds.) (1989). *Advances in motivation and achievement, Vol. 6: Motivation enhancing environments*. Greenwich, CT: JAI.

Maehr, M. L., & Braskamp, L. (1986). *The motivation factor: A theory of personal investment*. Lexington, MA: Lexington.

Maehr, M. L., & Fyans, L. J., Jr. (1989). School culture, motivation, and achievement. In M. L. Maehr & C. Ames (Eds.), *Advances in motivation and achievement, Vol. 6: Motivation enhancing environments* (pp. 215-247). Greenwich, CT: JAI.

Maehr, M. L., & Kleiber, D. A. (Eds.) (1987). *Advances in motivation and achievement, Vol. 5: Enhancing motivation*. Greenwich, CT: JAI.

Maehr, M. L., & Midgley, C. (1991). Enhancing student motivation: A schoolwide approach. *Educational Psychologist, 26*, 399-427.

Maehr, M. L., & Pintrich, P. (Eds.) (1991). *Advances in motivation and achievement, Vol. 7: Goals and self-regulatory processes*. Greenwich, CT: JAI.

Malmo, R. B. (1959). Activation: A neurophysiological dimension. *Psychological Review, 66*, 367-386.

Malone, T., & Lepper, M. (1987). Making learning fun: A taxonomy of intrinsic motivations for learning. In R. Snow & M. Farr (Eds.), *Aptitude, learning, and instruction: III. Conative and affective process analyses* (pp. 223-253). Hillsdale, NJ: Lawrence Erlbaum.

Manderlink, G., & Harackiewicz, J. M. (1984). Proximal versus distal goal setting and intrinsic motivation. *Journal of Personality and Social Psychology, 47*, 918-928.

Maratsos, M. P. (1973). Nonegocentric communication abilities in preschool children. *Child Development, 44*, 697-700.

Markus, H., Cross, S., & Wurf, E. (1990). The role of the self-system in competence. In R. J. Sternberg & J. Kolligian, Jr. (Eds.), *Competence considered* (pp. 205-225). New Haven, CT: Yale University Press.

Markus, H., & Nurius, P. (1986). Possible selves. *American Psychologist, 41*, 954-969.

Markus, H., & Ruvolo, A. (1989). Possible selves: Personalized representations of goals. In L. A. Pervin (Ed.), *Goal concepts in personality and social psychology* (pp. 211-241). Hillsdale, NJ: Lawrence Erlbaum.

Maslow, A. H. (1943). A theory of human motivation. *Psychological Review, 50*, 370-396.

Maslow, A. H. (1966). *Toward a psychology of being* (2nd ed.). New York: Van Nostrand.

Maslow, A. H. (1970). *Motivation and personality* (2nd ed.). New York: Harper & Row.

Maslow, A. H. (1971). *The farther reaches of human nature*. New York: Viking.

Masters, J. C., Barden, R. C., & Ford, M. E. (1979). Affective states, expressive behavior and learning in children. *Journal of Personality and Social Psychology, 37*, 380-390.

McCan, L. I., Sakheim, D. K., & Abrahamson, D. J. (1988). Trauma and victimization: A model of psychological adaptation. *Counseling Psychologist, 16,* 531-594.

McClelland, D. C. (1961). *The achieving society.* Princeton, NJ: Van Nostrand.

McClelland, D. C. (1985). *Human motivation.* Glenview, IL: Scott, Foresman.

McClelland, D. C., Atkinson, J. W., Clark, R. W., & Lowell, E. L. (1953). *The achievement motive.* New York: Appleton-Century-Crofts.

McCombs, B. L. (Ed.) (1991a). Unraveling motivation: New perspectives from research and practice. *The Journal of Experimental Education, 60,* 3-88.

McCombs, B. L. (1991b). Motivation and lifelong learning. *Educational Psychologist, 26,* 117-127.

McCombs, B. L., & Marzano, R. J. (1990). Putting the self in self-regulated learning: The self as agent in integrating will and skill. *Educational Psychologist, 25,* 51-69.

McDevitt, T. M., & Ford, M. E. (1987). Understanding young children's communicative functioning and development. In M. E. Ford & D. H. Ford (Eds.), *Humans as self-constructing living systems: Putting the framework to work* (pp. 145-175). Hillsdale, NJ: Lawrence Erlbaum.

McDougall, W. (1908). *An introduction to social psychology.* London: Methuen.

McDougall, W. (1933). *The energies of men.* New York: Scribner.

Meece, J. L., Wigfield, A., & Eccles, J. S. (1990). Predictors of math anxiety and its influence on young adolescents' course enrollment intentions and performance in mathematics. *Journal of Educational Psychology, 82,* 60-70.

Menig-Peterson, C. L. (1975). The modification of communicative behavior in preschool-aged children as a function of the listener's perspective. *Child Development, 46,* 1015-1018.

Mento, A. J., Steel, R. P., & Karren, R. J. (1987). A meta-analytic study of the effects of goal setting on task performance: 1966-1984. *Organizational Behavior and Human Decision Processes, 39,* 52-83.

Miller, A., & Hom, H. L., Jr. (1990). Influence of extrinsic and ego incentive value on persistence after failure and continuing motivation. *Journal of Educational Psychology, 82,* 539-545.

Miller, G. A., Galanter, E., & Pribram, K. H. (1960). *Plans and the structure of behavior.* New York: Holt, Rinehart & Winston.

Miller, I. W., III, & Norman, W. H. (1979). Learned helplessness in humans. A review and attribution-theory model. *Psychological Bulletin, 86,* 93-118.

Miller, J. G. (1978). *Living systems.* New York: McGraw-Hill.

Miller, N. E. (1944). Experimental studies of conflict. In J. McV. Hunt (Ed.), *Personality and the behavioral disorders* (Vol. 1, pp. 431-465). New York: Ronald.

Miller, N. E. (1951). Learnable drives and rewards. In S. S. Stevens (Ed.), *Handbook of experimental psychology* (pp. 435-472). New York: John Wiley.

Miller, N. E. (1959). Liberalization of basic S-R concepts: Extensions to conflict behavior, motivation and social learning. In S. Koch (Ed.), *Psychology: A study of a science* (Vol. II, pp. 196-292). New York: McGraw-Hill.

Mischel, W. (1968). *Personality and assessment.* New York: John Wiley.

Mischel, W. (1973). Toward a cognitive social learning reconceptualization of personality. *Psychological Review, 80,* 252-283.

Mitchell, T. R. (1982). Motivation: New directions for theory, research, and practice. *Academy of Management Review, 7,* 80-88.

Miura, I. T. (1987). A multivariate study of school-aged children's computer interest and use. In M. E. Ford & D. H. Ford (Eds.), *Humans as self-constructing living systems: Putting the framework to work* (pp. 177-197). Hillsdale, NJ: Lawrence Erlbaum.

Mook, D. G. (1987). *Motivation: The organization of action.* New York: Norton.

Morgan, M. (1984). Reward-induced decrements and increments in intrinsic motivation. *Review of Educational Research, 54,* 5-30.

Morgan, M. (1985). Self-monitoring of attained subgoals in private study. *Journal of Educational Psychology, 77,* 623-630.

Morris, L. W., Davis, M. A., & Hutchings, C. H. (1981). Cognitive and emotional components of anxiety: Literature review and a revised worry-emotionality scale. *Journal of Educational Psychology, 73,* 541-555.

Mowrer, O. H. (1939). A stimulus-response analysis of anxiety and its role as a reinforcing agent. *Psychological Review, 46,* 553-565.

Mowrer, O. H. (1952). Motivation. *Annual Review of Psychology, 3,* 419-438.

Mowrer, O. H. (1960). *Learning theory and behavior.* New York: John Wiley.

Murray, H. A. (1938). *Explorations in personality.* New York: Oxford University Press.

Murray, J. B. (1978). Psychologists and psychoactive drugs. *Genetic Psychology Monographs, 98,* 281-323.

Neisser, U. (1976). *Cognition and reality.* San Francisco: Freeman.

Neisser, U. (1985). The role of invariant structures in the control of movement. In M. Frese & J. Sabini (Eds.), *Goal directed behavior: The concept of action in psychology* (pp. 97-108). Hillsdale, NJ: Lawrence Erlbaum.

Nesselroade, J. R., & Ford, D. H. (1987). Methodological considerations in modeling living systems. In M. E. Ford & D. H. Ford (Eds.), *Humans as self-constructing living systems: Putting the framework to work* (pp. 47-79). Hillsdale, NJ: Lawrence Erlbaum.

Nicholls, J. G. (1978). The development of the concepts of effort and ability, perceptions of academic attainment and the understanding that difficult tasks require more ability. *Child Development, 49,* 800-814.

Nicholls, J. G. (1984a). Achievement motivation: Conceptions of ability, subjective experience, task choice, and performance. *Psychological Review, 91,* 328-346.

Nicholls, J. G. (1984b). Conceptions of ability and achievement motivation. In R. Ames & C. Ames (Eds.), *Research on motivation in education, Vol. 1: Student motivation* (pp. 39-73). Orlando, FL: Academic Press.

Nicholls, J. G. (1990). What is ability and why are we mindful of it? A developmental perspective. In R. J. Sternberg & J. Kolligian, Jr. (Eds.), *Competence considered* (pp. 11-40). New Haven, CT: Yale University Press.

Nichols, C. W. (1990). *An analysis of the sources of dissatisfaction at work.* Unpublished doctoral dissertation, School of Education, Stanford University, Stanford, CA.

Nichols, C. W. (1991). *Manual: Assessment of Core Goals.* Palo Alto, CA: Consulting Psychologist Press.

Nisbett, R. E., & Ross, L. D. (1980). *Human inference: Strategies and shortcomings of social judgment.* Englewood Cliffs, NJ: Prentice-Hall.

Nisbett. R. E., & Wilson, T. D. (1977). Telling more than we can know: Verbal reports on mental processes. *Psychological Review, 84,* 231-259.

Ogbu, J. U. (1981). Origins of human competence: A cultural-ecological perspective. *Child Development, 52,* 413-429.

Paris, S. G., Lawton, T. A., Turner, J. C., & Roth, J. L. (1991). Developmental perspective on standardized achievement testing. *Educational Researcher, 20,* 12-20.

Pattillo, J. R. (1990). *Predicting cardiac death in post-coronary patients: The depressive behavior pattern, explanatory style, and the Type A behavior pattern.* Unpublished doctoral dissertation, School of Education, Stanford University, Stanford, CA.

Pervin, L. A. (1983). The stasis and flow of behavior: Toward a theory of goals. In M. M. Page (Ed.), *Personality: Current theory and research* (pp. 1-53). Lincoln: University of Nebraska Press.

Pervin, L. A. (1989) (Ed.) *Goal concepts in personality and social psychology.* Hillsdale, NJ: Lawrence Erlbaum.

Pervin, L. A. (1991). Self-regulation and the problem of volition. In M. L. Maehr & P. R. Pintrich (Eds.), *Advances in motivation and achievement, Vol. 7* (pp. 1-20). Greenwich, CT: JAI.

Peterson, C., & Seligman, M. E. P. (1984). Causal explanations as a risk factor for depression: Theory and evidence. *Psychological Review, 91,* 347-374.

Peterson, C., Seligman, M. E. P., & Vaillant, G. E. (1988). Pessimistic explanatory style is a risk factor for physical illness: A thirty-five-year longitudinal study. *Journal of Personality and Social Psychology, 55,* 23-27.

Petri, H. L. (1991). *Motivation: Theory, research, and applications.* Belmont, CA: Wadsworth.

Petty, R. E., & Cacioppo, J. T. (1984). Motivational factors in consumer response to advertisements. In R. G. Geen, W. W. Beatty, & R. M. Arkin (Eds.), *Human motivation: Physiological, behavioral, and social approaches* (pp. 418-454). Boston: Allyn & Bacon.

Phares, E. J. (1976). *Locus of control in personality.* Morristown, NJ: General Learning Press.

Phillips, D. (1984). The illusion of incompetence among academically competent children. *Child Development, 55,* 2000-2016.

Phillips, D. A., & Zimmerman, M. (1990). The developmental course of perceived competence and incompetence among competent children. In R. J. Sternberg & J. Kolligian, Jr. (Eds.), *Competence considered* (pp. 41-66). New Haven, CT: Yale University Press.

Piaget, J. (1954). *The construction of reality in the child.* New York: Basic Books.

Pierce, J. L., Gardner, D. G., Cummings, L. L., & Dunham, R. B. (1989). Organization-based self-esteem: Construct definition, measurement, and validation. *Academy of Management Journal, 32,* 622-648.

Pinder, C. C. (1984). *Work motivation: Theory, issues, and applications.* Glenview, IL: Scott, Foresman.

Pintrich, P. R. (1989). The dynamic interplay of student motivation and cognition in the college classroom. In M. L. Maehr & C. Ames (Eds.), *Advances in motivation and achievement, Vol. 6: Motivation enhancing environments* (pp. 117-160). Greenwich, CT: JAI.

Pintrich, P. R. (1991). Editor's comment. Special issue: Current issues and new directions in motivational theory and research. *Educational Psychologist, 26,* 199-205.

Pintrich, P. R., & De Groot, E. V. (1990). Motivational and self-regulated learning components of classroom academic performance. *Journal of Educational Psychology, 82,* 33-40.

Pintrich, P. R., & Garcia, T. (1991). Student goal orientation and self-regulation in the college classroom. In M. L. Maehr & P. R. Pintrich (Eds.), *Advances in motivation and achievement, Vol. 7: Goals and self-regulatory processes* (pp. 371-402). Greenwich, CT: JAI.

Plutchik, R. (1962). *The emotions: Facts, theories, and a new model.* New York: Random House.

Plutchik, R. (1980). *Emotion: A psychoevolutionary synthesis.* New York: Harper & Row.

Porter, L. W., & Lawler, E. E., III. (1968). *Managerial attitudes and performance.* Homewood, IL: Dorsey.

Powers, W. T. (1973). *Behavior: The control of perception.* Chicago: Aldine.

Powers, W. T. (1989). *Living control systems*. Gravel Switch, KY: Control Systems Group.

Powers, W. T. (1991). Commentary on Bandura's "Human agency." *American Psychologist, 46,* 151-153.

Prigogine, I. (1976). Order through fluctuation: Self-organization and social system. In E. Jantsch & C. H. Waddington (Eds.), *Evolution and consciousness* (pp. 99-123). Reading, MA: Addison-Wesley.

Prigogine, I., & Stengers, I. (1984). *Order out of chaos*. New York: Bantam.

Privette, G. (1983). Peak experience, peak performance, and flow: A comparative analysis of positive human experiences. *Journal of Personality and Social Psychology, 45,* 1361-1368.

Rapaport, D. (1960). On the psychoanalytic theory of motivation. In M. R. Jones (Ed.), *Nebraska Symposium on Motivation* (pp. 173-247). Lincoln: University of Nebraska Press.

Raynor, J. O., & McFarlin, D. B. (1986). Motivation and the self-system. In R. M. Sorrentino & E. T. Higgins (Eds.), *Handbook of motivation and cognition: Foundations of social behavior* (pp. 315-349). New York: Guilford.

Revelle, W., & Michaels, E. J. (1976). The theory of achievement motivation revisited: The implications of inertial tendencies. *Psychological Review, 83,* 394-404.

Ridley, D. S. (1991). Reflective self-awareness: A basic motivational process. *The Journal of Experimental Education, 60,* 31-48.

Rogers, C. R. (1946). Significant aspects of client-centered therapy. *American Psychologist, 1,* 415-422.

Rogers, C. R. (1951). *Client-centered therapy: Its current practice, implications, and theory*. Boston: Houghton Mifflin.

Rogers, C. R. (1961). *On becoming a person: A therapist's view of psychotherapy*. Boston: Houghton Mifflin.

Rosenberg, M. (1979). *Conceiving the self*. New York: Basic Books.

Rotter, J. B. (1954). *Social learning and clinical psychology*. Englewood Cliffs, NJ: Prentice-Hall.

Rotter, J. B. (1966). Generalized expectancies for internal vs. external control of reinforcement. *Psychological Monographs, 80,* (1, Whole No. 609).

Rotter, J. B., Chance, J. E., & Phares, E. J. (Eds.) (1972). *Applications of a social learning theory of personality*. New York: Holt, Rinehart & Winston.

Ruble, D. N. (1983). The development of social comparison processes and their role in achievement-related self-socialization. In E. T. Higgins, D. N. Ruble, & W. W. Hartup (Eds.), *Social cognition and social development: A sociocultural perspective* (pp. 134-157). New York: Cambridge University Press.

Rumelhart, D. E., & McClelland, J. L. (Eds.) (1986). *Parallel distributed processing: Explorations in the microstructure of cognition*. Cambridge: The MIT Press/Bradford Books.

Ryan, R. M. (1982). Control and information in the intrapersonal sphere: An extension of cognitive evaluation theory. *Journal of Personality and Social Psychology, 43,* 450-461.

Ryan, R. M., Connell, J. P., & Deci, E. L. (1985). A motivational analysis of self-determination and self-regulation in education. In C. Ames & R. Ames (Eds.), *Research on motivation in education, Vol. 2: The classroom milieu* (pp. 13-51). Orlando, FL: Academic Press.

Ryan, R. M., & Stiller, J. (1991). The social contexts of internalization: Parent and teacher influences on autonomy, motivation, and learning. In M. L. Maehr & P. R. Pintrich (Eds.), *Advances in motivation and achievement, Vol. 7: Goals and self-regulatory processes* (pp. 115-149). Greenwich, CT: JAI.

Schein, E. H. (1985). *Organizational culture and leadership.* San Francisco: Jossey-Bass.

Schellenbach, C. J. (1987). Emotional development in infancy. In M. E. Ford & D. H. Ford (Eds.), *Humans as self-constructing living systems: Putting the framework to work* (pp. 81-120). Hillsdale, NJ: Lawrence Erlbaum.

Schermerhorn, J. R., Jr. (1986). Team development for high performance management. *Training and Development Journal, 40,* 38-43.

Schlenker, B. R., & Weigold, M. F. (1989). Goals and the self-identification process: Constructing desired identities. In L. A. Pervin (Ed.), *Goal concepts in personality and social psychology* (pp. 243-290). Hillsdale, NJ: Lawrence Erlbaum.

Schmidt, R. A. (1975). A schema theory of discrete motor skill learning. *Psychological Review, 82,* 225-260.

Schunk, D. H. (1982). Effects of effort attributional feedback on children's perceived self-efficacy and achievement. *Journal of Educational Psychology, 74,* 548-556.

Schunk, D. H. (1983). Ability versus effort attributional feedback: Differential effects on self-efficacy and achievement. *Journal of Educational Psychology, 75,* 848-856.

Schunk, D. H. (1984). Self-efficacy perspective on achievement behavior. *Educational Psychologist, 19,* 48-58.

Schunk, D. H. (1990a). Introduction to the special section on motivation and efficacy. *Journal of Educational Psychology, 82,* 3-6.

Schunk, D. H. (1990b). Goal setting and self-efficacy during self-regulated learning. *Educational Psychologist, 25,* 71-86.

Schunk, D. H. (1991a). Self-efficacy and academic motivation. *Educational Psychologist, 26,* 207-231.

Schunk, D. H. (1991b). Goal setting and self-evaluation: A social cognitive perspective on self-regulation. In M. L. Maehr & P. R. Pintrich (Eds.), *Advances in motivation and achievement, Vol. 7: Goals and self-regulatory processes* (pp. 85-113). Greenwich, CT: JAI.

Schutz, P. A. (1991). Goals in self-directed behavior. *Educational Psychologist, 26,* 55-67.

Schwab, D. P., & Cummings, L. L. (1970). Theories of performance and satisfaction: A review. *Industrial Relations, 9,* 408-430.

Scott, W. E., Jr. (1966). Activation theory and task design. *Organizational Behavior and Human Performance, 1,* 3-30.

Searle, J. R. (1981). The intentionality of intention and action. *Separata de Manuscrito, 4*(2), 77-101.

Seligman, M. E. P. (1975). *Helplessness: On depression, development, and death.* San Francisco: Freeman.

Seligman, M. E. P. (1991). *Learned optimism.* New York: Knopf.

Sexton, P. W. (1985). Trying to make it real compared to what? Implications of high school dropout statistics. *Journal of Educational Equity and Leadership, 5,* 92-106.

Shalley, C. E. (1991). Effects of productivity goals, creativity goals, and personal discretion on individual creativity. *Journal of Applied Psychology, 76,* 179-185.

Shantz, C. U. (1983). Social cognition. In J. H. Flavell & E. M. Markman (Eds.) & P. H. Mussen (Series Ed.), *Handbook of child psychology, Vol. 3: Cognitive development* (4th ed., pp. 495-555). New York: John Wiley.

Shevrin, H., & Dickman, S. (1980). The psychological unconscious: A necessary assumption for all psychological theory? *American Psychologist, 35,* 421-434.

Shure, M. B., & Spivack, G. (1978). *Problem-solving techniques in childrearing*. San Francisco, CA: Jossey-Bass.

Shure, M. B., & Spivack, G. (1980). Interpersonal problem solving as a mediator of behavioral adjustment in preschool and kindergarten children. *Journal of Applied Developmental Psychology, 2,* 211-226.

Silver, M. (1985). "Purposive behavior" in psychology and philosophy: A history. In M. Frese & J. Sabini (Eds.), *Goal directed behavior: The concept of action in psychology* (pp. 3-17). Hillsdale, NJ: Lawrence Erlbaum.

Simon, H. A. (1967). Motivational and emotional control of cognition. *Psychological Review, 74,* 29-39.

Skinner, B. F. (1953). *Science and human behavior*. New York: Macmillan.

Skinner, B. F. (1957). *Verbal behavior*. New York: Appleton-Century-Crofts.

Skinner, B. F. (1959). *Cumulative record*. New York: Appleton-Century-Crofts.

Skinner, B. F. (1974). *About behaviorism*. New York: Knopf.

Skinner, B. F. (1984). Selection by consequences. *Behavioral and Brain Sciences, 7,* 477-510.

Skinner, E. A., Chapman, M., & Baltes, P. B. (1988). Control, means-ends, and agency beliefs: A new conceptualization and its measurement during childhood. *Journal of Personality and Social Psychology, 54,* 117-133.

Skinner, E. A., Wellborn, J. G., & Connell, J. P (1990). What it takes to do well in school and whether I've got it: A process model of perceived control and children's engagement and achievement in school. *Journal of Educational Psychology, 82,* 22-32.

Slavin, R. E. (1981). When does cooperative learning increase student achievement? *Psychological Bulletin, 94,* 429-445.

Slavin, R. E. (1984). Students motivating students to excel: Cooperative incentives, cooperative tasks, and student achievement. *The Elementary School Journal, 85,* 53-63.

Slavin, R. E. (1987). Developmental and motivational perspectives on cooperative learning: A reconciliation. *Child Development, 58,* 1161-1167.

Slavin, R. E. (1989). Cooperative learning and student achievement: Six theoretical perspectives. In M. L. Maehr & C. Ames (Eds.), *Advances in motivation and achievement, Vol. 6: Motivation enhancing environments* (pp. 161-177). Greenwich, CT: JAI.

Smith, D. (1991, March 10). How to keep morale high in low times. *San Jose Mercury News*, p. 2PC.

Smith, R. P. (1981). Boredom: A review. *Human Factors, 23,* 329-340.

Snyder, C. R., Harris, C., Anderson, J. R., Holleran, S. A., Irving, L. M., Sigmon, S. T., Yoshinobu, L., Gibbs, J., Langelle, C., & Harney, P. (1991). The will and the ways: Development and validation of an individual-differences measure of hope. *Journal of Personality and Social Psychology, 60,* 570-585.

Sorrentino, R. M., & Higgins, E. T. (Eds.) (1986). *Handbook of motivation and cognition: Foundations of social behavior*. New York: Guilford.

Sorrentino, R. M., & Short, J. C. (1986). Uncertainty orientation, motivation, and cognition. In R. M. Sorrentino & E. T. Higgins (Eds.), *Handbook of motivation and cognition: Foundations of social behavior* (pp. 379-403). New York: Guilford.

Spence, J. T., & Helmreich, R. L. (1978). *Masculinity and femininity: Their psychological dimensions, correlates, and antecedents*. Austin: University of Texas Press.

Spence, K. W. (1956). *Behavior theory and conditioning*. New Haven, CT: Yale University Press.

Spence, K. W. (1958). A theory of emotionally based drive (D) and its relation to performance in simple learning situations. *American Psychologist, 13*, 131-141.

Spielberger, C. D. (Ed.) (1972). *Anxiety: Current trends in theory and research* (Vol. 1). New York: Academic Press.

Spivack, G., Platt, J. J., & Shure, M. B. (1976). *The problem-solving approach to adjustment.* San Francisco, CA: Jossey-Bass.

Sroufe, L. A. (1983). Infant-caregiver attachment and patterns of adaptation in preschool: The roots of maladaptation and competence. In M. Perlmutter (Ed.), *Minnesota symposium on child psychology* (Vol. 16, pp. 41-83). Hillsdale, NJ: Lawrence Erlbaum.

Sroufe, L. A., & Waters, E. (1976). The ontogenesis of smiling and laughter: A perspective on the organization of development in infancy. *Psychological Review, 83*, 173-189.

Staats, A. W. (1991). Unified positivism and unification psychology: Fad or new field? *American Psychologist, 46*, 899-912.

Steers, R. M., & Porter, L. W. (Eds.) (1987). *Motivation and work behavior* (4th ed.). New York: McGraw-Hill.

Stein, A. H., & Bailey, M. M. (1973). The socialization of achievement orientation in females. *Psychological Bulletin, 80*, 345-366.

Sternberg, R. J. (1990). Prototypes of competence and incompetence. In R. J. Sternberg & J. Kolligian, Jr. (Eds.), *Competence considered* (pp. 117-145). New Haven, CT: Yale University Press.

Sternberg, R. J., & Kolligian, J., Jr. (Eds.) (1990). *Competence considered.* New Haven, CT: Yale University Press.

Stipek, D. (1984). Young children's performance expectations: Logical analysis or wishful thinking? In J. G. Nicholls (Ed.), *Advances in motivation and achievement, Vol. 3: The development of achievement motivation* (pp. 33-56). Greenwich, CT: JAI.

Stipek, D., & Hoffman, J. (1980). Development of children's performance-related judgments. *Child Development, 51*, 912-914.

Stipek, D., & MacIver, D. (1989). Developmental changes in children's assessment of intellectual competence. *Child Development, 60*, 521-538.

Strang, H. R., Lawrence, E. C., & Fowler, P. C. (1978). Effects of assigned goal level and knowledge of results on arithmetic computation: A laboratory study. *Journal of Applied Psychology, 63*, 446-450.

Taylor, C. B., & Arnow, B. (1988). *The nature and treatment of anxiety disorders.* New York: Free Press.

Taylor, J. A. (1956). Drive theory and manifest anxiety. *Psychological Bulletin, 53*, 303-320.

Tesser, A. (1986). Some effects of self-evaluation maintenance on cognition and action. In R. M. Sorrentino & E. T. Higgins (Eds.), *Handbook of motivation and cognition: Foundations of social behavior* (pp. 435-464). New York: Guilford.

Tesser, A., & Campbell, J. (1985). A self-evaluation model of student motivation. In C. Ames & R. Ames (Eds.), *Research on motivation in education, Vol. 2: The classroom milieu* (pp. 217-247). Orlando, FL: Academic Press.

Thompson, R. (1991). Emotional regulation and emotional development. *Educational Psychology Review, 3*, 269-307.

Thoresen, C. E., & Pattillo, J. R. (1988). Exploring the Type A behavior pattern in children and adolescents. In B. K. Houston & C. R. Snyder (Eds.), *Type A behavior pattern: Research, theory, and intervention* (pp. 98-145). New York: John Wiley.

Tobias, S. (1979). Anxiety research in educational psychology. *Journal of Educational Psychology, 71*, 573-582.

Tobias, S. (1985). Test anxiety: Interference, defective skills, and cognitive capacity. *Educational Psychologist, 20*, 135-142.

Tolman, E. C. (1926). A behavioristic theory of ideas. *Psychological Review, 33*, 352-369.

Tolman, E. C. (1932). *Purposive behavior in animals and men.* New York: Appleton-Century-Crofts.

Tolman, E. C. (1938). The determiners of behavior at a choice point. *Psychological Review, 45*, 1-41.

Tolman, E. C. (1951). A psychological model. In T. Parsons & E. Shils (Eds.), *Toward a general theory of action* (pp. 279-361). Cambridge, MA: Harvard University Press.

Tolman, E. C. (1952). A cognition motivation model. *Psychological Review, 59*, 389-400.

Tolman, E. C. (1955). Principles of performance. *Psychological Review, 62*, 315-326.

Tomkins, S. S. (1962). *Affect, imagery, consciousness, Vol. I. The positive affects.* New York: Springer.

Tomkins, S. S. (1963). *Affect, imagery, consciousness, Vol. II. The negative affects.* New York: Springer.

Tubbs, M. E. (1986). Goal setting: A meta-analytic examination of the empirical evidence. *Journal of Applied Psychology, 71*, 474-483.

Tubbs, M. E., & Ekeberg, S. E. (1991). The role of intentions in work motivation: Implications for goal-setting theory and research. *Academy of Management Review, 16*, 180-199.

Urbain, E. S., & Kendall, P. C. (1980). Review of social-cognitive problem-solving interventions with children. *Psychological Bulletin, 88*, 109-143.

Urban, H. B., & Ford, D. H. (1961). *Man: A robot or a pilot?* Paper presented at the annual meeting of the American Psychological Association, New York.

von Bertalanffy, L. (1968). *General system theory.* New York: George Braziller.

von Bertalanffy, L. (1975). *Perspectives on general system theory.* New York: George Braziller.

Vroom, V. H. (1964). *Work and motivation.* New York: John Wiley.

Vroom, V. H., & Deci, E. L. (Eds.) (1992). *Management and motivation* (2nd ed.). London: Penguin.

Wadsworth (Winell), M., & Ford, D. H. (1983). Assessment of personal goal hierarchies. *Journal of Counseling Psychology, 30*, 514-526.

Walster, E., Berscheid, E., & Walster, G. W. (1973). New directions in equity research. *Journal of Personality and Social Psychology, 25*, 151-176.

Walster, E., Walster, G. W., & Berscheid, E. (1978). *Equity: Theory and research.* Boston: Allyn & Bacon.

Walton, M. (1986). *The Deming management method.* New York: Dodd, Mead.

Wehlage, G. C., & Rutter, R. A. (1986). Dropping out: How much do schools contribute to the problem? *Teachers College Record, 87*, 374-392.

Weiner, B. (1974). *Achievement motivation and attribution theory.* Morristown, NJ: General Learning Press.

Weiner, B. (1979). A theory of motivation for some classroom experiences. *Journal of Educational Psychology, 71*, 3-25.

Weiner, B. (1980). *Human motivation.* New York: Holt, Rinehart & Winston.

Weiner, B. (1985). An attributional theory of achievement motivation and emotion. *Psychological Review, 92*, 548-573.

Weiner, B. (1986). *An attributional theory of motivation and emotion.* New York: Springer Verlag.

Weiner, B. (1990). History of motivational research in education. *Journal of Educational Psychology, 82*, 616-622.

Weiner, B. (1991). Metaphors in motivation and attribution. *American Psychologist, 46*, 921-930.

Weiner, B. (1992). *Human motivation: Metaphors, theories, and research.* Newbury Park, CA: Sage.

Weiner, N. (1948). *Cybernetics: Control and communication in the animal and the machine.* Cambridge, MA: MIT Press.

Weisz, J. R., & Cameron, A. M. (1985). Individual differences in the student's sense of control. In C. Ames & R. Ames (Eds.), *Research on motivation in education, Vol. 2: The classroom milieu* (pp. 93-140). Orlando, FL: Academic Press.

Weisz, J. R., Rothbaum, F. M., & Blackburn, T. C. (1984). Standing out and standing in: The psychology of control in America and Japan. *American Psychologist, 39*, 955-969.

Weisz, J. R., & Stipek, D. J. (1982). Competence, contincency, and the development of perceived control. *Human Development, 25*, 250-281.

Wentzel, K. R. (1989). Adolescent classroom goals, standards for performance, and academic achievement: An interactionist perspective. *Journal of Educational Psychology, 81*, 131-142.

Wentzel, K. R. (1991a). Social competence at school: Relation between social responsibility and academic achievement. *Review of Educational Research, 61*, 1-24.

Wentzel, K. R. (1991b). Social and academic goals at school: Motivation and achievement in context. In M. L. Maehr & P. R. Pintrich (Eds.), *Advances in motivation and achievement, Vol. 7: Goals and self-regulatory processes,* (pp. 185-212). Greenwich, CT: JAI.

White, R. W. (1959). Motivation reconsidered: The concept of competence. *Psychological Review, 66*, 297-333.

Wicklund, R. A. (1986). Orientation to the environment versus preoccupation with human potential. In R. M. Sorrentino & E. T. Higgins (Eds.), *Handbook of motivation and cognition: Foundations of social behavior* (pp. 64-95). New York: Guilford.

Wicklund, R. A., & Brehm, J. W. (1976). *Perspectives on cognitive dissonance.* Hillsdale, NJ: Lawrence Erlbaum.

Wiggins, J. S., & Holzmuller, A. (1978). Psychological androgyny and interpersonal behavior. *Journal of Consulting and Clinical Psychology, 46*, 40-52.

Williams, R. B., Jr., & Barefoot, J. C., & Shekelle, R. B. (1985). The health consequences of hostility. In M. A. Chesney & R. H. Rosenman (Eds.), *Anger and hostility in cardiovascular and behavioral disorders* (pp. 173-185). Washington, DC: Hemisphere.

Winell, M. (1987). Personal goals: The key to self-direction in adulthood. In M. E. Ford & D. H. Ford (Eds.), *Humans as self-constructing living systems: Putting the framework to work* (pp. 261-287). Hillsdale, NJ: Lawrence Erlbaum.

Wlodkowski, R. J., & Jaynes, J. H. (1990). *Eager to learn: Helping children become motivated and love learning.* San Francisco, CA: Jossey-Bass.

Wood, D. N. (1990). *The development of responsibility schemata: Patterns of thoughts and feelings associated with older children's and adolescents' social responsibility.* Unpublished doctoral dissertation, School of Education, Stanford University, Stanford, CA.

Wood, R., & Bandura, A. (1989). Social cognitive theory of organizational management. *Academy of Management Review, 14,* 361-384.

Young, P. T. (1961). *Motivation and emotion.* New York: John Wiley.

Zajonc, R. B. (1980). Feeling and thinking: Preferences need no inferences. *American Psychologist, 35,* 151-175.

Zajonc, R. B. (1984). On the primacy of affect. *American Psychologist, 39,* 117-123.

Zand, D. E. (1972). Trust and managerial problem solving. *Administrative Science Quarterly, 17,* 229-239.

Zedeck, S. (1977). An information processing model and approach to the study of motivation. *Organizational Behavior and Human Performance, 18,* 47-77.

Zuckerman, M., Klorman, R., Larrance, D. T., & Spiegel, N. H. (1981). Facial, autonomic, and subjective components of emotion: The facial feedback hypothesis versus the externalizer-internalizer distinction. *Journal of Personality and Social Psychology, 41,* 929-944.

Name Index

Subject Index

About the Author

Martin E. Ford is a developmental and educational psychologist interested in the psychological and social processes that contribute to effective functioning and the development of competence in children, adolescents, and adults. His current work focuses on the motivational foundations of competence development. He is the creator of Motivational Systems Theory (Human Motivation: Goals, Emotions, and Personal Agency Beliefs), and has recently developed the Assessment of Personal Goals (with C. W. Nichols) and the Assessment of Personal Agency Beliefs (with Christopher Chase) to facilitate professional work and basic and applied research on motivational processes in human development, education, counseling, and business. He is also coeditor (with Donald Ford) of a volume designed to illustrate the utility of a living systems approach for scholars and practitioners in the human sciences and professions (*Humans as Self-Constructing Living Systems: Putting the Framework to Work*), and coauthor (with R. Christopher Barden) of *Optimal Performance in Education*, a volume designed to help undergraduate and graduate students apply principles of motivation and competence development to their academic achievement and career development efforts.

For his research Dr. Ford has received Early Career Contribution Awards from two divisions of the American Psychological Association (Developmental and Educational Psychology). He has also served on the editorial boards of several scholarly journals, and as

Associate Editor for the *Review of Educational Research*. In addition to his scholarly work, Dr. Ford consults widely with a diversity of agencies, organizations, and businesses on problems related to motivation and competence development.

Dr. Ford is currently Associate Professor of Education and Chair of the Committee on Psychological Studies in Education at the Stanford University School of Education.